EVERGLADES LAWMEN

True Stories of Game Wardens in the Glades

James T. Huffstodt

PINEAPPLE PRESS, INC.

Palm Beach, Florida

Inquiries should be addressed to:

Pineapple Press, Inc.
4501 Forbes Boulevard, Suite 200
Lanham, Maryland 20706
www.pineapplepress.com

Distributed by NATIONAL BOOK NETWORK

Library of Congress Cataloging in Publication Data

Huffstodt, James. T.
       Everglades lawmen: true stories of game wardens in the Glades /
           James T. Huffstodt.
                      p. cm.
           ISBN 978-1-56164-192-5 (pb)
           1. Game wardens—Florida—Everglades. 2. Florida Dept. of Fish
and Game—Officials and employees. 3. Wildlife management—Florida—
Everglades. I. Title.

HV7959.H84 2000
363.28 21—dc21   99–045717

Design by *osprey*design

Dedication and Acknowledgments

This volume is dedicated to the past, represented by my late brother, John "Jack" Huffstodt, of Peru, Illinois (1928–1995); and to the future, represented by my granddaughter, Jade Elise, five years old and full of promise.

The author thanks Susan Young of West Palm Beach, a wildlife artist and photographer, for suggesting this book about the intrepid game wardens of the Everglades and south Florida. Thanks as well to Steven "Tim" Lewis of Tallahassee, filmmaker, writer, and photographer, for his generous assistance in locating vintage photographs to illustrate the text. In addition, the following individuals generously provided photos from their personal albums: Dick Lawrence, Bill Ashley, John Reed, J. O. Brown, J. K. Davis, David Stermen, Jon Fury, Norman Padgett, Tom Haworth, and Jeff Ardelean.

Special appreciation is extended to the many individuals interviewed for this book project. The author is also indebted to June Cussen and Kris Rowland of Pineapple Press for their invaluable assistance, advice, and encouragement in fine-tuning the manuscript.

"Police work is dangerous under the best of circumstances, and to think about the special world of wildlife officers (game wardens) is to marvel that anyone would want to be one. They work mostly at night, because that's when the poachers are out. They work mostly alone. . . . They work in swamps and forests and fields . . . because that's where the animals are. Worst of all, their work requires them to be constantly accosting people who are armed to the teeth."

–Editorial, *St. Petersburg Times*, December 18, 1984

TABLE OF CONTENTS

Preface
Everglades at First Light

S awgrass marsh stretches horizon to horizon, a vast multicolored sea of brown, green, tan, and yellow. Cottonball clouds drift majestically in a vaulting sky as blue as the Gulf Stream. The emerging sun, rising in the east, bathes the splendid vista in a golden ethereal light.

We are flying inches above the surface of the marsh in a speeding airboat, plunging deep into the Everglades wilderness. A hundred yards ahead a brace of coots scurry into the sawgrass and a great blue heron takes to lumbering flight with slow-motion strokes of his powerful wings. Tiny bugs sting our faces as the wind whistles; even our ear plugs can't quite keep out the roar of the airplane engine that drives us at fifty miles per hour.

On many a fine day I have ridden aboard a thundering airboat piloted by the skilled, practiced hands of a game warden with the Florida Game and Fresh Water Fish Commission (GFC). It is an exhilarating and liberating experience, a flight to freedom, a journey into wilderness. Since 1986 I have served as the public information officer in the GFC's Everglades Region. This administrative designation encompasses ten counties of south Florida from Lake Okeechobee to Key West. The region's heart and soul is the seven hundred thousand acres of the northern Everglades lying just west of the metropolitan area that includes Miami and Ft. Lauderdale. To the south is Everglades National Park. The northern Glades are crisscrossed with canals and checkered with water-control structures and pump stations. Despite that intrusion, the area still retains much of its ecological integrity.

This wildlife-rich marsh is home to a variety of wildlife from

Everglades Lawmen

white-tailed deer and alligators to bobcats and wading birds. Its waters teem with largemouth bass and bream. It is a mecca for campers, canoeists, airboaters, hunters, fishermen, nature photographers, and tourists from Munich to Manila.

The tales told in this volume, with a few exceptions, take place in this strange country of contradictions—a wilderness remnant nearly encircled and increasingly menaced by a constricting band of concrete and condominiums. Bustling Miami's gleaming skyscrapers, cruise ships, and festive "Calle Ocho" (Eighth Street, the heart of Little Havana) are but an hour's drive from the peace and tranquillity of the Everglades. In terms of time and distance, it is a brief trip. But in another more fundamental sense, it is a long journey from today to a far distant yesterday.

The game warden is law in the Everglades. He is a cop, but a special cop whose sworn duty is to protect the state's wildlife resources from exploiters and poachers. One day in the Glades is never the same as another. Sometimes it is routine, consisting of nothing more than checking fishing licenses of the anglers whose boats dot the canals. On another occasion it might entail a search for an escaped felon seeking refuge in the wild country.

Many people are fascinated and intrigued with the mystique and romance of the Everglades game warden. The indelible image is that of a self-reliant, capable fellow, most likely a laconic and rangy man, as lean and taciturn as the late Gary Cooper. He is sun-baked and weathered as an old fencepost and likes to savor a chaw, which bulges under one cheek. Some wardens match the myth. Reality, however, is often far different. The man or woman at the joystick of an airboat is frequently a college graduate with a degree in law enforcement or wildlife biology. Some are Florida boys who grew up in the swamp and woods. Others were born in Philadelphia, New York City, or some small town in the Midwest. Most are hunters, fishermen, and outdoorsmen. Most are men, but a few women have joined the force. All are committed wildlife conservationists.

Danger comes with the badge and gun. A game warden warily approaching a campfire in the Everglades is never sure of what might lurk in the shadows. Are the men lit by the flickering flames simply law-abiding hunters resting after a day in the Glades? Or are they drug dealers waiting for a drop-off? Are they drunk? Are they high on drugs? Are they armed? Are they alligator poachers? Such

Shotgun Check. *A game warden checks a turkey hunter's shotgun to ensure that the magazine contains no more than the three shells allowed by state law. This was the early 1960s, a time of change, as many of the old-timers retired and were replaced by a new breed, often college educated and Northern born. (Florida Game and Fish Commission)*

Everglades Lawmen

questions are never far from the thoughts of a game warden who usually works alone, at night, and sometimes hours from the nearest back-up.

Everglades Lawmen is a series of true tales relating the exploits and adventures of Everglades game wardens from 1951 through 1998. The reader is invited to share the wilderness game warden's life with its serene beauty and its occasional, but deadly, violence.

This book—from first page to last—is a tribute to those indomitable men and women in green I have come to respect and cherish over many years of shared adventure and occasional danger.

—*James T. Huffstodt*

Author's Notes:

- Throughout this narrative I have chosen to describe these officers as game wardens, a time-honored designation more familiar to most readers than the official title of wildlife officer.
- The Florida Game and Freshwater Fish Commission, created in 1943, ceased to exist on midnight, June 30, 1999, ending a fifty-six-year history. Its personnel and resources, along with the Florida Marine Patrol, were incorporated into a brand-new agency, The Florida Fish and Wildlife Conservation Commission. The decision to create a single conservation agency for fresh and salt water was approved by seventy percent of the voters during a statewide referendum held in the fall of 1998.

Chapter 1:
The Chase

I remember flying through the air and landing in the shallow marsh. That's when my own airboat ran me down. Luckily there was just enough water that the boat crawled right over me. It sort of pushed me down into the soft muck. I came up choking and gagging. There was Everglades muck in my mouth, my ears, my nostrils. I couldn't see anything out of my left eye. I thought it had been knocked out, that I'd been blinded. There was the taste of blood in my mouth.

—Game Warden Dick Lawrence

Once the powerful aircraft engine sputtered into silence, the airboat slowly drifted to a stop in the middle of the darkened Everglades. Game Warden Dick Lawrence sat atop the boat, listening to the quiet music of the marsh—the croak of pig frogs, the weird cry of a distant limpkin, the graveyard hoot of a barred owl perched in a nearby cypress. Moments later the night echoed with the bellow of a bull gator sounding his primeval challenge. The deep bass sounded like the roar of a lion on the Serengeti Plain.

A man can't be any more alone than when he's out in the Glades long past midnight, swatting mosquitoes and hearing the constant drone of insects—a humming like that of some strange electric dynamo operating in the remoteness of one of America's last truly wild places. Above, the silver stars glitter against the backdrop of satin black sky while purple clouds sail the ocean sky like ancient ships bound for distant and exotic lands.

Everglades Lawmen

For the thirty-year-old warden it had been a long road that brought him to this lonely place. He had grown up in the Minnesota woods, hunted, camped, and fished there. He learned taxidermy in the Boy Scouts, discovering a talent for bringing to life the wildlife beauty he found so compelling. His life's path led to the U.S. Navy where his considerable athletic skills found expression on military baseball and football teams in such unlikely places as Morocco and Iceland. Before pinning on the gold badge of the game warden, Dick had been a successful Miami taxidermist. The swarthy, square-jawed extrovert could move with catlike grace and also played professional jai alai in his spare hours.

But now he had found his place in the world, patrolling the wild country and enforcing the game and fish laws, helping protect the wilderness world he loved so passionately. There is the soul of a poet in the heart of the game warden. He sees a lyrical splendor in the sight of a white-tailed buck flashing through a woods at dawn, or the watery explosion when a trophy bass strikes a lure like aquatic lightning. The world of the game warden is one of stillness and dramatic sunsets, echoing with the screech of a bobcat or the sweet song of the Carolina wren. Lawrence had heard the intoxicating melody and was hopelessly addicted. "They were paying me to go out into the woods and have fun!" he said.

In the fall of 1973, he had been working as a warden for three years, learning the varied skills and absorbing the knowledge necessary to carry out his mission of protecting the wilderness and its wild creatures. Lawrence had a good teacher in Captain Tom Shirley, who had grown up at a fish camp in the Glades and knew its secrets and its history. Some of the gator and deer poachers were his childhood friends; they had hunted and fished this vast marsh together. Shirley knew the critters that lived in the marsh and their ways, and he knew the men who hunted them. Through the years, Shirley had passed on much of his precious knowledge to Lawrence, who was winning attention within the Florida Game and Fresh Water Fish Commission as a warden with energy, drive, initiative, and guts. Lawrence was an eager and quick learner.

As Lawrence waited in the shadows, he felt confident in his knowledge, skills, and abilities. He was proud of being a game warden and cherished this job that paid him to patrol the wild places. Lawrence brought to the task a boundless enthusiasm, a gregarious nature, and utter fearlessness. The dangerous game of chasing poachers in the depths of the Glades was, to him, an adventure and a challenge that gave him the same exhilaration he had felt in running for touchdowns or hitting home runs. This was just a different kind of game, more important and infinitely more dangerous. Most men might pause, hesitate, reflect. But Lawrence loved the game and thrived on a diet of adrenaline and danger.

Alligators were still an endangered species at this time in the early 1970s, their decreasing numbers completely protected by state and federal laws. But the severe penalties didn't deter hard-core Everglades outlaws. They saw gators as money in the bank. Prices were high and profits lucrative. The possibility of being caught and prosecuted only made the venture more enticing because, in many ways, most poachers roaming the Glades were lovers of danger just like Lawrence. Most of them played by informal rules known by the lawman and lawbreaker, based on the understanding that poaching wasn't something to kill or be killed over. But there were renegades, bone-bad men who would murder a game warden in blood as cold as a gator's if they had the opportunity.

As Lawrence waited in darkness, perhaps his thoughts turned to one of his first days in uniform when he had entered a country store at the edge of the wilderness. He was making a purchase when a tall, heavy man in a faded work shirt and tattered jeans rose from a bench where he'd been drinking a soda and talking with several other men.

"You Dick Lawrence? The new game warden?" he asked in a deep drawl. His face was sun-burned and creased. His speech and appearance spoke of a rugged, outdoor life. He was shoeless.

"Yes, I am," Lawrence replied, trying to hide his surprise that a stranger would know him on sight.

"Well, my name is Jimmy Deeds. Lived here in the Glades my whole life. I hunt gators to feed my family. Thought we might talk. I want you to know that I won't hurt you if you don't hurt me. Can we make a deal?"

"That's not a problem," Lawrence replied. "I don't want to hurt anyone, but I will enforce the law."

"Understood," the big man said with a shake of his head and then shambled back over to the bench and his friends.

Everglades Lawmen

Lawrence later encountered Jimmy several times in the Glades but had never caught him gator poaching. Perhaps the big man was out there tonight moving quietly in the night, listening for the approach of a game warden's airboat.

A brief beam of light glowed in the distant marsh for a few seconds and then darkness returned. Lawrence watched and waited. The beam of light flashed again for a few moments and then nothing but a black curtain. By now, the warden's eyes were accustomed to the night. He could see the shadowy outlines of tree islands and the spidery airboat trails that wound through the vast sawgrass marsh. The Everglades was a dark labyrinth, but overhead the charcoal sky was perforated with silver stars that faintly illuminated the wilderness. Now Lawrence heard the throaty growl of an airboat engine starting. From the sound, it was close, perhaps less than a quarter-mile away.

Once the quarry started his engine, Lawrence started his own and pointed his airboat to the place on the horizon where he'd seen the glimmering light. The brief duration of the light was an indicator that this was no legal hunter come to gig frogs from his airboat. Legal sportsmen would keep their lights on as they prowled the lily pads for big bullfrogs. But a poacher in search of protected alligators or a deer out of season rarely left his light on for more than a second or two.

"They usually had a pretty good idea of where the gator or deer might be found at night," Lawrence said. "A poacher would flick on his light and then move on in the darkness until he was ready to snap it on once more. If there was a deer or gator in the beam, all the warden heard was a bang and then the light vanished. It doesn't take more than a few seconds. It's a game of cat and mouse."

Every few minutes Lawrence cut his engine and listened. As long as he could hear the poacher's engine, it was safe to proceed. The roar of the engine drowned out any other sound in the marsh including that of another airboat. In this manner, Lawrence closed the gap until he could see the spidery outline of the poacher's airboat engine cage drawn sharply against the evening skyline. They were only several hundred yards apart, both engines off, listening and watching for one another. Suddenly the Glades reverberated with the roar of an aircraft engine when the poacher "showered down" at full power. He had seen Lawrence. No doubt of it. The

A Good Night's Work. *Game wardens love catching night hunters illegally shooting deer frozen in the glare of a spotlight. J. K. Davis (left) and Jimmy Lanier seized this small arsenal of weapons and a gutted deer from poachers one productive night in 1956. Lanier was one of the original game wardens hired in 1943 when the agency was created. (J. K. Davis)*

chase was on. Lawrence's boat thundered after the fleeing quarry. Soon they were running at sixty to sixty-five miles per hour with no lights through the shadowy Glades. All that Lawrence could see was the silver wake of his quarry's boat and the reddish glow rippling from the exhaust pipes. He gradually closed the gap until he was only a dozen yards behind the fleeing poacher.

"I had the advantage," Lawrence said. "The poacher had to find the trail and stay in the grass as he picked his way through the marsh. He did all the work for me. If his boat slid through, I knew mine would too. I just hung on his tail and kept the throttle wide open."

The game warden saw that they were nearing the Cypress Trail on the western edge of the Everglades.

"I didn't want to lose him among the cypress trees," Lawrence remembered. "But there was no way to cut him off. And then we were going like hell, weaving in among the trees." The game warden's heart was pounding as fast as the cylinders of his straining aircraft engine.

He slid around one turn; the stern's starboard side smashed into a cypress. The boat shuddered and ricocheted from tree to tree like a steel ball bearing in a pinball machine. Another collision sent Lawrence catapulting head over boots through the air, sailing far ahead of his pilotless craft. Lawrence belly-flopped into the shallow marsh in a few feet of water. Moments later, his rampaging pilotless airboat came thundering right over him.

"There was enough water that the airboat crawled right over me, sort of pushed me down into the muck," Lawrence recalled. "I came up choking and gagging. There was Everglades muck in my mouth, my ears, my nostrils. I couldn't see anything out of my left eye. I thought it had been knocked out, that I was blinded. I could taste blood running into my mouth.

"Then I reached up and felt my left eyeball. It was still there, but I couldn't see a thing. That's when I realized that the boat had struck a glancing blow to my forehead. It had left a deep gash running from the bridge of the nose to the end of the left eyebrow. The skin had been sliced open like a ripe tomato, and the flap of bloody skin fell across the eye like a black curtain. I don't remember any pain at all."

Lawrence spotted the boat, which had foundered in the shallows about forty yards away. The hull was submerged, but the superstructure with the all-important radio was still clear of the water. The injured warden held his slashed-open forehead with one hand and gripped the radio mike in the other. Luckily, he was able to raise somebody, and help was dispatched from a Miami hospital.

The bleeding stopped a few minutes later. Lawrence sat atop the sunken airboat awaiting rescue. It was nearly an hour before he heard the thwap-thwap-thwap of chopper blades slashing the night air. Like some great, brilliantly lit butterfly, the Bell helicopter came to his light like a moth to flame. They lowered a stretcher, and Lawrence clambered into it and was winched up to the open door and pulled inside the cabin. The medics applied a butterfly clamp to the jagged cut as they roared off into the night.

In the hospital emergency room, the doctor used sixty stitches inside and out to close the gaping wound over Lawrence's left eye. The injured warden lay there in his soaking wet uniform stinking of

Everglades muck. He joked with the doctor as the wound was sewn shut. Another warden arrived an hour later to take him home.

This time the poacher escaped. Perhaps the outlaw would not be so lucky the next time he came to the Glades in search of endangered alligators and the hard cash their skins brought on the black market. Wardens like Dick Lawrence were sure to be there prowling the wilderness shadows—vigilant protectors of the vast marsh and its wildlife riches.

Chapter 2:
Men Were Taller Then

You mess with one game warden and the rest of us were going to come lookin' for you. There would be retribution. No doubt of that!

—Game Warden J. O. Brown

It was a different world back in 1950 when J. O. Brown pinned on a badge and became a deputy game warden in the Everglades. Like many of his contemporaries, the twenty-one-year-old rookie warden had walked the other side of the street. He had done some deer poaching and gotten away with it—good credentials for a game warden in those simpler times. J. O. knew the Glades and the outlaws who made their illegal living there. That was enough.

A game warden wasn't even considered a bona fide law enforcement officer. They were empowered only to enforce the game and fish statutes. They bought their own guns and uniforms, worked one-hundred-hour weeks during the hunting season, and earned every dollar of their two hundred-dollars-a-month pay. There was no formalized training, few had college diplomas, some hadn't finished high school, but they all—at least the ones who stayed—had more than a fair portion of grit and determination. That was essential when a game warden, almost always alone, ventured at night into outlaw country.

The quarry was often quite formidable. Everglades outlaws were a tough, unfettered lot who roamed the wild places in search of gator and deer. Most of them would challenge and test any game warden who stood in their way. They were resourceful, skilled

Poachers on the Run. *This 1958 photo apparently shows two Florida game wardens chasing their quarry in an Everglades marsh, although the scene may have been staged. Bob Brantley, a retired agency director, came on board in 1957 and remembers how the wardens had to buy their own guns and uniforms and worked 100-hour weeks during deer season. "They wouldn't even let us have a heater in the car," he says. "They wanted us to keep the window rolled down even in the coldest weather so we could hear gunshots." (Florida Game and Fish Commission)*

hunters, as at home in the Glades as the water moccasins and alligators. Some were a lot more dangerous than the natural predators and had that "go to hell" frontier spirit, which was once commonly found where men made their homes in the wilderness. They were tough, stubborn, and sometimes violent men.

Back when J. O. came on, there were only seven wardens in all of south Florida. Today, there are sixty. The toughest of the old timers was Lt. J. P. Hodgis, who grew up a country boy in Pahokee on the shores of Lake Okeechobee. A lot of Florida boys went by initials in those days. Brown remembers Hodgis as "all man" with nearly black hair, a large head, and piercing blue eyes framed by thick eyebrows. He stood a shade under six feet and carried 175 pounds of muscle on his bones.

"J. P. didn't know what fear was and didn't back down from

anybody," Brown recalled.

One day after coming in from the woods, Hodgis went to a juke joint in Belle Glade, met a pretty girl, and danced with her. Another man didn't like it, picked a fight, and got whipped. J. P. and the girl stayed on and danced through the night. The jealous and enraged rival came back with a 9mm German Lugar and shot J. P. four times in the stomach. Despite his wounds, the game warden staggered toward his attacker, wrestled the gun from his hand, and was going to kill him when he collapsed.

Surgeons took three feet of intestine out of J. P., but he lived thanks to a rugged constitution and an indomitable will. In a few months, he was back patrolling the Glades. Outlaws didn't like J. P. and most feared him, but all respected him.

When J. O. Brown signed on, Hodgis told him: "You all know what the job is. Now go out and do what you have to do." Deputy wardens were unpaid volunteers who worked under the direction of the regular game wardens. Brown took to the life right off and relished matching wits with the renegades who roamed the vast Glades.

The life came naturally to J. O. He had grown up in Dania in the late 1930s and early 1940s. He and his friends would ride their bikes out to the Glades and shoot coots in the canal running along Alligator Alley. J. O. was about twelve when he came home with a croker sack full of coots shot out of season.

"My old man was hard about things like that," J. O. said. "Dad got on the phone and called this old game warden. They worked for the county back then. Well, he came over and gave me a lecture, told me I'd end up in jail if I ever pulled anything like that again. I remember that warden clearly. He only had one arm."

As a young man, J. O. made his living as a cabinetmaker but spent every spare hour running the Glades in his homemade airboat powered by a four-cylinder Chevy car engine. He hunted hogs and deer and gigged frogs at night. Sometimes he poached.

One day he and some friends were out on a swamp buggy and shot a deer out of season. The game wardens were out that day in a little Piper Cub and came to investigate. Brown told his friends to bury the deer carcass and wash their hands of blood in a nearby gator hole.

Just as he thought, the game wardens met them about 11 P.M. as they came out of the Glades. Game Warden J. P. Hodgis and another warden searched their buggy and inspected their clothes and hands for blood stains. The pilot had tipped them off that some poachers were coming out of the Glades.

Hodgis knew they had been up to no good, and they knew he knew. The game warden suggested they start a fire and warm up some coffee so they could talk. They drank coffee and played the game until the wardens let them go around 2 A.M.

"After I hired on as a warden, one of the first things J. P. asked me was where had I hid the deer. Making an ex-poacher a warden wasn't all that unusual back in those days. I ended up hiring a few myself years later. They usually either did good or were problems. No in-betweens. That deer I buried in the Glades was the last illegal deer I ever took."

J. P. used to come by and drink coffee with J. O. and his wife in their Ft. Lauderdale apartment. Brown made five hundred dollars a month as a cabinetmaker but was happiest when out in the swamp or woods. However, when Lieutenant Hodgis asked him to sign on as a full-time game warden, Brown said, "Ain't no damn way! Not enough money. Not with a wife and three kids."

After Hodgis left, J. O.'s wife told him, "If you really want that job, take it. We'll learn to live on the salary." J. O. still had misgivings, but the next time Hodgis paid a visit, he relented. "I guess your wife made the decision for you," J. P. told him.

The Glades was outlaw country back then. The poachers were a rough bunch, most hot-tempered and inclined to fight any game warden who got in their way. They were defiant, hard-muscled men who were handy with gun and knife. A few, Brown recalled, were probably crazy. Those were the ones to fear if you valued your life.

In the years ahead, J. O. came to know the Hall brothers well. Frank and T. J. were professional gator poachers with a contempt for game laws and a preference for the wild and free life back in the most remote corners of the Everglades.

"Frank was tough as a nail but just a normal guy," Brown recalled. "But his brother T. J. was pretty close to crazy. Most people were afraid of him. If you came up to him at the boat landing and asked him how he'd done, he often would snarl back: 'None of your damn business, you son-of-a-bitch!' and then chase you down the levee with a machete in his hand. T. J. would fight men twice his

Everglades Lawmen

Outlaw Country. *This 1950s game warden visits a wilderness hunt camp. Most people he encountered were law-abiding sportsmen. A minority were game law violators. A handful were violent, lawless renegades. (Florida Game and Fish Commission)*

size. Everybody in the Glades was afraid of him."

Brown remembered T. J. as a small man, but strong and wiry and "mean as hell." The game warden arrested him four times and had to fight him each time. That was just the way it was. A game warden had to scrap or he couldn't show his face in the Glades again. This was the frontier code. It didn't allow for fear or weakness.

T. J. sometimes used an old home-built pole boat or Everglades skiff on his forays into the deep wilderness. One night, he and his ten-year-old son—one of thirteen children—poled out of the marsh with a load of gator hides. They loaded their hides into the back of their "skeeter," an old sedan cut down to serve as a make-shift pickup truck. Brown and two brand-new wardens were waiting on the road, sitting in their patrol vehicle with the lights out. Brown recognized the "skeeter" right off as belonging to T. J.

"You boys listen to me and do what I tell you," Brown told his young wardens. "This old boy is bad. Pure bad. You're liable to get hurt if you don't listen."

They flashed their lights, and T. J. came to a stop, but he quickly locked all the doors and refused to come out as ordered. Brown told one of his officers to stand in front of the truck, draw his revolver, and aim at the ground.

"If T. J. starts comin' at you, fire into the ground, and then, if that doesn't stop him, jump clear. Don't fire into the truck. I don't want that little boy gettin' hurt," Brown ordered.

Brown walked up to the driver's side and smashed the window in with the barrel of his revolver. The game warden threw open the door and grabbed T. J., who was fumbling under the seat for a loaded double-barreled shotgun.

The gun and T. J. came flying out of the car and out onto the road. "I wasn't too dainty about it," Brown remembered.

Enraged, T. J. scrambled to his feet, drew out a folding case knife from his back pocket, and charged Brown. One of the young wardens yelled for Brown to get out of the way so he could kill T. J.

Brown shouted, "Don't shoot! Don't shoot!"

The game warden hit the oncoming poacher on the side of the head with his gun barrel, knocking T. J. to the ground. The knife fell from his grasp. All the fight was out of him; it was time to go to jail.

It was 1958 when Brown, a blunt-spoken man with the steady eyes of one who means what he says, told Judge Tompkins in a

Broward County courthouse that he would have to kill T. J. if he came at him again with a gun or a knife. "One day only one of us is going to walk out of that swamp, and I intend it to be me."

The judge turned to T. J. and asked the defendant if he heard what the officer just said.

"I did, Your Honor," T. J. said.

"Well, then," the judge replied. "I'd advise you to be as meek and humble as could be in your dealings with that man. I know him pretty well, and it's easy for me to believe what he's saying."

Norman Padgett was another outlaw Brown scrapped with on many a day and sent to jail on several occasions. The game warden remembers Padgett as being "rough as a cob, mean as hell, and determined to ignore the game and fish laws no matter what."

"One day I told Norman he had two choices," Brown remembered. "He was going to jail one way or another. Either vertical or horizontal. It was his choice. He seemed to calm down then."

It was early on, around 1953, when Lieutenant Hodgis and Brown were driving their airboats down the Miami Canal one night when they encountered Padgett. Hodgis pulled up nose to nose with the outlaw's boat and grabbed hold of the gunnel. Brown cut his engine and drifted in alongside.

"I'm coming aboard, Norman, to search your boat," Brown said.

"No, you're not," Norman replied and picked up the four-pronged, eight-foot-long frog gig from the bottom of the boat.

Brown slapped the spear away with one hand and jumped into the boat. J. P. Hodgis was furious and threatened to whip Norman's ass. But tempers cooled, and after finding nothing, the wardens let Norman go on his way.

Like many wardens, Brown respected Padgett. "There was a lot of man to him," he would say later. "Norman was hard, not a bit of fat on him, and he would scrap with the best of them."

Years later, when Brown was a major based in the Lakeland office, his secretary told him there was a man waiting in the lobby who wanted to talk with him. Major Brown didn't recognize Padgett until he introduced himself, said he had gotten straight with the Lord, and had come to apologize for all the trouble he'd caused the game wardens through the years.

"Hell, I don't hold grudges, so we shook hands and talked about the old days in the Glades," Brown said. "Norman told me if I ever wanted to use one of his airboats just to drop by and pick it up at his house in West Palm Beach. And, you know, he meant it too. He was man enough, all right."

Another game warden, Don Arnold, once told Brown: "The only difference between you and Norman Padgett is that one of you went one direction and the other in the opposite direction. He was an outlaw. You were a game warden. Except for that you were just alike."

Of all the Everglades outlaws, Brown remembers the "Homestead bunch" as the wildest and most dangerous. They were originally saltwater commercial fishermen in Flamingo until Everglades National Park was created and they were evicted. Like a lot of men who live in the back country, they didn't care to be told what to do.

There is a story that some of the Homestead bunch once smashed up a game warden's brand-new Ford patrol vehicle and poured hot tar onto the seats. Word got around who had done it, but there wasn't proof to take them to court.

Well, the story tells how this game warden later on came upon a swamp buggy belonging to the Homestead boys hidden in a clump of willow trees. They say this warden settled the score by emptying his revolver into the buggy's gas tank. This same warden, the story goes, walked up to the Homestead boys a few days later and told them he'd heard about their buggy. He said it sounded like it must have been the same son-of-a-bitch who had smashed his patrol car to pieces.

Brown can't swear to the truth of the story, but it's very possible. Game wardens in those days took care of business, and that some-times meant ignoring the letter of the law.

Both outlaws and wardens played rough. One night in 1954, Game Warden Lubbie Kirkland caught a few boys from Immokalee with a deer out of season and wrote them up. A week or so later, four of them caught him in the woods alone and beat him badly, putting Lubbie in the hospital.

Not long afterwards, the outlaws were at a square dance in Immokalee when some strangers picked a fight with them. After a little shoving and a few hard words, they all stepped outside to settle the matter. The three strangers beat the outlaws bloody with blackjacks and left them battered and bruised. There are some who will tell you that the strangers were off-duty game wardens, but there is no proof of that. It's only a story. The Everglades is home to a lot of stories. Some are true and others are not.

"It might well have happened," Brown admits. "We were like a family back then," he said. "You mess with one of us and the rest of us were going to come lookin' for you. There would be retribution. No doubt of that."

Brown tangled with some of the toughest. A lot of times that meant a scrap. The poacher always went to jail, although Brown admits that sometimes it would be difficult to tell the winner from the loser. And on two occasions, Brown was shot while enforcing the game laws.

The first time was on the Hillsborough Canal in 1955. Brown and Game Warden Charlie Snelgrove were hiding in the underbrush as two suspicious airboats nosed up to the landing. When the boats touched shore, the game wardens came running out of hiding. One of the airboat operators stood up, grabbed a bunch of gator hides, and threw them over the back of the boat. Then he gunned the engine, hoping the prop blast would force the hides underwater.

But the other man came up with a .22 rifle. The wardens never really learned what he intended, whether he was trying to throw the rifle overboard or was set on shooting it out. In any event, the rifle went off. A bullet clipped Brown's finger on his left hand, gouged out a chunk of flesh, and went screaming off into the Glades. The game warden wrapped up his wound in a handkerchief and never did go to the hospital. It was like that in those days.

Another time, around 1957, Brown came up on some good old boys drinking heavily and shooting rats around an old concrete building they used for a camp. It was between Snake Creek and US 27, which was marsh back then. Now it is all developed like so much of what used to be wild country. One of them, an old-timer, was well into his drink and shooting rats with a .38 revolver when Brown came walking around the edge of the building in the dark.

The drunk saw movement in the shadows and said: "There goes one of those SOBs now!" and pulled the trigger.

"Well, the old man got the wrong SOB," Brown recalled. The bullet dug a furrow along his hip and creased the inside of Brown's holster.

"He didn't mean to shoot me," Brown said. "He was just a drunk old man. He said he was sorry and carried on crying and sobbing like drunk people do. It wasn't much to tell, really."

When prisoners escaped into the Glades or other dangerous fugitives fled into the wilderness, Sheriff Quill Lloyd of Broward County always called the game wardens. They knew the country better than anybody, and they could handle even the most dangerous felon.

The night began with hard words exchanged between two men drinking at a black juke joint at the edge of the Glades. One man drew a knife, stabbed another man, and killed him. Then the murderer, still in a rage, went to get a shotgun. He came back into the tavern moments later and killed a second man with a blast of buckshot. Before the gun smoke cleared, the shooter went out the back door and disappeared into the dusky Everglades.

It was a bright, moonlit night as Game Wardens Brown, Bill McClelland, and T. O. Morris, along with two sheriff's deputies, moved in a long ragged line through the dried-up marsh.

Maybe thirty minutes later, about six hundred yards west of the juke joint, Brown's flashlight revealed a black boot in the palmetto bushes. He looked closer and saw another. His light traveled up along the legs and chest of a man and then illuminated his face.

"Don't you even flinch or I'll kill you!" Brown shouted. "Now come up with your hands out where I can see 'em. Move slow and easy."

The man rose up slowly as if he were growing out of the ground like a giant tree. Brown stepped back and realized the fugitive stood six feet, five inches tall and weighed nearly three hundred pounds. The shotgun was nowhere to be seen. Brown told him to turn around and tried to handcuff the hulking suspect. He couldn't. The Smith and Wesson cuffs wouldn't fit around the huge wrists.

"All right, you just walk ahead of me with your hands in the air, and don't try running," Brown said. "If you make a move, I'll shoot you dead."

"Yes, sir," the suspected murderer replied and moved out obediently.

In 1957, two prisoners escaped from the road prison near Belle Glade and headed south into the Glades. Game Wardens Brown, Tom Shirley, and Louis Freeman came driving up towing airboats near Andytown when they saw dozens of patrol cars along the road.

"Never saw so much law in all my life," Brown remembered. "There were highway patrol, convict chasers, sheriff's deputies. They had dogs and an airplane up in the sky.

"Sheriff Lloyd saw us and said he was glad we were there," he said. "One of the convict chasers made some smart remark that they didn't need any help from any game wardens. Sheriff Lloyd told us to ignore the remark and join in the hunt."

Shirley drove the pickup while Brown and Freeman stood in the back scanning both sides of US 27. They stopped several times when they thought they had seen signs along the shoulder. Nothing panned out. Then Brown spotted the matted grass leading into the flooded Glades. Several people had beaten down a path not long before. He pounded on the roof of the truck cab, and Shirley pulled over.

The wardens waded out into the marsh and found the two convicts asleep in a clump of myrtles. They drew their revolvers and told the fugitives to get up slowly and keep their hands where they could see them.

"We took them back to Andytown and walked them up to Sheriff Lloyd," Brown said. 'Is this what you been lookin' for, Sheriff?' Lloyd just laughed."

Brown left the Glades in 1962 and became regional manager in Lakeland. He retired with the rank of lieutenant colonel in 1993. He is one of the old timers, one of the few who remember the Everglades the way it used to be, back when a game warden had to be just as tough as the wilderness outlaws he pursued.

•   •   •

"We pretty well called our own shots in those days," recalls retired Game Warden J. K. Davis, seventy-four, who now runs a chicken farm in north Florida. Those days were from 1953 through 1980, a time of change and challenge for this taciturn and quiet man. Born in Georgia, he grew up in little South Bay on the edge of the Glades in the 1930s.

During World War II, J. K. served in the U.S. Navy as part of an armed guard detachment assigned to civilian merchant ships. The sailors manned the deck guns onboard as a defense against marauding Axis aircraft and submarines. J. K. spent most of four years at sea, served in several ships in both the Atlantic and Pacific Oceans, and visited twenty-nine countries.

After the war, this quiet man worked as a farmer, construction worker, tile layer, and drill operator before Game Warden Ernest Williams talked the young Navy veteran into pinning on a badge.

"Didn't pay nothin', but it sounded like fun so I went along," J. K. said. He was an avid hunter and fishermen, a good tracker, and at home in the Glades.

It was a free outdoor life where a game warden pretty well was his own boss. On the other hand, the days and nights were long, especially during hunting season. Lieutenant Jimmy Lanier, Williams, and J. K. often spent four or five days in the woods or swamp, cooking their meals over campfires and sleeping under the stars.

Old-time game wardens were often legendary figures among the hunters, anglers, and campers in the Glades. One time in the 1950s, Williams learned from an informant that turkey poachers would be working a head in the Big Cypress one night.

"Ernest drove his jeep out there, hid it in a tree island, and picked out a likely spot for turkeys," J. K. said, remembering the story. "Well, it gets dark and pretty soon a pair of headlights come down the road. Several hunters get out of the jeep, load their shotguns, and fan out through the woods.

"Well, one of these old boys from Clewiston sighted a turkey roostin' in a tree and started to draw a bead on it," he said. "Just before he squeezed the trigger, Ernest came up out of the darkness and tapped him on the shoulder. 'Now don't shoot that turkey, son. It's against the law,' he said in a quiet voice."

The boy from Clewiston nearly jumped out of his skin. This game warden had come out of nowhere like some ghost. Somehow, the law had known just where and when he intended to poach wild turkeys. It was enough to make a man believe game wardens could read minds and tell the future.

There was another game warden whose marksmanship with a Winchester .30-30 lever-action rifle was talked about for many years by wardens and outlaws alike. J. K. can't remember the man's name anymore, but this game warden won recognition during an encounter with outlaw Norman Padgett, who had a well-known reputation for poaching gators and scrapping with game wardens.

"One night several of our wardens spotted Norman Padgett out in his airboat and put the light on him," J. K. said. "There was Norman wearing a lantern on his head similar to what coal miners wear. Well, there were words exchanged, and Norman pulled out a revolver. That's the story I heard.

"Norman was wavin' his gun around, cussin' and makin' threats when this one game warden decided he had just about had enough," J. K. said. "He aimed that thirty-thirty and shot the light right off Norman's head. That quieted Norman down considerable."

The old game wardens taught J. K. Davis a valuable lesson. "If the man you arrest is nice, you be nice. If he turns mean, you be meaner." For nearly three decades in the Everglades, the soft-spoken game warden from South Bay lived by that motto.

Arresting a gator poacher was a feather in your cap, but the trick was to nail the middleman. In the late 1950s, Davis learned from several sources that the brother of a county sheriff was running a big operation out of a little farmhouse. Evidently, his kinship with the local law gave him a feeling of security. He didn't know that J. K. and Lieutenant Jimmy Jordan didn't care who his brother was. They were going to bust 'im.

J. K. wore some old U.S. Army surplus pants and a well-worn shirt on the day he drove up to the hide buyer's farmhouse. He walked up to the porch, knocked on the door, and was greeted by a large, suspicious man who asked what he wanted.

"Just to talk a little," J. K. said. "Maybe you and I can do some business?"

They went into the house, and J. K. told his story. He was a dragline operator lookin' for a little extra cash money and had heard the big man bought alligators with no questions asked.

"The man was real leery and cautious," J. K. said. "He looked me straight in the eye and said, 'Well I don't buy gator hides from game wardens, if that's what you're askin.' "

J. K. tried to look innocent and surprised that the man would make such an outlandish accusation. "Lord, I hope I'm not any game warden," he replied. "Mercy, no."

This was no game. The hide buyer had a reputation for violence and had reportedly shot a cab driver a few years back in Ft. Myers. So J. K. wasn't too surprised when the suspect walked over to a table and picked up a revolver. There were no threats. He just held the revolver pointing at the floor, but the message was blunt and clear.

"Hey, I didn't come here lookin' for trouble, Mister," J. K. said. "If you don't trust me, I'll get out of your hair right now. There's no reason to go threatenin' people with a gun."

The undercover warden did some fast talking, and gradually the hide buyer became convinced. He set down the revolver and walked out with J. K. to his jeep where he had several gator hides. At first the buyer said he didn't pay cash. He would write out a check and mail it to him. J. K. changed his tune and played the tough guy, telling the man he knew where he lived and would get his money one way or the other. The buyer finally just handed J. K. the check, and they parted friends. J. K. promised he would return with more hides soon.

"We wanted him to make two buys so we could establish that there was a pattern," J. K. said. "That would be important in court if he claimed this was the only time he'd ever bought gator hides."

A few weeks later, Davis and another young game warden, both in work clothes, drove up to the buyer's house in a jeep loaded down with nine hides for sale. Not far away, Lt. Jimmy Jordan and several other wardens waited in concealment. They were going in like the cavalry in exactly fifteen minutes, which should give the undercover officers time to make the sale.

"I had a smoke grenade in the jeep," J. K. adds. "If we ran into trouble and needed help immediately, I was to ignite the grenade. Jimmy and the others would come runnin' as soon as they saw the smoke."

The other undercover game warden was young and headstrong, "a big, strong man who could throw people around if it came to that." Lieutenant Jordan told the youngster to let Davis do the talking and follow the older warden's lead.

The two wardens drove up to the gate, dismounted, and walked up to the main house. The hide buyer came to the door and suggested they walk over to an outbuilding where he had his business. Once they entered, they saw an unskinned, ten-foot gator carcass on a long table. On the floor were several big bags bulging with skins. This was a big operation. Shutting it down would make a real impact on poaching in the Everglades.

Unfortunately, the younger warden got excited and forgot the script they had agreed upon. He reached into his jeans, pulled out his badge, and blurted: "I'm a game warden, and you're under arrest!"

"Where did you get that?" the astonished hide buyer replied, staring at the badge.

"Don't worry, it's for real," the youngster said.

"That's when things started to get serious," J. K. recalled. The hide buyer was angry, and the look in his eyes showed fight.

"Now don't make it any worse than it already is," J. K. said, trying to defuse the tense confrontation. "Now let's go outside."

The buyer suddenly let out a yell, and another man burst into the room. "What the hell's goin' on, Dad?" he yelled. The son was as big as or bigger than the father. They were both "bowing up," as the country boys say. A fight looked likely.

"They arrestin' me," the hide buyer shouted to his son.

The son disappeared around the corner and came back in a few seconds, brandishing a pump shotgun. J. K. grabbed the father. They wrestled around the room while the son danced around trying to get a clear shot at the undercover warden. J. K. maneuvered his opponent so that his bulk would shield him from the shotgun blast. It was total chaos. The men slammed into each other. J. K.'s young partner shouted for the son to drop the gun. J. K. shoved the hide buyer against the son, who lowered the shotgun barrel long enough for the other warden to grab it. J. K.'s partner and the son fell to the ground, grappling for the shotgun between them.

"It was a real brawl," J. K. said. "I reached down with one hand into my pants, feelin' for the small pistol I was carrying. Somebody was going to get hurt or killed if the fight kept goin'."

Somehow J. K. broke loose of the father and jumped on the son, who was on top of the other warden. J. K. shoved the gun barrel into the son's back.

"Turn loose of that shotgun or you're a dead man!" J. K. shouted.

The man continued to battle the other warden for the shotgun, but the father realized his boy was in real danger. He screamed, "He's got a gun in your back, son. Turn that shotgun loose or he's going to shoot you for sure."

"Damn right," J. K. added. "I'm serious and my patience is about to run out."

The son slowly got off the other warden, and the fight was over. In a few minutes, Jordan and the other wardens arrived, and they later took the two suspects off to county jail. They had seized sixty-eight alligator hides in the little outbuilding.

Being the brother of the sheriff didn't count for as much as some might have thought. The suspects negotiated a plea, paid a big fine, and were sentenced to long probations.

"One of the big outdoor magazines got hold of the story somehow and ran the whole report," J. K. said. "I think it was *Field and Stream,* but I don't remember for sure."

The quiet game warden was establishing a reputation as someone who was all business and didn't back down. He roamed the Glades at night like a phantom, searching out the deer and alligator poachers even in the deepest and most remote corners of the Everglades. Old timers warned him about Norman Padgett. The incorrigible gator poacher was considered a violent and dangerous man who had no respect for the game laws or the men who enforced them.

Padgett was known to test a game warden just to see if he could get him to back down. Some did, but not J. K. The old warden remembers hiding in the underbrush one night at a boat landing waiting for Padgett to come ashore. The poacher cut his engine and drifted close to shore. He drew out his pistol and started firing randomly into the darkness.

"Norman was just trying to intimidate me," J. K. said. "I just stayed where I was, and let him waste his ammunition. Later I told him he'd better make that first shot count, and remember that he couldn't see me, but I could see him."

J. K. doesn't hold any grudges against Norman or any of the other outlaws he arrested. "If I hadn't been in law enforcement, Norman and I could probably have been friends. Those outlaws weren't mean all the time. You could be friends with them some of the time."

Padgett is not so forgiving. To this day, Norman is bitter, convinced that Game Warden J. K. Davis deliberately shot his half-brother with a .357 Magnum without just provocation.

J. K. remembers it differently. It was back in the 1960s, and Norman's half-brother, Ray Watson, was following the family's outlaw tradition. One of his favorite hobbies was poaching gators in the Loxahatchee National Wildlife Refuge, one hundred thousand acres of Everglades that occupy a big chunk of western Palm Beach County.

There were big gators in the refuge, and Ray Watson was one of those who came secretly in the night in search of a little fun and easy money. No damned game warden was going to keep him from sneaking into the refuge any time he damn well pleased. Ray Watson and one of his brothers were putting a johnboat in the canal that encircles the refuge around 9:00 one night when Game Wardens J. K. Davis and Jim Cook caught them. Both men ran and hid in the thick undergrowth, but the wardens rousted them out a few minutes later. One outlaw had a .22 pistol.

J. K. told the two brothers that he was taking them to jail for being in the refuge after hours and for carrying a gun within the refuge. That wasn't as good as catching them killing alligators, but it would have to do.

The Watson boys seemed pretty cooperative, so Warden J. K. Davis told Ray to drive his own pickup to county jail. J. K. rode behind the cab just to make sure the driver didn't get lost on the way. It looked like the quick-tempered Watson was going to stay cool for once. When they got to West Palm Beach, Watson pulled into an A&W root beer stand, and asked if he could use the pay phone. J. K. agreed and waited while the suspect made his call. Everything was going smoothly until J. K. told Watson he would ride up front with him the rest of the way to jail.

"No son-of-a-bitch game warden is riding in my truck," Watson shouted, locked the door, and quickly began rolling up the driver's side window.

J. K. thrust his arm through the gap and tried to unlock the door. The suspect grabbed his arm and twisted it. The game warden had to back off. All the while, according to Davis, Watson ranted and raved.

"You're already under arrest, Ray," J. K. shouted. "Now roll the damn window down!"

The poacher kept up his litany of oaths. It was a standoff, but then J. K. drew out his Colt .357 Magnum.

"I hit the window vent with the barrel hard, but it didn't break," J. K. said. "It appeared to me that Watson was getting ready to grab the gun once the window broke. He was just crazy."

The game warden hit the vent again, but the glass only cracked. A third blow shattered the vent. J. K.'s revolver went off with a thunderous report. The bullet went completely through Watson's forearm and lodged in his metal belt buckle. The only reason the bullet didn't penetrate was that J. K. had loaded the cylinder with wad-cutters that carried a relatively small powder charge.

Warden Cook had pulled up into the drive-in parking lot in the middle of the altercation and witnessed it all. Now he called for an ambulance. Watson was bleeding badly and still cussing for all he was worth.

J. K. regrets what happened that night. He insists it was an accident. "I was a pretty fair shot," J. K. points out. "By that I mean I usually hit what I was aiming at. If I wanted to deliberately shoot Ray Watson, I wouldn't have aimed at his arm."

The court found Warden J. K. Davis liable for Ray Watson's injuries and ordered him to pay the defendant thirteen thousand dollars. The Florida state legislature passed a bill authorizing payment of the judgment so J. K. never had to spend a dime of his own money. However, the ill-feelings born that night in the A&W parking lot have festered for nearly three decades. Norman Padgett is convinced J. K. Davis deliberately shot his half-brother for nothing more serious than refusing to roll down a car window.

During his years in the Everglades, J. K. perfected and refined his considerable tracking skill. That ability to read signs allowed a posse to capture an escaped felon who had brutally beaten and assaulted a woman in her South Bay home. That woman was J. K.'s wife.

It was a routine day in 1972. J. K. was riding in his patrol vehicle to Ft. Lauderdale to file some cases with the state's attorney's office. About halfway there, radio dispatch sent him a message to stop and call the Everglades Regional Office in West Palm Beach. Something was up. Davis knew there was a reason radio dispatch hadn't just given him the message over the air. He pulled over and called from a pay phone.

The dispatcher on the end of the line told him not to get upset. "Your wife is all right now, but she's in the hospital in Belle Glade. She's been assaulted and is bruised up pretty bad."

J. K. leaped into his patrol vehicle, turned on the blue light, and headed north. When he ran into his wife's hospital room, he was aghast. Her pretty features were black and blue with contusions, her nose had been broken, and her eyes were swollen shut.

She managed to tell the story. After J. K. had left for work, she had dropped her mother off and returned home. She entered the bedroom and was startled by the presence of a large man in a light blue shirt and white pants. There was real fear in her heart, but she tried to brazen her way through.

Everglades Lawmen

"What you doin' in my house, boy?" she demanded, trying not to tremble or show fear. "You get out! You get out right this instant!"

The man started coming toward her with a terrible look in his eyes. She turned and ran, but he caught her in the kitchen and threw her to the floor. He was big and powerful with sledge-hammer fists. He struck her in the face. Again and again, he pounded that rock-hard fist into the woman's face, shattering the delicate facial bones like fragile porcelain. Blood spattered and rained on the floor, the walls, and even the ceiling.

When the woman was able to get up, she staggered to the door and ran to a shop where they sold pumps. The man in the store, a friend she saw nearly every day, didn't even recognize J. K.'s pretty wife. Her face had been beaten into a bloody mush.

That was the story she told her husband. J. K. was numb as he heard the words. A man's worst nightmare had entered his home and savaged a gentle woman who had never hurt a soul. She was going in and out of consciousness due to the painkillers and didn't say much more.

Assured by the doctors that his wife would live, J. K. left the hospital and drove to South Bay. Perhaps he could help with the search that was already under way. When he arrived, the game warden entered his home, now crowded with sheriff's deputies and plainclothes detectives. He saw with his own eyes the terrible splashes of blood in the kitchen, graphic and obscene testimony to his wife's recent ordeal. J. K. also informed the detective that a small .22 pistol was missing from the bedroom.

One of the detectives told him that they had followed the attacker's tracks along the edge of a nearby sugarcane field to where they ended near a rubber tire print on the pavement. "We think somebody stopped and gave him a ride," the detective explained.

Despite his personal anguish, Warden Davis kept his mind clear and insisted he be allowed to join the search. "Let's go take a look at that tire track," he told the detective.

They took him to the place where the tracks ended. J. K. looked at the sign with the eyes of a game warden skilled and practiced in the art of trailing wild animals and men through the Everglades. There had been a heavy dew early that morning. He could tell that the tire track had been made long before the footprints in the dirt. He walked slowly up and down both sides of the road, staring intently, hoping to pick up the fugitive's trail.

A few minutes later, he saw the faint outline of a boot print in the grass. J. K. waved to a nearby sheriff's deputy and highway patrolman to follow him. The trail led through the huge cane field and out onto another road. The other officers noted that the road led back into South Bay and assumed that was where the attacker had fled.

But the game warden kept up his slow and meticulous search, looking for the telltale sign that would show him the way to his wife's attacker. He walked alongside a narrow, six-foot-wide canal and looked intently on the other side. J. K.'s keen eyesight detected a small patch of grass mashed down flat. The hunt resumed. J. K. took a running start and jumped the canal. He studied the mashed grass, saw that it was fresh sign, and then picked up the fugitive's trail a few feet into the cane field.

"Somebody's been over here!" he yelled to the other officers. "This here is fresh sign!"

The three officers fanned out as they moved through the sugar-cane. J. K. took out his revolver and cocked it. There was no point in taking any chances. The fugitive might rise up out of the cane any moment with a gun in his hand. A man had to be ready.

They moved slowly. Take a step or two and look. Take another step and look again. Then J. K. saw a patch of blue in the sugarcane a few feet away. He knew instantly that he'd found the man who had beaten his wife almost to death a few hours before. He also knew that he would shoot the man dead if he bolted from his hiding place.

"Come out of there right now!" J. K. yelled, his revolver aimed at the patch of blue. The attacker rose up out of the sugarcane and J. K looked the man in the eyes. His finger tensed on the trigger.

The man in the blue shirt didn't have a gun. He was standing there defenseless in the gunsights of his victim's husband. But J. K. eased off on his trigger finger and called the other officers over.

"You want to beat on me for a while?" J. K. asked the big man.

"I would probably have worked him over good if the others hadn't come up then. One of them said, 'It's okay now. We'll take care of him, J. K.,' " he recounts.

They searched the suspect and handcuffed his hands behind his back. They marched him through the cane fields until they came to the canal. The handcuffed prisoner fell into the water, flailing about, swallowing a good bit of water, and no doubt wondering if the officers were ever going to fish him out.

They did, but not immediately. Not right off. They waited a bit so he could think about things for a while.

In time, J. K.'s wife's wounds healed over, although the incident left invisible psychological scars. Her attacker, who had been out of prison just three days after serving a sentence for burglary, was given another five years, a small price for the suffering and anguish he had inflicted on two people he didn't even know. The author asked J. K. if he'd come close to killing his wife's assailant out there in that cane field.

"It wouldn't have taken much," was his clipped reply. "No, it wouldn't have taken much at all."

Chapter 3:
Echoes of Gunfire

He just came up drinking a fifth of Jim Beam with one
hand and shooting the revolver with the other.
                              —Game Warden Bruce Lawless

O n either side of the road, the Glades marsh glimmered in
midday. The orange sun and white clouds reflected like a
painting in the burnished mirror of the "River of Grass," as
Marjory Stoneman Douglas described it in her famous 1947 book on
the Everglades. Florida Game Warden Bruce Lawless was driving his
patrol vehicle down US 27 through the northern Everglades west of
Ft. Lauderdale. The date was November 20, 1984. Opening day of
deer season was only a few days off.

This remnant of frontier wilderness was his beat. For more than
a decade, Lawless had studied the Glades and those who came there
to hunt, fish, camp, and boat. Lawless loved the Glades and loved
the life. Every day was different and every week brought new adventure. He patrolled for gator and deer poachers, enforced the game
and fish laws, rescued stranded boaters, and stepped in to enforce
the peace when men's passions turned violent.

This was a strange place for a kid from the streets of north
Philadelphia, where Lawless had grown up in Germantown, the
scene of an American defeat during the Revolutionary War and now
a blue-collar community. In the 1950s, Bruce played stickball in the
streets and hung out with guys in the neighborhood pool halls.
Bruce's father, an infantryman who had stormed ashore at
Normandy during the D-Day invasion of Nazi-held France, drove
one of the city's trolley cars. It was a pleasant and uneventful life,

far removed from the alligators and panthers of the Everglades wilderness.

Bruce probably would have stayed in the city and become a cop like one of his uncles, if not for a chance encounter with Karl Robinson in a local pool hall. They shot a game, and the older man told fifteen-year-old Bruce about his passion for fly-fishing. The boy was intrigued. A friendship and lifelong hobby began there in the cool, dark pool hall. In the years ahead, Karl taught the boy the ancient art of fly-fishing in lakes all over New Jersey. "Best damned fly-fishermen I ever knew," Bruce remembers. Bruce became a member of the Boy's Club, which sponsored fishing trips. He loved being outdoors with a fishing pole in his hand, enjoyed the feel and the smell of the wild places or at least what still passed for wild in those urbanized surroundings.

When his family moved to Ft. Lauderdale in the 1970s, Bruce came to visit and ended up as a mate on a charter fishing boat. He sailed south to the Keys and west to the Bahamas in pursuit of sailfish, marlin, dolphin, and other big game fish. A few years later he learned that the Florida Game and Fresh Water Fish Commission was hiring new game wardens. He applied and was accepted. His life would change dramatically.

In July 1973, the twenty-six-year-old Philly kid graduated from the GFC Wildlife Officer Academy in Tallahassee and was assigned to Broward County and the northern Everglades. Now the kid who played stickball and shot pool in Philly patrolled the vast wilderness in pursuit of gator poachers, deer poachers, and fugitives from justice. He relished the outdoor life and enjoyed his daily contacts with the hunters, fishermen, froggers, and campers. It was, by and large, a quiet and serene existence with a great deal of personal freedom.

Sometimes it was easy to forget how violence could erupt with the speed, shock, and deadliness of a lightning strike in the marsh. Passion could turn reasonable men into dangerous predators. On one occasion, a young man and his girlfriend had a bitter fight on the dock at the Everglades Sawgrass Fish Camp. The enraged man pointed a .30-30 Winchester at the girl. He threatened to kill her just when Warden Lawless walked out onto the wooden dock.

"Throw the gun down! Right now!" Lawless ordered, holding the man in the sights of his .357 Magnum revolver. After a moment's hesitation, the boy carefully laid the rifle down. A tragedy was averted, both for the man with the rifle and the girl he was threatening. But incidents like that were rare. The Glades was usually quiet and peaceful, the silence and serenity only broken by the sound of crickets, frogs, and the occasional bellow of a bull gator. But Lawless was to see a day when the marsh rang with deadly gunfire.

Lawless pulled off the highway and drove into a Florida Division of Forestry facility to pick up a swamp track. Hunting season opened in two days, and he was going to tow the vehicle on a trailer to the S-140 Pump Station where they would position it for opening day.

"That was standard procedure," he said. "That way we wouldn't waste time on opening day morning. The track was ready to go. We would just head out there in the predawn, and it would already be in place. We could just mount our vehicle and start our patrol."

A track or airboat was a necessity, both for sportsmen and the game wardens. The tracks were ungainly, home-built affairs that ran on steel treads, not unlike the Sherman tanks that had gone ashore with Bruce's father at Normandy. The track's truck engine was mounted almost eight feet up from the wheels and the undercarriage, allowing the vehicle to easily traverse even the deepest portions of the marsh. The wardens perched on an elevated steel platform that gave them an excellent view of the surrounding sawgrass.

Normally, Bruce would have hooked the track trailer to a pickup truck they kept nearby, but not today. One of the pickup's tires was flat, and Lawless didn't want to bother fixing it that day. He would tow the track and trailer with his Dodge Ram Charger. It was a decision that might have saved his life. There was no radio in the pickup; there was one in his patrol vehicle. A long time later, he commented, "Maybe God was with me that day. Maybe I had an angel in my pocket."

But he didn't know the implications of the decision when he drove the track up onto the trailer and secured it with chains. A few minutes later, he pulled out of the Forestry parking area bound for the S-140 Pump Station some twenty miles away.

Twenty minutes later, Lawless drove up the levee road to the pump station facility, a huge building maintained and manned by the South Florida Water Management District to control water level and flow in the northern Glades. The station itself was a multistoried building that loomed high above the surrounding marsh and the long straight canals that crisscrossed the wilderness. The entrance road was blocked by a late-model white sedan with a man sitting behind the steering wheel.

Lawless stopped and left his vehicle. He walked up to the gray-haired, slightly bald man in the car. The man was drunk and had been sitting in his car for some time with a whiskey bottle and a .22 revolver on the seat behind him. For years he had suffered unremitting headaches resulting from an industrial accident in 1977. Later, his wife would tell the Grand Jury that her husband had left the house that day in a dark and suicidal mood.

But, at this point, Lawless was unaware and unconcerned.

"I said 'Sir, please pull your car over to the side so I can get around,' " Lawless said. "He didn't speak. He just looked at me. It was a strange look. The man never really acknowledged my presence. Just stared at me hard."

The driver pulled up a few feet, but there still wasn't room for Lawless to pass with the huge track trailer.

The game warden dismounted and approached the sedan once again. "Pull over like I asked," Lawless said. "I've got to get this trailer into the pump station parking area."

The man, dressed in a white T-shirt and brown slacks, only cursed and stared back with that strange look.

"Sir, look, I don't want any problems from you today," Lawless said. The game warden couldn't smell the booze or see the gun. "Just pull your vehicle over like I said."

Lawless turned his back and returned to his vehicle. This time the man pulled over and Bruce passed him on his way to the L-28 Levee where he would leave the track.

When he dismounted, he saw that the white car had followed him, but he didn't pay too much attention. The man probably was just pulling into the lot so he could turn around and leave.

Lawless was standing beside the trailer, undoing the chains that secured the huge track. The man in the white car pulled to within twenty-five yards and parked. The game warden glanced over and then turned his back to finish unsecuring the track from its carrier.

"The first shot went right past my ear," Lawless said. "It was a singing, whistling sound. It was the sound of a bullet. Once you hear it, you know what it is. Nobody has to tell you."

Lawless spun around. The man was still sitting behind the wheel with the car pointed towards the game warden. There was no gun in sight.

"I could see his face as plain as day," Lawless said. "He didn't say anything. There was just that strange stare again." Lawless thought the man had been the shooter but wasn't absolutely sure. The officer sprinted around the trailer, using it as cover, and ran to his patrol vehicle.

Lawless grabbed his twelve-gauge pump shotgun from its rack inside the vehicle and then unhooked his radio mike. The long extension cord allowed him to lie on the ground and talk. He could see the white vehicle beyond the track and would see the possible assailant's feet if he got out of the car to ambush him.

"Shots fired at the S-140 Pump Station," Lawless told the radio dispatcher. "Send me backup now! I'm taking cover!"

Strange, disturbing thoughts went through his mind. Would he live to see another day? Would he ever speak with his wife and kid? Would he ever see his parents again? Despite those concerns, he remained calm and steady. It was a dangerous situation, but he was determined to act cool, use good judgment, and carefully plan his moves.

He moved toward the front of the truck, crouching with the shotgun at the ready. There was still uncertainty in his mind. The shot could have been fired by plinkers killing snakes or birds a mile away down the levee. It was unlikely but still possible. "The last thing I wanted to do was kill an innocent man," Lawless later recalled.

He peered around the bumper. Lawless could see the probable shooter sitting behind the driver's wheel facing him.

"Get out of the vehicle, and put your hands in the air! You are under arrest!" Lawless shouted and drew a bead on the suspect. He was confident that the .00 Buck would shatter the windshield and kill the man instantly.

The man in the white T-shirt was silent. He just stared for a few moments, then stuck a black revolver out the window with his left hand. Lawless saw the flash from the barrel and an instant later heard the bullet scream nearby.

Three workers from the pump station were loitering outside in the parking area behind the shooter, watching the confrontation like some action movie. If Lawless returned fire, he might hit one of the bystanders. There were also several fishermen in a boat out in the marsh who could become casualties if the game warden over-shot his target.

"Go inside! He has a gun!" Lawless screamed at the onlookers. A minute or two passed before the men finally turned away and ran back to the pump station building.

The man in the car fired again. Lawless was still reluctant to shoot because of the fishermen, but then their boat motored from his direct line of sight. The game warden now had a clear field of fire. Lawless fired five shotgun blasts at the car's front windshield. The buckshot ricocheted off the window and whistled off into the sky. Lawless was stunned. Apparently, because he was shooting at an angle from a kneeling position, the buck shot—the size of .38 caliber bullets—couldn't penetrate the glass. Most of the pellets carved furrows through the glass, but that was all.

Except for the final shotgun blast. The man slumped over onto the seat, sinking from sight.

Was the gunman dead or just wounded? Lawless didn't know for sure. He reloaded his shotgun and returned to the radio mike, keeping the gunman's vehicle in sight at all times.

"I'm 10-4, but I think he's 10-7," Lawless told the dispatcher. In plain language: "I'm alive. The shooter's probably dead."

Lawless returned to the front of the patrol vehicle and peered around once more.

"I was startled to see the man appear again. He just came up drinking a fifth of Jim Beam whiskey in one hand and shooting the revolver with the other. To my utter amazement, the man appeared unhurt.

"At that point, I unholstered my own revolver and took aim. I shot once," Lawless said. "The man sagged back against the seat and then slumped over the wheel. He was somewhat heavyset and the wheel kept him from falling over."

Lawless kept behind cover. The man had come up shooting once before. It could happen again. There was no sense taking a chance. That's when Lawless turned and saw other officers emerge from the pump station building and run down a steel catwalk. Lt. John West, Lt. Charlie Dennis, and Sgt. Jimmy Sistrunk, all fellow game wardens, were coming to his aid, along with a sheriff's deputy.

"I was so relieved to see them," Lawless said. "I started to feel pretty good at that point. I was alive and unhurt and reinforcements were here."

Lawless heard his rescuers discussing their assault tactics. They were going to split up into two groups and rush the car. Concerned that he might be caught in a crossfire, Lawless scurried down the

On Target. *Sgt. Bruce Lawless knows from personal experience that skill with firearms can mean the difference between life and death for an Everglades game warden. (Jim Huffstodt)*

levee, keeping his patrol vehicle between him and the shooter.

He ran and then doubled back to join the other game wardens. West and Sistrunk came up on the passenger side; Dennis and the deputy rushed the driver's side. Lawless was right behind them.

Dennis flung open the car door and grabbed the shooter around the chest in a bear hug. "I was ready to tear his head off if he moved," Dennis later said. He is a big, powerful man who teaches hand-to-hand combat tactics to the other game wardens. It was not just talk.

At the instant Dennis opened the door, Lawless saw the gun still in the shooter's hand. He lunged by Dennis and stripped the gun away in one quick motion.

"I got the gun, Charlie," he said to Dennis.

"Where did you come from?" Dennis replied in surprise.

"What? You think you guys risk your lives to save me, and I won't be there to back you up?" Lawless replied.

The shooter was dying. He had been hit the first time with one buckshot pellet in the chest. The revolver bullet also hit him in the heart area. The gunman was bleeding, barely breathing and gurgling deep in his throat.

"The man was in the process of dying," Lawless said. "But he had one round in the gun's cylinder. It's possible he might have got that last shot off. It only takes a second, and then it would have been all over for Charlie."

• • •

Oscar Pablo Duran was a dangerous man who knew many ways to kill. He'd been trained by the best—the American CIA. Hidden within his beat-up Chevy station wagon was a small arsenal of guns and ammunition. There was a Walther P-38 9mm automatic in a secret compartment along with fourteen loaded clips. A .30-.06 automatic rifle was concealed under the front seat. Two other rifles and hundreds of rounds of ammunition completed the rolling arsenal. Duran was also carrying a concealed .22 Magnum revolver on his person.

The Cuban-American from Hialeah had been a lieutenant in Alpha 66, the fanatic anti-Castro commando unit that launched repeated rains on the Communist-held island during the 1960s. Duran was a man fascinated with guns and violence. The slightest incident could snap his hair-trigger temper. Most of the Alpha-66 commandos trained in the Everglades wilderness and knew the country well.

Darkness had come to the Everglades on the evening of August 22, 1972. Duran's battered 1956 Chevy crunched gravel as it rolled along the L-5 Levee road. The occupants had killed a deer illegally at night and were hoping to slip out without encountering suspicious game wardens. Duran rode in the front passenger seat, a friend was driving, and a teenage boy was in the backseat. On the floor of the backseat they had hidden several freshly butchered deer hams rolled inside some carpet cushion.

The night suddenly lit up with flashing blue lights directly ahead. They had driven right into the hands of the law. Game Warden Conley Campbell got out of his patrol car and walked with his flashlight in one hand toward the station wagon. He was accompanied by his brother-in-law, an unarmed civilian in plain clothes who had come along to see what a game warden's life was like. Within minutes the lives of five people would be changed forever.

Friends called the two-hundred-pound, six-foot-one-inch-tall Campbell "Big Al." This easygoing Florida boy had pinned on his badge three years before. The game warden's life was a natural one for a man who had grown up fishing and hunting in Florida. The

Campbells were old Florida. His grandfather and a number of uncles had been market hunters long ago. Campbell could trace his pioneer ancestors back to Christmas, Florida, where they settled in 1828.

As in most law enforcement jobs, a game warden's days were often routine, even monotonous. There had been some excitement on occasion—high-speed airboat chases after deer poachers and the like—but Campbell had never encountered anybody like Lt. Juan Oscar Duran.

As Campbell and his brother-in-law, Clayton Wilkes of Miami, walked toward the station wagon, Duran opened the door and got out.

"How you doin'?" Campbell asked.

"Fine."

"What you doin' out in the Glades this time of night?"

"Fishing."

"Did you have any luck?" Campbell asked.

"Hadn't caught a thing," was the answer.

That was a little peculiar, Campbell thought to himself. Even the most inept fisherman should come away with at least a few fish from the bass-rich marsh. The game warden got a little leery and guessed that deer, not bass, had brought these two men and the boy into the Glades that night.

"Can I look in your vehicle?" Campbell asked.

"Yes."

Campbell walked to the rear of the Chevy station wagon. After Duran pulled down the tailgate, Campbell shined his light into the interior. The inside was cluttered with cushions, groceries, several fishing rods, and assorted junk. The game warden took special care to inspect the spare tire wheel well, a favorite hiding place for illegal deer meat. He found nothing.

"Have any guns in there?" Campbell asked.

"No," replied Duran, a twenty-six-year-old, out-of-work carpet-layer. Campbell thought the man looked hard and rough in the glare of the flashlight. But he didn't know this dark and brooding stranger had murder in his heart.

Duran was closing up the back gate of the station wagon as Campbell walked toward the front of the car. The warden shined his light into the backseat where a fifteen-year-old boy sat.

"That boy looked scared to death when I shined the light on him," Campbell said. "He was almost shaking. He was that scared."

Everglades Lawmen

At that point, Campbell directed his light on the car floor where he could see deer hair protruding from a rolled-up section of carpet padding. He had himself a deer poacher.

Campbell asked the man behind the wheel to step out.

"I don't speak English," was the reply.

Campbell turned to ask Duran to interpret and saw the Alpha 66 commando pull his revolver and drop into a combat shooting stance, just like he'd been taught by the CIA.

"He didn't say a thing, just started shooting. Pow! Pow! Pow! One shot after another. Just that quick!" Campbell said.

The muzzle of Duran's gun spouted yellow flame in the dark, "like old-fashioned camera flash bulbs exploding." Campbell screamed in pain as multiple bullets pierced his body. He was trying to get low and slide his Colt .357 Magnum revolver from its cross-draw holster.

"Each time a bullet hit me, it was like getting hit with a baseball bat," Campbell said. "It hurt. I'm tellin' ya'."

One bullet passed through his right forearm. Another hit him in his right upper arm, the hollow point fragmenting into hundreds of pieces. Three other slugs hit him in the right side. The most dangerous wound was low in his stomach just above his gunbelt.

Campbell was now on his back on the road. He drew his revolver and emptied the six-shot cylinder as fast as he could. When the hammer snapped down on an empty cylinder, he rolled off the dike and tumbled about ten feet down the sloping bank into the marsh.

He knelt in the water, shucking his empties, and fumbling for his "bullet-keepers" for a quick reload. He jammed four cartridges into the cylinder, but his trembling hands dropped the others in the marsh. His right side was numb as if shot full of novocaine.

Once loaded, the dangerously wounded game warden pointed the gun toward the top of the dike. Perhaps the gunman would come to finish him off. If he did, Campbell would have the shooter silhouetted at the top of the dike against the lighter evening sky. Campbell cocked his piece and waited.

Then he heard Duran moan and say: "Let's go!" Perhaps he'd been hit too?

The car moved slowly down the levee road. It was about a hundred yards away when Campbell scrambled out of the marsh and started shooting. He emptied one cylinder, reloaded, and then emptied another cylinder. One shot burst a tire. Campbell felt sure other bullets had struck home. The vehicle speeded up and disappeared into the night.

"Adrenaline and just plain bein' mad kept me goin' that night," Campbell said.

A few moments later, his brother-in-law climbed out of the marsh where he too had fled.

"You hit?" Campbell asked.

"Yeah, in the hand."

The game warden examined Clayton's hand in the beam of his patrol car headlights. It was only bullet crease from a slug that had gone completely through Campbell's body.

"You hit too?" his brother-in-law asked.

"Yeah, all over," Campbell answered. (Later he described it as "one big numbness." Investigators at the shooting scene the next morning would find a huge blood pool on the road that looked as if somebody had shot a deer there with a high-powered rifle.) Ignoring his five bullet wounds, Campbell got on his car radio. He prayed another warden was out and listening.

In those days the radio dispatch center was manned only during working hours (8 A.M.–5 P.M.), and the primitive system was unable to raise other law enforcement agencies. If you were out in the woods or swamp without any other wardens nearby, you were on your own.

But this night, Campbell heard the reassuring voice of Warden David Albury who was at a ranch about twelve miles distant. Campbell told him he'd been shot and gave a description of the shooter and the car. They agreed to meet at the Terrytown truck stop on US 27.

Albury had been talking with a ranch security guard just when Campbell came on the radio. That was another lucky break. The guard used his radio telephone to alert the Florida Highway Patrol Headquarters in Pahokee. A BOLO (Be On the Look Out) was flashed to dozens of police units.

Campbell started to drive, but his brother-in-law realized the wounded officer was in no condition to be behind the wheel.

"Slide over," he said. "I'll drive."

Ten minutes later, they pulled into the truck stop. An old man came toward the car as the bloodied officer got out.

"The old man just went nuts when he saw me," Campbell said. " 'Jesus Christ! What happened to you?'," the old man said, waving his arms and jumping around.

"Calm down! Calm down!" Campbell told him. "Just tell me, did a station wagon with a flat rear tire just go back by?"

"Flat? Hell, there was no rubber on that rim at all," the old man replied.

"Which way did they go?"

"South," the old man said.

Campbell knew there was no way to turn off US 27 for another twenty miles until the Andytown crossroads. There was a good chance one of the oncoming police units could set up a roadblock before Duran got there, especially since he would have to stop somewhere and change a tire. That's when Game Warden David Albury came barreling down the L-6 Levee on the other side of US 27.

"David was really movin'. I'm tellin' ya'," Campbell later recalled. "He didn't stop to unlock the levee gate. David just smashed through it like so much kindling wood."

Albury screeched to a stop near the wounded officer. Steam poured out of his truck's radiator, and a severed deer leg jutted out of the busted grill. Albury later said he'd hit three deer during his wild ride down the levee.

An ambulance was on the way from Plantation by now, but Campbell was beginning to feel the effects of his wounds. "I was shaky, clammy, had the dry heaves," he said. "Having gone through emergency first aid training, I could tell I was going into shock."

Albury was keyed-up with excitement and adrenaline.

"Let's go get the bastards," he said.

"I'm empty, David," Campbell replied.

"Hell, don't worry. I got plenty of bullets," Albury answered.

As they talked, a small crowd had gathered around the vehicle. One of them was a young man who had just got back from service as a U.S. Navy medical corpsman in Vietnam.

The Navy vet came forward to provide what help he could. He was talking to Campbell when the bleeding officer began to slide down on the car's front seat.

"Don't lay down!" the medic ordered. "I've seen wounded Marines in Vietnam do that, and they were dead a few minutes later."

"Oh, Jesus!" Campbell moaned. "Help me get back up then."

Albury suggested they start driving south to meet the ambulance. It was obvious that a few minutes might mean the difference between life and death. Albury drove Campbell's patrol car with the blue light flashing. "We were really goin'," Campbell said. "I'm tellin' ya'."

Incredibly, Campbell remained conscious. There was no doubt in his mind that he was going to survive. In a few minutes, he saw the flashing lights of the oncoming ambulance. Albury pulled over to the shoulder, where they made the transfer.

The ambulance turned around and ran back south with its wounded passenger.

Not long after, they came to the Andytown junction.

"I see blue lights ahead," the ambulance driver said. "Lots of them. Looks like they must have got your shooter."

"Stop there for a few minutes," Campbell told the driver. "I want to see if they got the right guy."

"No way, buddy," the driver replied. "You need to get to the hospital right now. No time for stopping."

"Well, slow down then when we go by," Campbell asked.

They slowed down. The wounded warden saw the old station wagon parked along the roadside, its left side riddled with his bullets.

"They got 'em," Campbell said and fell back down on the gurney. At the hospital emergency room, the nurses stripped off his boots and clothes. His right boot was half-filled with blood. They inserted probes into the wounds and wheeled the wounded officer to X-ray. All three nurses, Campbell later learned, were married to law enforcement officers.

The surgeon came up and told him the bullet in his stomach was life-threatening. "We're going to go in there and get it," the doctor said. "You'll be fine. Don't worry about it."

Campbell woke up in a hospital bed. He would fade in and out of consciousness for some time. The doctor told him one bullet had exploded against the upper right arm bone. Tiny shards of bullet were embedded in the warden's back like so much artillery shrapnel. A larger piece of the bullet was lodged dangerously near a nerve. The doctor decided to leave it there rather than risk the officer losing all movement of his right arm.

Ten days later he was discharged from the hospital. Three months later he was back in the Glades. But it was never the same.

"There was no psychiatric counseling for officers back then in the Game and Fish Commission," Campbell said. "You just went back out there and put on a badge and a gun like nothin' ever happened. But something like that leaves a mark. Work wasn't fun anymore. I withdrew from society, became a loner. Just didn't enjoy it anymore."

Duran lived too, despite a .357 Magnum slug in his right leg just below the hip. The trial for attempted first-degree murder took place in Broward County Courthouse in Ft. Lauderdale. The defendant claimed Campbell had "lost his mind" and pulled out his gun first and started shooting. He pleaded self-defense.

The jury found Duran guilty of attempted second-degree murder, but the judge hit him with fifteen years in prison, the minimum sentence for first degree. Even so, Duran would spend only five years in state prison.

"One year for each bullet that went into my body," Campbell said.

Years of mental turmoil, nagging pain, and four more operations followed for the wounded officer. He left the GFC and opened a taxidermy shop in Okeechobee. Later he went to college, studied mortuary science, and became a funeral home director in Belle Glade.

Six years after the shootout on the levee, he got a call from a Hialeah police lieutenant.

"I've been trying to track you down for a long time," the officer said. "And I'm goin' to make your day."

"How's that?" Campbell asked.

"Duran, the man who shot you, got out of prison last year. We found him on the street blown in half by a shotgun blast. Thought that just might make your day."

• • •

The Everglades has echoed to the sound of gunfire many times since the white man came. In the early years of this century, the wading bird rookeries of the Everglades were invaded by rifle-toting poachers who killed birds by the thousands. They left the carcasses to rot and took only the beautiful and delicate feathers. The breeding plumage gave the snowy egrets, roseate spoonbills, and other wading birds an almost ethereal beauty.

The plume hunters left devastation and the stench of decay in their wake. Even some of the hardened shooters were soon sickened by the brutal execution. One plume hunter, who would later quit the bloody trade, was consumed by guilt as he surveyed the hideous aftermath of an hour's work:

"The heads and necks of the young birds were hanging out of the nests by the hundreds," he wrote. "I am done with bird hunting forever!"

These men were not meat hunters or sport hunters. They slew indiscriminately for money. The beautiful feathers were worth twice their weight in gold. The millinery industry paid top prices for these feathers, which adorned the sweeping hats worn by women of fashion strolling the boulevards of Paris, London, and New York.

Conservationists, like pioneer ornithologist Frank M. Chapman of the New York Museum of Natural History, were horrified. The museum's bird expert had made his reputation in Florida where he cruised and camped every year in search of beautiful birds.

Deep in the Everglades lay the Cuthbert Rookery, a beacon which drew Chapman again and again into the swampy wilderness. On three trips he failed to find the fabled rookery, until, on the fourth expedition, he encountered Guy Bradley. This young man was a Cracker, had hunted and fished the Glades all his life, but he was different from the others. He had turned away from the lure of easy money offered to rapacious plume hunters and become Florida's first game warden. He'd been hired by the Audubon Society to guard the Cuthbert Rookery from the men who slaughtered beautiful birds for money and left the orphaned chicks to die from heat exposure, starvation, or predation. It took a brave man to defy these violent and reckless Everglades outlaws. Bradley was that kind of man.

Bradley guided Chapman to the Cuthbert, perhaps the one remaining major refuge in the Glades that hosted thousands of resplendent breeding wading birds. The raucous cries of the nesting birds reverberated through the tangled underbrush of the tree islands. In the water below, dozens of alligators patiently waited for a weakened chick to fall from its perch. The adult birds flew in and out on foraging missions to feed their young. It was a wilderness scene that John James Audubon would find familiar. It was old Florida. It was paradise. Ornithologist Frank Chapman was resigned to the fact that the rookery would be exterminated soon. Warden Bradley was also a realist. He predicted that the plume hunters would eventually murder him. It was only a matter of time, he told Chapman.

A few stalwart souls stood against the plume hunters. They knew that continued plume hunting would soon exterminate several wading bird species. Extinction was a real, even likely, possibility. Some researchers believed that over a twenty-year period the plume

Everglades Lawmen

When Slaughter Was in Fashion. *This elegant Pensacola woman shows off a hat decorated with the beautiful plumage of a wading bird, circa 1890. Florida plume hunters killed several million birds before tough laws and changing styles rescued several bird species from imminent extinction. (Florida State Archives)*

hunters, in relentless pursuit of money, slaughtered more than one million birds in the headwaters of the Shark River Slough in the Everglades alone. Ornithologist William Hornaday claimed in a 1913 magazine story that plume hunters had killed seventy-one percent of the wading birds in the Everglades between 1881 and 1898. The total butcher's bill will never be known. The state's treasure of beautiful wading birds faced a crisis of survival unless fundamental change took place.

The shot-out rookeries were stinking bird graveyards, and the plume hunters poled their skiffs deeper and deeper into the Everglades in pursuit of the golden feathers. Few doubted that the plume hunters would turn their guns on anyone foolish enough to try to stop the killing. The plume hunters were convinced that the rookeries would never be depleted. They had the ignorant confidence of the buffalo hunters who, only a few decades earlier, had come dangerously close to exterminating that species. Greedy men contemptuously spurned the warnings of conservationists. They thought there would never be an end to the wading birds of the

Everglades, just like there never would be an end to the buffalo, the prairie chicken, or the passenger pigeon.

Guy Bradley, the quiet man from Flamingo, saw it differently. Even though he had grown up in the heart of the Glades and had once been a plume hunter, he had the vision to foresee the terrible inevitable. He loved the land and the wild things that lived there. And he was ready to risk his own life in the defense of the besieged Cuthbert Rookery. The senseless slaughter had to stop.

Author Marjory Stoneman Douglas described Bradley in her classic work, *Everglades: River of Grass,* as a "pleasant, quiet young man, not tall, with blue eyes, always whistling and a pretty good violinist. He wasn't wild like a lot of those other boys. He had an easy courage."

This was still a frontier where violence made its own brutal law. Capt. Walter Smith, a Confederate veteran who had been a noted sharpshooter in the long-ago war, had a son who was arrested for plume hunting by young Bradley.

"You ever arrest one of my boys again, I'll kill you!" Smith told the warden.

On July 8, 1905, the sound of gunfire drifted across the waters of Florida Bay to Bradley's home in Flamingo. Somebody was shooting up the Cuthbert Rookery. The warden slipped his .32 caliber revolver into his pocket, said goodbye to his wife, and pushed his small sailing skiff into the water.

Bradley found Smith's sailboat, the *Cleveland,* anchored off the rookery. The old Confederate's sons were loading dead birds aboard their vessel. Bradley lowered sail and let his boat drift in close.

"I want your son, Tom," Guy Bradley called out.

"Well, if you want him, you've got to have a warrant," Captain Smith yelled back.

Bradley told him that Tom had been breaking the law by killing birds, and that act precluded the need for a warrant. He was there to arrest Tom and would tolerate no argument.

"Well, if you want him you have to come aboard this boat and take him," Captain Smith said with rifle in hand.

There was at least one shot. Maybe two. Hundreds of startled egrets and herons flooded the sky and filled the air with the sound of their flapping wings and calls of alarm. The old Confederate sharpshooter had murdered Guy Bradley in cold blood. Fishermen

Everglades Lawmen

Golden Feathers. *An Everglades plume hunter displays his trophy, circa 1890. Breeding plumage was in demand as adornment for the huge hats of that era. Prices rose steadily until the feathers were worth twice their weight in gold. (Florida State Archives)*

found the drifting skiff later with Bradley's body on board. His revolver was in his pocket, still loaded and unfired.

Smith told the Grand Jury in Key West that he had fired in self-defense and pointed to a bullet hole in his boat's mast as evidence. They believed him and set him free. Then again, perhaps they knew Smith's guilt but feared his retaliation, or maybe they thought Warden Bradley should have just minded his own business. The old rebel, Captain Smith, would in later years introduce himself proudly as the "man who killed Guy Bradley."

Bradley's tragic murder galvanized wildlife conservationists across the nation who intensified the campaign for an end to the reign of the plume hunters. Times were changing. Many were revolted at the slaughter of the wading birds for the whims of fashion. A turning point came in 1910 when the New York Legislature passed the Audubon Plumage Act outlawing the plume trade. Other states quickly passed similar laws. Congress soon

Fallen Warden Remembered. *A park ranger pays his respects at the stone memorial to Guy Bradley, a Florida warden murdered in 1905 by a plume hunter. The plaque reads: "Guy Bradley 1870–1905. Faithful unto death. As game warden of Monroe County, he gave his life for the cause to which he was pledged." (Florida State Archives)*

followed by banning the import of hats decorated with bird plumes.

Ironically, the wading birds of the Everglades were finally saved by the changing demands of style and fashion. Increasingly, the feathered hat was losing popularity among the fashion conscious. Only street walkers and women of low character clung to the fashion. Gradually the sound of gunfire faded in the remote haunts of the plume hunters.

Today's Florida game wardens revere the memory of Guy Bradley. They regard the Audubon warden as the patron saint of conservation law enforcement in the Sunshine State. The spirit of the quiet man from Flamingo lives on in their hearts. As the game wardens of the Florida Game and Fresh Water Fish Commission patrol the state's wilderness, they remember the man who defied the ruthless plume hunters almost a century before.

Perhaps Bradley still lingers in the wilderness swamp that gave him birth and for which he gave his life. Sometimes in the early morning mist of the Everglades, people have seen a man pole an old-fashioned skiff through the marsh. Some believe it's the shadow of Guy Bradley still guarding his precious birds.

Chapter 4:
Sky on Fire

You could see he was beaten—all wet, chewed up with insect bites, his eyes almost swollen shut. He had thrown away the shotgun somewhere in the swamp. Just stood there in the glare of the spotlight. Didn't run. You knew immediately he was ready to surrender.

—Game Warden John Reed

Crimson and yellow plumes of flame vividly lit the night sky as Game Wardens John Reed and Richard Dubberly drove their patrol pickup down the levee road toward the isolated Everglades hunt camp. They knew only that there had been trouble in the little community of tents, campers, and motor homes, which sprang up each year within the Holey Land Wildlife Management Area.

"We could see a massive red glow in the sky," Reed recalled. "It was unbelievable. Flames shot one hundred feet into the air. It seemed like the whole camp was burning. People were standing around the blazing motor home, swamp buggy, and pickup. There must have been a hundred people out there."

Only later would Reed and Dubberly learn all about the tragic series of events that had led to this conflagration. The story that unfolded was one of passion, jealousy, and murderous revenge. It had begun when a young man in Ft. Lauderdale suggested to his girlfriend that they visit his best friend at the Everglades hunt camp.

She agreed, and they drove out to the camp, where the friend asked them to go along on a track ride into the wilderness. They journeyed four or five miles out into the marsh, and there was some drinking. It was a beautiful day in the Glades, December 12, 1978.

What we do know is that the girlfriend became interested in her boyfriend's best friend. Her actions and words ignited a firestorm of jealousy. Hard words were traded. Tempers flared. Fists flew. The hunter threw the boyfriend off into the marsh.

"Here you have this guy standing in the marsh fuming while his best friend rides off into the sunset with his girlfriend," Reed said. "He has to wade and trudge through three or four miles of swamp to reach the camp, stumbling and falling in the dark, plagued by insects, and probably fearful of walking up on a big gator."

Hours later, the boyfriend showed up at his best friend's motor home. He heard the unmistakable sounds of lovemaking from within. He pounded on the door. The girl and his friend emerged, and the two men fought once more. Not only did the bedraggled boyfriend take another beating, but this time his ex-girlfriend struck him in the face with a two-by-four.

The couple returned to the motor home while the beaten man staggered off to a nearby campsite occupied by a man everybody called "Pops." There is a Pops in almost every hunt camp, an older man who no longer hunts but likes the atmosphere and camaraderie. Pops is always there with a cup of coffee and a yarn or two about the good old days.

The boyfriend told Pops he was cold and needed to start a fire. Did Pops have any matches? The old man handed him a pack of matches without any inkling as to what the angry and humiliated young man was contemplating.

There were several jerry cans of gasoline on his former best friend's track trailer. The jealous rival hefted one of the gasoline cans and splashed gasoline all over the motor home, the trailer, the track, and the pickup. He then jerked open the motor home door. His ex-girlfriend, clad only in panties, was sitting at a table. Her new lover was in the bathroom. The boyfriend sloshed gasoline into the interior, threw the can inside, lit a match, and ignited a conflagration. The fire was so intense that law enforcement officers searching the burned-out hulk the next morning found the gas can welded to the motor home's refrigerator.

"The whole camp exploded into flames," Reed said. "People in the surrounding camps heard the girl scream when she came running out of the flaming motor home. She was a human torch.

Everglades Lawmen

Several hunters knocked her down, rolled her over on the ground, and extinguished the flames. She was badly burned." The new lover was largely shielded by the bathroom door but did receive major burns on the soles of his feet where the flames licked under the door's bottom edge.

When Wardens Dubberly and Reed arrived, the bystanders told them what had happened. The boyfriend had fled into the Everglades marsh, but only after stealing a loaded shotgun from one of the camp sites. He was out there lurking in the dark somewhere, half-crazy with anger, desperate, and armed.

"We thought it highly unlikely that the fugitive would stick to the swamp," Reed said. "We figured that he would turn up sooner or later on one of the levee roads."

But they couldn't discount the possibility that the man was still hiding in one of the unoccupied camps. For the next hour, they searched dozens of camps. It was a tense and taut experience for both young wardens. They expected to confront a shotgun-toting maniac every time they drew back a tent flap or threw open a camper door.

"It was very stressful," Reed said. "One of us would go in low and the other high. The one man had the shotgun, the other the light and a revolver. We must have checked fifty camps. Most of the occupants were out watching the fire, which raged long into the night."

Deputies from Palm Beach and Broward Counties were also on the scene along with other game wardens. It was now past midnight; various police vehicles were running up and down the levee roads, flashing their spotlights into the surrounding marsh.

Only one escape route still lay shrouded in darkness, a levee leading to US Highway 27. Reed knew it well. The track was rough and strewn with rocks and boulders that required even heavy-duty vehicles to proceed at a snail's pace or risk ripping out their undercarriage.

Reed drove while Dubberly played a spotlight out the window. They moved slowly and cautiously, staring intently into the pool of yellow light that lit up the shadows of the swamp. They saw nothing for about forty-five minutes.

"Oh, God! There he is!" Dubberly suddenly shouted.

They both saw a bare-chested man wearing only a soaked pair of Levi's standing along the fringe of the levee about twenty yards away.

Both wardens leaped from the truck. Reed aimed his riot gun at

Land Flying. *Game Warden John Reed prepares to "shower down" and patrol the great sawgrass marsh, circa 1977. The airboat is to the Everglades game warden what the mustang was to the American cowboy. (Florida Game and Fish Commission)*

the fugitive, and Dubberly drew his .357 Magnum revolver.

"You could see he was beaten—all wet, chewed up with insect bites, his eyes almost swollen shut," Reed said. "He had thrown away the shotgun somewhere in the swamp. Just stood there. Didn't run. You knew immediately he was ready to surrender."

"Come up with your hands in the air!" Reed ordered.

The fugitive came out blinking at the glare of the truck's headlights.

The wardens ordered him to lie on the ground, arms and legs spread. After frisking him down, Dubberly cuffed the suspect. They turned him over to sheriff's deputies, and later that morning the jealous lover was charged with attempted murder and arson.

The suspect later accepted a plea bargain agreement to serve a twelve-year sentence. His ex-girlfriend lived but had to endure a number of painful treatments and operations. Her face had been ravaged and terribly wounded.

Incidents like this happen only rarely. One of the joys of the game warden's life is that he normally deals with nice people interested only in enjoying their sport in the great outdoors. Most stops are just opportunities to share a common interest with the hunter, angler, or camper. Some people become insistent that the game warden check their hunting or fishing license; they want to show that they have invested in the game and fish management effort that keeps their sports viable. They are disappointed if the warden doesn't ask for a license.

For whatever reason, however, John Reed found himself in series of incidents throughout his career far removed from the routine of the typical game warden. These encounters were frequently dangerous and sometimes bizarre.

Not long after graduating from the Wildlife Officer Academy in Tallahassee in 1977, this Indiana native learned about a bizarre cult that called itself the Zion Coptic Church. The group's coupling of drugs and religion brought intensive news coverage. Their leader and prophet called himself Brother Love.

In the late 1970s this cult promoted a religious belief whose sacraments involved drug use. They believed specifically in the spiritual power of smoking marijuana. They even encouraged drug use among their own children. Some dope-smokers were only seven years old.

Reed's first close encounter with the Zion Coptics took place in a Miami federal courtroom. The game warden was moonlighting as a deputy federal marshal—courtroom security was his main responsibility.

The self-styled Brother Love was in court that day with his retinue of lawyers. The cult leader faced charges of smuggling marijuana into Florida from the Caribbean. The cult maintained a small airstrip in the middle of the Everglades for this very purpose, or so it was rumored.

Brother Love was a very tall individual, six feet, eight inches, with a charismatic personality and a fondness for flamboyant and unconventional dress. Even in court he wore a long flowing robe like some Eastern potentate.

The cult's activities were the focus of considerable media attention in south Florida. Reed had often seen television news reports on the group and its leadership. The Zion Coptic Church, headquartered in Ft. Lauderdale, was a holdover from the hippie era of the late 1960s.

Sometime after the trial ended in acquittal, Reed was enjoying a bright, early morning drive, bound for airboat patrol in the western Glades. The big Dodge Ram Charger easily pulled the airboat trailer as Reed drove Alligator Alley. The surrounding marsh was flooded in the blinding white of the Florida sun. A motorist waved Reed over to the shoulder of the road and reported he had seen the wreck of a large aircraft north of the alley in what was essentially a flooded cow pasture.

Game Warden Ray Green came from the other direction, and the two met up near the crash site. The plane was about a quarter mile from the road. It was a twelve-passenger, twin-engine Cessna.

"You could plainly see the aircraft," Reed recalled. "It had bellied down with the landing gear up but looked intact from the road."

The two game wardens unloaded their airboats and sped off to the crash site. As they drew closer, they saw that the aircraft had indeed suffered massive destruction.

"The whole right side of the aircraft had been torn away as if struck by a giant cleaver," Reed said. "The damage extended from the cockpit on back to the tail. You could see right into the interior of the aircraft."

Reed and Green brought their airboats to a stop, dismounted, and waded to the wreck. The cockpit was a hideous and macabre sight. A corpse slumped in the copilot's seat with the right side of his head completely torn away. Blood and brains spattered the interior. The game wardens removed the body of the passenger, who, they soon learned, was a member of Brother Love's legal defense team.

Back in the rear of the aircraft, the wardens found fifty bales of marijuana. The wreck was only three miles short of the Zion Coptic airstrip along the L-28 Interceptor. They had obviously stumbled on to the aftermath of a drug smuggling mission gone bad.

The pilot had escaped the crash. Reed followed his tracks through the muck and quickly found a cache of aeronautical maps hastily hidden under a rock near a stand of cabbage palm.

Deputies from the Broward County Sheriff's Department were soon on the scene. They spearheaded the investigation, which eventually shed some light on what had occurred that night in the sky over the Everglades.

"Evidently, the aircraft was flying in the dope from the Bahamas, trying to come in low through a gap in the radar coverage between the Ft. Lauderdale International Airport and West Palm Beach International Airport," Reed said. "They also found pieces of the aircraft at the base of a radio tower in Boca Raton. The aircraft probably hit one of the tower's ground cables. The steel cable sliced through that airplane like a hot knife through butter."

"That pilot must have been good," he added. "Despite the serious damage to the fuselage, he kept it airborne and came pretty close to landing at the Zion Coptic strip in the Glades. He had the skill to land it wheels-up in that flooded field."

Brother Love and his Zion Coptic Church have since disappeared from the south Florida cultural scene. Warden Reed has no regrets about their departure.

"They were nothing but drug smugglers posing as a legitimate religion," he said. "Brother Love was no different in his manipulation of his followers than Charlie Manson or Jim Jones."

● ● ●

Most people come to the Glades to flee the hectic, noisy hubbub of modern urban life. They come to fish, hunt, camp, and canoe. But there are a few who come for another reason: they come to hide.

Sky on Fire

The blue Chevy Nova was parked, blocking the gate across one of the Everglades levee roads. Game Warden John Reed drove up early that morning. He walked over to the car and observed two disheveled, dirty, long-haired men sleeping in the front and back seats.

The California plate on the rear bumper set off that warning radar all good law enforcement officers possess. It didn't match up with the current Florida safety inspection sticker on the window.

Reed returned to his patrol vehicle and called radio dispatch in West Palm Beach. He asked them to run the tag on the National Criminal Information Center (NCIC) computer and advise. A few minutes later, the dispatcher asked if the car's occupants were 10-12—the radio call signal for with or nearby.

"That's affirmative," Reed replied. "They are in the car sleeping."

"Extreme signal O" was the crackled response from radio dispatch. That meant extreme danger. The officer was to proceed with caution!

The dispatcher also called the Broward County sheriff's office for backup. In the interim, Reed took his riot shotgun from the rack, made sure it was loaded, then checked his .357 Magnum revolver. Inside that car, according to the dispatcher, were suspects wanted in the murder of an assistant school superintendent in San Bernardino, California, and another killing in Houston. They were believed to be armed and dangerous.

Help was slow in coming. This was in the early morning just as patrol shifts were changing. The minutes dragged by. Finally, Reed radioed dispatch.

"10-50," he said. The dispatcher knew he was going in alone. If he didn't radio back in fifteen minutes, the dispatcher would automatically "call out all the troops." At that moment, a county sheriff's deputy drove up to join Reed. The two officers, both carrying loaded shotguns with the safeties off, slowly approached the vehicle.

Reed was worried about the man in the back. He had been sleeping on his stomach with his hands under his body. It was possible he was holding a knife or gun. The other slept on his back, spread-eagled. He appeared unarmed.

The tactical situation wasn't ideal. The car sat up on the levee in the open. The sides of the levee were covered with short-grass. There was no cover for the two officers. If it came to a shoot-out, they would be naked targets.

The officers came up on each side of the vehicle; they aimed their riot guns against the windows. Reed covered the man in the back seat, the one who might be concealing a weapon.

"Get out of the car! Police!" the warden and deputy shouted. They pounded on the car windows with their shotguns butts.

The two occupants crawled out. Reed had the barrel pressed against the man who rolled out of the back seat with empty hands. Clad in a ratty T-shirt and Levi's and a pair of scruffy tennis shoes, he crouched on all fours like some hunted animal.

The suspect vomited on the ground. The sickly sweet odor of alcohol scented the morning air. He was obviously drunk.

"What's up? What's up, officer? What's goin' on, man?" The suspect seemed bewildered, dazed.

Reed replied, "You're wanted for the murder of two people, one in San Bernardino and the other in Houston, Texas."

Without hesitation, the suspect blurted out: "I never killed two people. I only killed one."

"It was a spontaneous utterance," Reed said. "There was no doubt in my mind that he was telling the truth."

During an interrogation by homicide detectives from San Bernardino, the same suspect asked to speak to Game Warden Reed. The tape recorder was turned off and one of the detectives brought Reed in from the adjacent room.

"Listen, my buddy had nothin' to do with any of this," he told Reed. "Will you see that all charges are dropped against him if I cooperate?"

Reed told him he would do what he could but couldn't promise specifics. That would be up to the state's attorney and the judge.

The brief exchange over, the detectives turned the tape recorder back on and resumed the interrogation.

The suspect gave a full confession. It was a sordid and ugly story that began in the San Bernardino bus station, where he was selling himself for sex to the homosexuals who congregated there. One of his tricks was a large man who happened to be the county assistant superintendent of schools. The prominent educator didn't realize that the young man he picked up was carrying a heavy steel curtain sash weight in his pocket and planned to kill and rob him.

As they engaged in sex in the front seat on a lonely dark road, the suspect struck the victim hard with the sash weight. The big man fought back hard. In the violent struggle, the victim kicked out repeatedly and smashed the dashboard. Blood spouted from his head wound. Slowly his struggles subsided as the attacker tightened his grip on the man's throat. After the victim ceased to struggle, the assailant placed the apparently dead victim in the back seat and drove off looking for a place to dump the body.

Sometime later, the attacker heard gurgling noises from the back seat. The victim was still alive. The defendant pulled over and strangled him again until he was dead. Police later found the body along a country back road.

The defendant told police that he drove the victim's one-year-old Mustang to Houston, picked up his friend, then came to Ft. Lauderdale, where they sold the car to a junk-dealer for seventy-five dollars. They then stole a Chevy Nova whose owner had left the keys in the ignition. Their mistake was bolting on the California plate. That evening they went to drink at Big Daddy's Liquor Store and Lounge in Ft. Lauderdale. After a night of booze, they drove out to the Glades to sleep it off. It was a safe haven, far from any suspicious lawman, or so they thought. That's when Game Warden Reed appeared on the scene.

The Mustang was recovered from the junk dealer, who at first denied he had the car. When pressed, he took Reed and the homicide detectives to the rear of the junkyard. The victim's car sat under a tarpaulin. Dried blood, a quarter-inch thick, plastered the front seat. The stench was overpowering. The smashed dashboard gave further evidence to the violence of the deadly struggle.

"It must have been a terrific battle," Reed said. "Blood was everywhere."

Reed asked the junkyard dealer if he hadn't been suspicious when the men brought in a blood-stained, year-old-car and sold it for seventy-five dollars.

"Hey, people do weird things," was his cryptic reply.

Reed was later flown to San Bernardino to testify in the preliminary hearing and subsequent trial. The public defender argued that California state law forbade turning off the tape recorder during an interrogation without certain safeguards. This law was conceived to protect defendants from police battering during questioning.

Everglades Lawmen

"It was very specific," Reed said. "The law required you to record why the tape recorder was being turned off, who was present, and the time. Then the same procedure was to be followed when the tape recorder was turned back on."

The judge threw out the entire confession, ruling that it had been obtained illegally, that the information provided had been tainted under the "fruits of the poisoned tree" principle. In the subsequent trial, the state's attorney could not even mention the confession or any evidence obtained related to it. The defendant now pleaded self-defense, claiming he had accepted an offer of friendship from the victim, who then tried to attack and rape him.

The killer walked free.

•   •   •

Two unwitting girls in their early twenties were picked up on the Ft. Lauderdale beach by several burly members of the Outlaws motorcycle gang. It was during the early 1980s, and they were just girls having some fun. Their new friends took the unsuspecting young women out to the Everglades for a little sightseeing.

After parking on a remote levee road, the Outlaws repeatedly raped, abused, and tortured the two girls at knife point. The ordeal continued throughout the night. One of the girls did manage to break free and fled into the wilderness.

"Come back here right now, bitch!" the Outlaws yelled in the darkness. "If you don't get your ass back right now, we will cut your friend up into little pieces."

The terrified girl returned. Her tormentors ground burning cigarette butts into her flesh. They also beat both women severely, subjecting them to a night of terror.

That next morning Game Warden John Reed was standing by the roadside talking with a Florida State Trooper. They were parked near a colorful little place called the Andytown Bar just off the intersection of Alligator Alley and US 27.

The radio dispatcher came on the air with a priority BOLO ("be on the lookout") for motorcycle members driving a beat-up Ford Falcon. Earlier that morning at a restaurant further up the road, a woman had noticed the frightened look on two women emerging from the ladies restroom. Written in smeared lipstick on the bathroom mirror was the desperate plea: "Help us!"

Within moments of the BOLO, the two law enforcement officers saw the very same Falcon pull away from the intersection. Inside were two women and two bearded men dressed in biker leather. The officers leaped into their patrol cars, flicked on the blue lights, and pulled the suspects over a short way down the road.

"We both pointed our shotguns at the occupants and ordered them to get out and lie spread-eagled on the road," Reed said. "This one poor girl came running up to me, completely hysterical, crying, and trying to kiss my hands. 'Look what the SOBs did to me,' she cried, pulling her pants down to show the terrible burns."

Both bikers posted bond and promptly—and predictably—bolted. One man was later killed in a knife fight in a New Jersey bar. The other, as far as Reed knows, is still running free.

Dangerous encounters with felons were not always a frequent occurrence for an Everglades game warden. A lot of that changed in the 1960s when the drug culture bloomed. Drug runners flew in at night and landed on deserted fields in the heart of the Glades, like the infamous "Road to Nowhere." Others made aerial drops to accomplices in airboats waiting in the marsh.

Several little fishing communities became corrupted by the easy money that came with the drug trade. Drug use spread throughout all elements and levels of society. Game wardens started using the term "Broward County can of worms" or "Dade County can of worms" to describe Game and Fish arrests that ended up turning into felony drug charges, weapons charges, or other serious crimes. Many suspects were wanted for serious crimes on outstanding warrants from all over the country. During the 1970s, game wardens like John Reed routinely recovered the bullet-ridden bodies of "cocaine cowboys" from Miami who had been murdered in the ongoing drug wars.

The enduring Robin Hood–inspired myth that the game poacher is only a poor man feeding his family was increasingly out of tune with reality. Deer and gator poachers were often arrested in possession of drugs, paraphernalia, and/or stolen boats, motors, or all-terrain cycles.

The "poor man feeding his family" usually turned out to be an outlaw driving a twenty-thousand-dollar, four-wheel drive vehicle, using a CB radio to locate game wardens, and carrying expensive weaponry. In these cases, the deer meat went to the black market, where it brought a pretty penny. Poachers were in the game for one reason—profit.

Drugs played a pivotal role in one of the strangest cases that ever took place in south Florida. South Florida drug dealers often like to parade around their estates with exotic predatory pets like ocelots, mountain lions, or, in one case, even a Bengal tiger. The big cats were part of their intimidating, flashy, macho image.

That was certainly the case with a drug smuggler who lived in an armed compound in a rural area east of Naples, Florida, where roaming black bears were as common as the daily school bus. On the morning of October 24, 1992, the suspect slept late in his back bedroom. His loaded MAC-10 submachine gun lay within easy reach while two of his six pet mountain lions lounged in bed with their master.

The house was encircled by an eight-foot-high fence tipped with electrified barbed wire. Within the compound were the trappings of a flamboyant, free-spending lifestyle—a luxurious motor home, a twenty-six-foot cabin cruiser, an Electro-Glide motorcycle, a classic 1950s' convertible, a Piper Cub aircraft, and three all-terrain cycles.

But outside the wire hid a team of U.S. Customs Agents and game wardens. The wardens—Lt. Tom Quinn, Lt. John West, and Sgt. Eddie Lee Henderson—were present to deal with the cougars. West and Quinn were specially trained wildlife inspectors who dealt every day with exotic wildlife, from spitting Mamba snakes slithering through a Miami suburb to a rhino rampaging in a south Florida orange grove.

This bust was the culmination of a two-year investigation by U.S. Customs. They had gathered extensive evidence implicating the man in the house with the smuggling of three hundred thousand pounds of marijuana into Florida aboard his fishing boat.

Everything was planned to the minute. The takedown would be executed when the suspect left for his morning papers and coffee, as he did every morning at the same time. The only problem? The normally punctual suspect chose this particular morning to sleep in. An hour elapsed, and the suspect hadn't appeared.

If the agents waited much longer, they risked detection. That's when Lieutenant West made his suggestion. He told the agent in charge that he knew the suspect well, having visited numerous times to check the mountain lions. This was routine procedure when people keep large predators as personal pets.

"Lieutenant Quinn and me, along with two of your agents wearing game warden jackets, can drive up to the gate without inciting suspicion," West said. "I know the wife will let us in the compound. Once inside, I will pretend to find a problem with one of the cats kept in one of their outside cages and ask her to bring her husband outside. That's when we hit them."

The plan went perfectly. West drove up, the wife came to the gate with a smile, and he introduced the other officers as new game wardens interested in seeing her big cats. She undid the lock and chain without hesitation. They were in.

As planned, West looked over the cats and almost immediately found a problem. One of them looked a little underweight. Could her husband come out to discuss it? She nodded ascent and quickly returned with the main target of the impending bust.

The husband was sleepy and covered his eyes against the sun. The agents and wardens were as taut as bow strings. They knew the suspect was usually armed and knew that he kept weapons in almost all his vehicles and boats.

At one point, the man reached in his pocket. Quinn let his hand rest on the butt of his holstered revolver. A second's hesitation could spell death or serious injury for himself or any of the other officers.

A moment later, Quinn breathed easier and let his hand fall away from the .357 Magnum on his belt. The suspect's gun had turned out to be a comb, which he ran through his hair. It had been close. Very close.

That's when the agent-in-charge gave the signal. The agents jumped and cuffed the two suspects. Both were carefully frisked for weapons. It went smoothly, but now it was time to clear the house of the two mountain lions kept inside.

As the three wardens entered the home, they noticed a crude cardboard sign telling intruders that the premises were booby trapped and guarded by vicious mountain lions. When the game wardens opened doors into the various rooms, they didn't know what to expect: an armed drug dealer, the explosion of a booby trap, or the snarl of an enraged mountain lion.

Quinn cracked open the back bedroom door just an inch. All he could see were "teeth and eyes." They had found the cats. The

Not Always So Friendly. *Lt. John West (above), with the help of Lt. Tom Quinn, once had to capture two cougars like this one roaming the hideout of a major drug dealer. (Jim Huffstodt)*

wardens slowly entered the room with their catch poles. The cats were nervous, jumping all around from the bed to the chair, and even on top of a television. The machine gun lay on the floor, another possible danger should the officers inadvertently step on it or kick it.

Suddenly an agent blundered into the bedroom. The biggest cat, a 150-pounder, saw his chance for escape. He bounded into the air, striking Quinn in the chest, knocking the six-foot-two-inch game warden flat. The cat coiled and leaped off the prone officer, its back claws shredding his uniform shirt. Quinn would have been disemboweled except for the protective bulletproof vest he habitually wore. The tawny animal dashed through the house past astonished customs agents. Quinn was up on his feet in pursuit, shouting: "Don't shoot the cat! Don't shoot the cat!"

The brown blur headed out the door into the fenced compound. In the bedroom, West had gotten his noose over the other cat's neck, guided it into the adjoining cage, and quickly slid the door shut.

Outside, Quinn had gotten his noose around the other cat and was leading it back into the house when the agitated animal squirmed free and went inside a small closet.

"He was definitely angry," Quinn said. "He was in the classic attack posture—hissing, snarling, and with the ears laid back on the head."

West soon came to assist Quinn. And after another harrowing encounter, they got the noose back on the cat.

It was neither the first nor the last time game wardens played a key role in a major drug bust. It was just part of doing business in south Florida.

•   •   •

A game warden never knows when a routine stop may turn into a life-or-death confrontation.

It was opening day of dove season in Palm Beach County in 1983, and the game wardens were out in force. Capt. Eddie Wheeler, a tough little man who had once been a gator poacher himself in younger and wilder years, directed the operation from overhead in the GFC helicopter.

On the ground Game Warden Monte Moye heard the distinctive crack of a .22 rifle being fired in a nearby field outside Delray Beach. Shooting doves with a rifle in Florida is illegal, primarily for human safety concerns. Moye drove down a dirt road to investigate.

He came upon two young men and two children, a boy and a girl, all standing next to a car. One of the men, dark and scowling, was holding an automatic .22 rifle in his hands. Moye got out of the car and started walking toward the individuals. He had said nothing at this point.

The man aimed the rifle at the officer. "Get out of here or I'll kill you."

Moye sensibly backed off, got in the car, and alerted Sgt. Dick Lawrence. Lawrence rendezvoused with Moye. They discussed the situation, and then both officers drove back down the road, each in his own patrol vehicle. Lawrence was in the lead. Captain Wheeler was also informed, and he ordered pilot Jimmy Jordan to immediately fly to the location.

"I stopped the car about forty yards from the suspect," Lawrence remembers, "took the snap off my holster, got out, and stood behind the door."

The man stood there with the rifle in his hand. The other man and the two children were nearby.

"Put the gun down!" Lawrence ordered.

The man replied with an obscenity.

"Put the gun down, sir. Right now!"

"No! Leave us alone! Get the hell out of here!" the man shouted back.

Lawrence drew his revolver and rested it between the door and the vehicle body, taking careful aim at the rifleman. He pulled the hammer back; the metallic click had a menacing and frightening sound.

"Put the gun down!" he repeated, trying to use the command voice he'd been taught.

Lawrence heard the chilling metallic snap as Moye, standing beside his car, also cocked his piece. The slightest touch on either trigger would send a .357 Magnum bullet into the rifleman.

The man didn't point his rifle at the wardens, but he refused to put it down and continued shouting obscenities.

"It seemed like an eternity while this exchange was taking place," Lawrence said. "The palms of my hands were sweating. I remember that clearly. If he points that gun at us, I thought, it means I'll have to kill him. But I can't let him fire first either; he may kill one of us. Those were the thoughts racing through my mind at that instant."

Lawrence repeated his order to lay the gun down. And finally, for some inexplicable reason, the rifleman lowered the rifle barrel.

"Put the rifle in the car trunk!" Lawrence yelled. The man slowly complied.

"Now, step away from the car!" As he spoke, Lawrence heard the rhythmic beat of the helicopter as it hovered nearby in preparation to land.

Lawrence and Moye approached the man with drawn revolvers. Lawrence quickly walked over to the car and slammed the trunk shut. Then the wardens holstered their pieces.

"Just what were you thinking?" Lawrence asked the suspect. "Why did you throw down on my officer? What for? He hadn't even said a word to you."

"I just got out of the Army, and I'm tired of taking orders," the man replied curtly and with defiance. He was angry and highly agitated, obviously not in complete control.

"Well, what were you doing?"

"Nothin'. Just target practice," he answered.

"Why did you point a rifle at a police officer then? If you weren't doing anything wrong, what was the point?"

The man sullenly responded that he was tired of people in uniforms telling him what he could or couldn't do.

Captain Wheeler and pilot Jordan came walking up. A tough little man with a quiet voice, the older Wheeler was adept at defusing tense situations. He told the suspect not to make things any worse than what they were already. He asked him to just think it through and stay calm.

The suspect pushed Wheeler away roughly.

Lawrence took off his sunglasses and placed them on the car roof. "Gentlemen, you're now going to jail. Please turn around."

Both suspects turned around. Moye snapped one handcuff on. Suddenly, the man who had pointed the rifle turned and swung a looping punch.

In the wild melee, the shooter backhanded the GFC pilot with the dangling handcuff, split his lip, and sent him dazed to the ground. Moye, a slender man, briefly struggled with the other suspect, who hurled the game warden bodily into the bushes. Wheeler grappled with the main suspect, then drew his revolver and slammed the barrel down hard on his skull. The man sank to the ground. Lawrence was trading punches with the other individual, a tall, heavy man with an Afro haircut.

During Lawrence's struggle, the man shouted to the children to "grab their guns." As he fought, Lawrence slapped away the hand of one child reaching for his holstered revolver.

Everglades Lawmen

The man with the Afro finally backed off. Moye had regained his feet and helped Wheeler secure the main suspect. The pilot, Jimmy Jordan, was still on all fours, long gouts of blood spewing from his mouth.

Lawrence carefully eyed the big man with the Afro. "He actually pawed the ground like a bull in the bull ring," Lawrence said.

Lawrence drew his revolver and ordered: "Calm down or I'm going to separate your head from your shoulders."

"Okay, okay," the man answered.

The dazed pilot was between Lawrence and the other man. Lawrence holstered his sidearm and walked toward the second suspect. The man with the Afro charged him.

"I pushed the pilot out of the way, sidestepped, and grabbed the man by his hair with one hand and by the back of his shirt with the other," Lawrence said. "I just continued his momentum and slammed his head into the car trunk."

The man collapsed to the ground, unconscious. Lawrence quickly cuffed him. He took a deep breath. In just a few minutes he had come close to killing or being killed, had fought a vicious fight with two men, and all over a minor incident.

The suspects and officers went to a nearby hospital. The rifleman's skull was fractured from the blow with the revolver; the other man was cut. Warden Moye had been bitten on the arm, and the pilot took several stitches to close the wound to his lip.

"Why? I just want to know why?" Lawrence asked the two men later. "Don't you realize that you could have been shot and killed? Don't you realize those children could have been seriously hurt or killed? What for?"

The men were silent. The suspects, who turned out to be brothers, were charged with resisting arrest with violence and aggravated battery on a police officer. Both jumped bond a few days later. Reports indicated they had fled to their native Mexico. Just a routine day in the life of a game warden in south Florida. Routine that almost erupted into senseless tragedy.

Chapter 5:
Everglades Cowboys

*A motorboat equipped with aerial propellers . . . yes-
terday successfully made her first trip on waters . . .
during harvest home festival. We have named her the
Ugly Duckling and hope she will turn out to be a swan.*
                              —Alexander Graham Bell, 1905

T he Everglades game warden roaring through the sawgrass
        marsh aboard his airboat is as much a part of the American
        myth as the Western cowboy astride his mustang on the
Great Plains. Not surprisingly, harrowing airboat pursuits and sometimes fatal wrecks are part of the reality concealed behind the glam-
orous facade.

Most wardens revel in the speed and power of their airboats and
take joy in the easy access it provides to the heart of the wilderness
marsh. Before his deadly gun duel, Conley Campbell spent many
days piloting his airboat through the Glades. Those were the joyful
times spiced with the tang of adventure.

The big man was at home in this wild and strange land. His roots
go deep into the pioneer past. Florida wilderness is in his blood.
Conley's people arrived in Christmas, Florida, around 1828, eight
years before the outbreak of the bloody Second Seminole War. Not
many can trace their Florida roots back that far, and Conley has a
quiet pride in his family's history. His grandfather and uncles were
market hunters back around the turn of the century, stalking the
woods and swamps near Wolf Creek in search of otter, bear, turkey,
gators, and deer. Family legend claims grandpa once had five
hundred gator hides salted and stored for sale.

Everglades Lawmen

Ugly Duckling. *Alexander Graham Bell's research team in Nova Scotia constructed the ancestor of today's airboat as an aircraft engine test bed that would be a safe alternative to in-flight experiments. Bell, a pioneer inventor in many fields, called his 1905 creation the* Ugly Duckling. *(Drawing by Peggy Perkerson)*

Conley is a large man, over six feet tall, packs about two hundred pounds, and has the reputation of being a "game warden's game warden." The Everglades was his backyard from 1969 to 1977. The experience left him with a voluminous collection of anecdotes that he tells in a deep drawl befitting a Florida native. The brown-haired, blue-eyed Conley spent his early boyhood hunting and fishing in the Ft. Pierce area. His teen years were spent in Miami, but his heart stayed in the woods. So it was no surprise when he pinned on a game warden's badge and began patrolling the Everglades.

One hot night around 1970, Conley and Game Warden Buzz McIntire went out in separate airboats checking frog hunters to keep 'em honest. After a few hours, they stopped in a slough with their lights out and waited. They soon heard the drone of another airboat running dark. Both wardens turned on their lights almost at the same time, bathing the oncoming airboat in the harsh yellow glow. The strange boat idled to a stop, and the two wardens maneuvered to either side. McIntire had just turned off his engine when one of the two occupants in the airboat alongside reached out and kicked the warden's boat back several feet.

In seconds the strangers "showered down." That's how Crackers describe starting their engines and the way the whirling propeller creates a shower of spray in its wake. Conley gunned his engine and sped off in a wild pursuit that wound its way through the grass, down sloughs, and past tree islands, thundering under the starlit sky.

Conley was so close he was showered with spray from the fleeing airboat's spinning propeller. He could hardly see as he closed to within a few yards, and then the suspects glided to a stop. When Conley's airboat gently glided into theirs, one of the occupants leaped off onto the game warden's craft.

"I drew my weapon and pointed it at him," Conley recalled. "God only knows what he thought he was doing."

"Don't shoot! Don't shoot!'" the man yelled.

"Get on back to your boat!" Conley ordered.

The man jumped back. Then Game Warden McIntire came riding up in his airboat, drifted to a stop, and shut down his engine.

"They threw out something while you were chasing them," McIntire told Conley.

"Do you think you can go back and find it?"

"Yes."

McIntire turned around and retraced his steps. It was easy to follow the wet trail of the boats through the grass in the yellow moonlight.

He came back fifteen minutes later. He pulled up to Conley's boat and showed him a little yearling deer wrapped in a tarp. The tarp had kept the deer from sinking and sealed the fate of the two poachers.

One of the poachers asked Conley, "Why were you chasin' us?"

"Why were you runnin'," Conley replied.

"Well, we thought you were goin' rob us for sure," the poacher replied.

"Son, we don't get many armed robbers out here in the Glades. That's somethin' you find back in town."

The man shrugged and confessed. They had run the deer down in their airboat and killed it with a machete.

Everglades Lawmen

"Never did figure what that boy thought he was doin', jumpin' on my boat like that," Conley said. "Could have got himself shot."

• • •

Airboat chases in the Glades are the stuff of legend and lore. People are captivated by the drama and excitement of powerful airboats roaring through the marsh and skittering over the tall sawgrass. Tourists visiting south Florida invariably want to do two things: take an airboat ride and see an alligator.

The game warden piloting his speeding airboat through the labyrinthine vastness of the Everglades strangely evokes in the public imagination the mythic vision of the Western cowboy riding his half-wild mustang across the Montana plains. Both images, although vastly different, inspire similar dreams of romance and adventure that are uniquely American. Both are symbols of man in the wilderness, conveying a sense of individual freedom that is a

Mythic Vision. *The Everglades game warden skimming the marsh in a thundering airboat is as American as the cowboy galloping the plains on his mustang. This publicity photo was probably taken sometime in the late 1950s. (Florida Game and Fish Commission)*

part of the American psyche and character.

Airboats opened the door to the wilderness treasures of the Everglades. Access to the interior prior to the advent of the airboats in the 1930s was strictly by poling either an Everglades skiff—sometimes called a push boat—or a Seminole dugout hewed from a single cypress tree. It was not a task for the delicate or the easily discouraged.

Adventurer Hugh L. Willoughby penetrated the heart of the Everglades in 1896 and wrote about his adventures in his book *Across the Everglades—A Canoe Journey of Exploration.* The Rhode Island native was familiar with paddling canoes in the lakes and rivers of New York, Maine, and Canada. He soon discovered that poling was the only way to traverse the great sea of sawgrass.

"When the rock is near the surface, with little soil, this sawgrass grows to a height of about four feet, but where the soil is deeper it has very little water around its roots and reaches a height of ten feet. This is the great barrier to Everglade travel; it pays better to go twenty-five miles around than half-a-mile through," Willoughby wrote.

He continued: "What makes this grass so formidable and so much to be dreaded is the saw-like edge which it is armed on three sides. If you get a blade between your hand and the pole, it will cut you to the bone, with a jagged gash that takes long to heal. The nose and face suffer much. When very thick, pushing through it becomes almost impossible."

Two men of vision and ideas developed the world's first practical Everglades airboat. They were Alexander Graham Bell, inventor of the telephone, and Glenn Curtiss, one of the early pioneers of the air, whose exploits rank with the Wright brothers, Louis Bleriot, and Santos-Dumont.

Bell and Glenn were both of an elite fraternity of geniuses who were busy inventing the future in the early decades of the twentieth century. Oddly enough, the ancient ancestor of the modern Everglades airboat first took to water at Cape Breton Island in Nova Scotia. This was the site of Bell's sprawling northern estate he christened Beinn Bhreagh, which is Gaelic for "beautiful mountain."

Glenn Curtiss was one of Bell's idea men. They had come to this barren place to create machines that would carry man across the sea and sky. The hydrofoil boat in 1919 was only one of the innovations

Ahead of Its Time. *Pioneer aircraft pilot and designer Glenn Curtiss built the Scooter in 1920. The craft boasted an enclosed cockpit, aerodynamic lines, and a top speed of 70 miles per hour. (Historical Association of Southern Florida)*

that took shape at this lonely and remote laboratory.

In 1905 Bell penned a letter to his daughter and son-in-law, describing a novel new boat design intended as a safe test bed for aircraft engines: "A motorboat equipped with aerial propellers . . . yesterday successfully made her first trip on the waters . . . during harvest home festival. We have named her the *Ugly Duckling* and hope she will turn out to be a swan."

Gilbert H. Grosvenor, the publisher and editor of *National Geographic,* photographed Curtiss at the controls of the *Ugly Duckling* during tests on Baddeck Bay in the summer of 1907. This was undoubtedly the world's first practical airboat, differing from today's craft mainly in being pulled across the water by the propeller rather than being pushed.

The possibilities of the *Ugly Duckling* lay fallow in Curtiss's inventive brain for several years. He immersed himself in designing, building, and flying increasingly more sophisticated aircraft. But one day Curtiss was lured south by magical Florida, where he founded the community of Opa-Locka near Hialeah.

An avid hunter and fishermen, Curtiss made many forays into the sawgrass wilderness of the Everglades. He soon concluded that there had to be a faster, easier mode of transportation than laboriously poling a skiff or dugout through the endless grass. Conventional outboard engines weren't the answer. Propellers quickly locked in a tangle of grass after only a few minutes' progress. That's when Curtiss's fertile mind returned to the potential represented by the *Ugly Duckling.*

The world's first true airboat gradually took form in his imagination. *Scooter* was the child of his genius. This enclosed airboat, using a pusher prop, was photographed in 1920 by a Miami native as it was towed across Biscayne Bay. The picture reveals a sophisticated, aerodynamic craft that used aerial rudders for steering. Scooter could carry a half-dozen passengers at speeds up to fifty miles per hour; a lighter version later reached a speed of seventy miles per hour.

Strangely, Curtiss never patented his airboat idea and evidently moved on to other more enticing projects. During the Great Depression, a couple of backwoods mechanics, who made their living gigging succulent Everglades frogs for the restaurants of Miami, followed in the footsteps of Bell and Curtiss.

The record is silent on whether they were aware of Curtiss's *Scooter.* They may well have come to the same conclusions on their own. Their first creations were undoubtedly airboats, although powered by heavy car engines and driven by crude propellers tediously carved from cypress logs.

These craft were heavy and slow, going no more than ten miles per hour through the grass. Froggers used them to haul equipment and supplies to their isolated camps deep in the Glades. Once there, they continued to hunt frogs from push boats using a gig or spear.

An unsigned and undated monograph of early frog hunters, discovered in a dusty file in the archives of the Florida Game and Fresh Water Fish Commission, is the only record we have of these Depression-era airboats:

About 1935, Mr. Willard Yates was the first man known to use an airplane engine in his airboat which he used for frogging. He used a sixty-five horsepower engine. The airboat was still steered by ropes attached to the rudder like reins on a horse. No seats were used yet and the pilot of the airboat stood by the engine and operated the throttle manually. Later, a stick control similar to that used in small aircraft was attached to the rudder ropes. It was several years later before a high seat and foot stand with gas pedal and rudder control bar were devised.

The high seat permitted the airboat pilot to see over high grass and bushes and to avoid rough or dangerous obstacles and dry spots. Mr. Willard Yates was mortally wounded in an airboat accident when his engine supports came loose from the floor and the whirling propeller blade came forward to mutilate him.

Airboats used today by the Everglades game wardens and biologists are lighter, sleeker, more powerful, and much faster than the early boats. Tour companies take visitors into the Glades on huge airboats that carry forty or more passengers. The pioneer vision of Bell and Curtiss is now an everyday reality in south Florida.

Despite the advances, the modern airboat is not for the fainthearted. Piloting one takes a great deal of manual dexterity, coordination, and courage. Game Warden Dick Lawrence is brave, damn near fearless, but even he admits he was more than a little apprehensive the first time he cranked up that huge twelve-hundred-horsepower aircraft engine.

"Learning to operate an airboat is an experience. Let me tell you," Lawrence said. "You have to remember that I'd never seen an airboat until they took me out to the Glades. Never seen one in my entire life.

"It was very scary when that engine began to turn over," he said. "These things got my attention right off. Yes, sir. Remember they go awful fast and don't have brakes. Make a mistake when you're flying along at sixty-five miles per hour, and you're a dead man."

Few laymen appreciate that the airboat pilot has little or no control over his craft once he shuts the engine down. That's because the airboat is steered by rudders that deflect the blast of air rushing by in the same manner as the tail rudder of an aircraft.

"One of the first lessons you learn is to keep the throttle a little open when you're coming to a stop so you can maintain steerage," he said. "Once you turn that prop off, you don't have any more control. It's very important to keep control until the last few seconds so you can avoid a thick clump of sawgrass, a log, or other obstacle.

"Once the engine is off, you can turn the rudder, and the airboat will continue to go straight. When you're out there in the grass, you don't slow down when you encounter a tree, you give it the throttle and maneuver around the obstacle."

Lawrence learned the technique and art of piloting an airboat in the venerable school of on-the-job training. He learned the basics with his hand on the rudder bar while a veteran officer stood alongside. Slow and apprehensive at first, Lawrence gradually worked up his confidence and speed. Fear was now replaced by exhilaration.

"It's pretty simple really," Lawrence said. "You push the rudder forward and the boat goes right. You push the rudder stick back and it goes left. They teach you how to use the throttle, how to load the boat up and equally distribute the weight, and demonstrate basic maintenance like changing the oil and spark plugs."

Lawrence says all game wardens go through the same learning stages as they progress from raw beginner to skilled operator. The early hesitancy and trepidation is soon replaced by a budding confidence in developing skills.

"You go solo and slowly build up speed, taking easy turns," he said. "Then you get a little braver and start pushing the rudder bar all the way forward or back which causes the boat to spin three hundred sixty degrees around. Spinning around like that is doing a 'donut.' By now you're thinking you're pretty slick."

As an airboat turns, it slides across the top of the water. Beginning operators are usually afraid of making sharp turns. A sharp turn is inherently dangerous because the boat literally is slipping sideways across the grass.

"You hit something going sideways and that boat will flip," Lawrence said. "You learn to avoid that as you progress through what I call the cowboy phase. The final stage is when you achieve a combination of skill, judgment, and a respect for the airboat. Remember, piloting an airboat is like riding a seven-hundred-pound engine, bucking-bronco style."

Sooner or later airboat pilots either sink their craft or are jettisoned from the seat for a spectacular swan dive into the marsh. "Anybody who has driven an airboat for any amount of years who says he never sank one or took a dive is lying," Lawrence said.

Everglades Lawmen

Storm over the Glades. *Game wardens confer before an airboat patrol into the marsh while storm clouds gather on the horizon, circa 1979. From left: Bill Ashley, David Thompson, and John Carter. (Bill Ashley)*

Sinking an airboat is easy. It usually happens when the operator goes from the shallow marsh into a deep-water canal. As he slows, the airboat's wake catches up and flows over the stern. There is little freeboard, and the boat will rapidly fill and go to the bottom.

"When that water starts pouring in, you're going straight to the bottom like a submarine, like the U.S.S. Nautilus," Lawrence joked. That means getting a track or swamp buggy back into the Glades, attaching a tow-rope on the sunken craft and hauling it out. Following that are hours of draining the oil, cleaning the engine, and fighting rust.

One of Lawrence's most memorable airboat adventures in the Glades happened when he ran his craft up on a willow head—a small island covered with young trees—during a driving rainstorm. Storms come fast in the Everglades. The bright blue sky quickly turns charcoal; the rain drops splatter down like watery machine-gun bullets. Lightning streaks like skeletal hands in the darkness.

"That day we didn't even have time to get our rain gear on," he said. "It was just a black wall of rain."

Despite zero visibility, Lawrence and his partner, Game Warden Johnny Manning, kept pushing on towards the boat ramp where they planned on loading up equipment and supplies for their advance camp. Hunting season was scheduled to begin the next day, and the wardens wanted to catch "any early birds out there the night before." They were feeling their way through the rain when the boat ran over something and came to a wobbly stop.

"I could just make out that we were sitting on top of a willow head," Lawrence said. "We had driven up onto an island. At first we tried rocking the boat off. Finally, I told Johnny to get off the boat, not realizing how high up we were. We both stepped off and fell down six feet or more into the water."

The embarrassed wardens used machetes to cut down the willows to allow the boat to settle slowly onto the island proper. Once on the ground, Lawrence gave it the gun, moved the rudders back and forth, and wiggled the machine off into the marsh.

"We just sat there until the rain stopped," he admitted sheepishly. "Then we resumed our trip back to the landing. You might say that we had learned a lesson from hard experience."

Danger comes with the exhilaration and excitement of piloting an airboat. GFC records documented twenty-five airboat accidents during 1997. Three people died. During the first six months of 1998, there were twenty-one accidents with five fatalities. These represent only accidents investigated by GFC wardens, not those investigated by other agencies.

"Airboats are dangerous. You bet!" Lawrence said. "Very dangerous! There was an accident in the Glades early this year where the pilot flipped the airboat and caused the propeller to spin off. The man was cut right in half by the whirling blade."

Few appreciate the risks inherent in operating airboats like Jon Fury does, a GFC fisheries biologist with fourteen years working the swamp. The Pennsylvania native labors alongside the game wardens in the immense Everglades marsh. In the space of two years, Fury was involved in two serious airboat mishaps. Either incident could have ended in death.

It happens in an instant. Fury was at the controls with wildlife

Survivor. *Fishery Biologist Jon Fury, a lanky and sardonic Pennsylvania native, has escaped two near-fatal airboat accidents in his fourteen years in the Glades. (Jon Fury)*

biologist Jim Schuette as passenger, buzzing through the Everglades through what appeared to be open grass. They didn't realize that the high vegetation concealed the nearby canal levee. They hit with tremendous impact. Fury flew out of the seat like a rocket, turning over and over again. "All I remember is seeing the water, then the sky, then the water, then the sky," Fury said.

Investigators estimated that Fury flew nearly forty feet before slamming onto the levee. The huge airboat came hurtling behind him and dug into the levee only a few feet from the injured airboat pilot. He had come very close to being crushed by his own boat.

The airboat rolled over on its side and came to rest upside down. The engine cage was crumbled and the propeller had shattered in an explosion of huge wooden splinters. Somehow the two men escaped being sliced apart by these airborne missiles.

Schuette was the luckier of the two. "I didn't have my glasses on and was looking down to avoid getting hit by the tall sawgrass," he remembered. "Suddenly I started to see annual grasses which only grow on dry land. Then I felt the first bump, followed quickly by a second."

The wildlife biologist rolled out of the airboat right at impact. He remembers scrambling out of the way as the heavy boat, weighing fifteen hundred pounds, rolled over with a tremendous crash. Schuette was in pain and suffered severe bruises, but was able to go to the assistance of Fury, who lay seriously injured on the levee. A few moments later, another airboat containing GFC wildlife biologists sputtered to a halt. They radioed for help. Both injured men were picked up by helicopter and flown to a Miami hospital. Schuette was released in a few hours with relatively minor, although painful, injuries. Fury was in much worse shape with a fractured rib and collapsed lung. He spent ten days in the hospital.

Only a few weeks before the crash, Schuette had escaped another potentially fatal airboat accident when the gas filter came loose from the engine as he sped through the grass. The filter went through the cage and splintered the prop into a thousand pieces. The biologist walked anyway without a scratch.

Two years later, Fury was not so fortunate. He was piloting another airboat through the Glades with a young woman from the United States Geological Survey (USGS) sitting in the passenger seat nearest the engine. A GFC fisheries biologist and another USGS employee rode in another airboat.

Their mission that day was to sample small fish, water, and plants for mercury concentrations and undertake radioisotope studies for the USGS. Water levels were lower than Fury ever remembered, only a few inches in some areas. Not surprisingly, Fury ran out of water and stuck the craft fast in the tall grass. The men from the other boat got out and stood on either side of the bow of Fury's craft. When he started gunning the engine, they would rock the boat back and forth, helping him break free. This was Fury's passenger's first airboat ride, and she may have felt a little apprehensive as the engine revved up and the craft began trembling.

Bang! Fury felt like some big man had struck him in the back with a two-by-four. A motor mount had cracked, dropping the engine down so the spinning propeller started gouging into the deck, which quickly exploded into so much wooden shrapnel. The fragments ripped through the cage and tore out pieces of steel mesh that became flying missiles.

It was as if a terrorist bomb had suddenly exploded aboard. Fury dismounted and was alarmed when he saw a wire fragment sticking out of the back of his passenger's life jacket. Luckily, the wire failed to penetrate the kapok and the woman's flesh.

Fury wasn't so lucky. He was bleeding from the back where he'd been struck by propeller and cage fragments. One of the other men told him that a two-inch-long piece of steel caging was protruding from his back. The man jerked it loose, and the bleeding quickly subsided.

"I don't think it was that deep," Fury said with stoic indifference. He also suffered a bad cut on his upper arm and severe abrasions, which the others treated as best they could under the conditions.

Fury quietly insisted they continue the sampling mission. After driving nearly an hour into the Glades, he didn't want to go back without getting the job done. An hour later, they all left aboard the other airboat. Game Warden Chris Sella took Fury to a hospital in Plantation. When the doctor examined him in the emergency room, he asked when Fury last had a tetanus shot.

"Oh, about two years ago, right after my other airboat accident," Fury replied.

"Maybe you should stay away from airboats," the doctor suggested with a touch of irony.

Actually, Fury was most concerned whether the splinter of steel had ruined the tattoo of a Chinese dragon on his back. That kind of almost indifferent calm is a characteristic of most GFC biologists and game wardens. They tend to be a rather fatalistic bunch.

Few risks discourage those who use airboats on a daily basis. They accept the danger as part of a trade-off for the privilege of seeing the legendary Everglades as few ever experience them. You might say danger is simply part of the ticket price for admission.

One of the most graphic and insightful accounts of an airboat trip into the Everglades was written by T. H. Watkins for an article titled "Men in Green," which was featured in *Audubon Magazine* in 1980.

Lt. Jerry Lord is a veteran game warden who long ago fled the tedium of office life at a finance company for the freedom and far horizons of the Florida wilderness. He served as Watkins' guide into the endless marsh south of Alligator Alley. Watkins wrote:

Sitting in the catbird seat of an airboat, I quickly learned, was like being strapped to the wing of a DC-3. The noise of the prop and engine obliterated quite completely every other sound in the world. At fifty-five to sixty miles an hour, we slithered and bumped across the sedges and sawgrass with no more than three or four inches of water as our traveling cushion, turns made with a wide, slipping slide, following vague airboat trails. . . . Ahead of us, as we sped along, great shining-white clouds of common egrets rose outraged from the grass; great blue herons took awkwardly to the air, flapping and coasting, long necks folded into an 'S' between their wings, looking like China clippers; wood ducks scampered in panic; and once a year-ling doe leaped from a hiding place just before we slammed over it, bouncing off across the sawgrass with astonishing speed.

Lord took the writer to an isolated Everglades cabin whose owners gladly welcome any who wish to stay, as long as they leave it as they found it. Watkins was impressed by a dish of Lord's special chili; afterwards they reboarded the airboat for a moonlit ride through the shadowy maze of wilderness marsh and tree islands.

"After half an hour, we coasted to a stop somewhere in the middle of the Glades, turned off the engine, and listened," Watkins wrote. "A light breeze lapped waves against the hull, but that and the eternal frogs calling among the duckweed and bladderwort were the only sounds in all that inland sea."

"It can get pretty lonely out here when you're by yourself," Lord said. "But it's a good place to think, when you got some thinking to do. . . . I get bored once in a while, particularly when things get . . . I get slow . . . But whatever I do, I remember those days in the finance company."

In some ways most of those who come to the Everglades are fleeing some tedious office or the congested, harried turmoil of modern life lived in the dark shadows of the city's concrete canyons. The airboat is their magic carpet to a quieter, simpler, and more beautiful place. This is a wilderness world inhabited by gator, deer, and even an occasional endangered Florida panther.

Today, the throaty growl of a distant airboat is as much a part of

Endless Vista. *Nature writer T. H. Watkins described his airboat ride through the Glades "like being strapped to the wing of a DC-3." (Jon Fury)*

the Everglades as the bellow of a bull gator or the weird cry of the limpkin. This invention, ironically born in the Canadian northland, has opened wide the gate to myriad wilderness wonders for people who otherwise would never know the remote and previously almost inaccessible beauty of the Everglades.

Chapter 6:
Good Guys and Bad Guys

I could take out my knife, stick you between the eyes and
kill you before you ever get that gun out of the holster!
—John the Snake

The Green Frog, a ramshackle tavern off Tamiami Trail, was a familiar landmark for the game wardens patrolling the surrounding Everglades. Many of the tavern's patrons used drugs, dealt drugs, or were involved in other crimes. These outlaws were a mix of rednecks from the country and tough urban punks. Some were felons, some ex-cons, some thieves, some deer and gator poachers. A few were violent and profane outcasts—dangerous men. Disputes were sometimes settled with fists, boots, or knives.

"Hell, I was afraid to go in there by myself," Game Warden Lawless admits. "A game warden walking in there? Much less a Yankee game warden? That just wouldn't have cut it with those good ol' boys. Believe me, the Green Frog was rough, a place to avoid.

"When I drove by on the highway I always gave the Green Frog a careful look. One day I took special note of a black pickup driven by a clean-cut white man with brown hair. I saw him get out and walk into the tavern. He just didn't look like the kind of outlaw that place attracted. Then again, looks can be deceiving."

Several nights later, Lawless and Warden David Melvin were briefed by their sergeant about a professional gator poacher who had been working the Glades hard for several weeks. In 1973, the alligator was an endangered species found on both the state and federal list. Killing a gator was a felony that carried heavy fines and possible jail time. But the money was good for the outlaw willing to take the risk.

This latest wave of gator poaching was apparently the work of one or two men who knew their trade well. They were meat hunters and took only gator tails. The tailless gator corpses were left to rot in the marsh or canal where they'd been killed. It was quick and easy money. A six-foot gator tail might provide fifty pounds of meat, which went for big money on the black market.

That night the wardens drove their patrol vehicle down the Tamiami Trail and pulled off to the right near the southern terminus of the L-67 Canal in the northern Everglades. Across the road to the south lay the fourteen-million-acre Everglades National Park. To a Philadelphia kid this was something out of an adventure novel. Here he was, only a few weeks out of the Wildlife Officer Academy, sitting in the dark waiting for signs of an alligator poacher. Somewhere out there in the darkened marsh the poacher might be killing a protected gator.

Not five minutes had passed when the two wardens saw the faint glimmer of a light in the National Park. Saw it for only an instant. Then the curtain of blackness drew shut. They drove across the road to one of the park entrances, where they found a black pickup.

The wardens quietly padded their way into the park until they came to the edge of a levee overlooking a canal. The shadowy Shark River Slough stretched out beyond, a place where you found huge gators and sometimes encountered the men who hunted them.

Most poachers see themselves in a romantic light. They believe they are living the tradition of frontier America, walking in the paths of Crocket, Boone, and other legendary hunters of the golden past. Laws are for weak, domesticated city boys. They were men who made their own law and their own way. They didn't like authority, didn't like other men telling them what they could or couldn't do in the swamp.

The wardens stood there on the levee peering through their binoculars. They saw little except shadows and the black waters of the canal that ran parallel to the levee.

"No moon. No stars. Pitch black," Lawless remembered. "It was a spring night and cool. No bugs. Very pleasant. We just waited there several minutes in silence. To this point, we hadn't heard a shot or anything to indicate the light marked a gator poacher. It was prob-

Glades Hunt Camp. *Wardens J. O. Brown (left) and J. P. Hodges shoot the breeze with hunters along the old "Mud Canal" north of Alligator Alley in Broward County in November 1954. (Lt. Col. J. O. Brown, Retired)*

ably just a lost fisherman trying to find his way home."

That's when they heard the noise: a wheezing, labored breathing. A few seconds later, they glimpsed the silhouette of a man trotting along the edge of the canal below them. Lawless snapped on his flashlight. The man below suddenly froze. He was a slender, brown-haired, clean-cut man in his late twenties wearing a T-shirt, jeans, and boots. The poacher wore a .44 Magnum revolver on his hip. Over one shoulder, he carried the seven-foot tail of a huge gator. The tail alone probably weighed more than a hundred pounds.

The wardens covered the suspect with their .357 Magnum revolvers. There was nowhere to run, nowhere to hide. The poacher was caught in the harsh glare of the game wardens' flashlights. His face was a blank mask.

There was an unreality in all this that sent strange thoughts running through the mind of Warden Lawless, the rookie from north Philly who had never seen a poacher or a bloody alligator tail before. Perhaps it was a dream, or a scene from some old movie, or even a passage from some barely remembered adventure novel?

"This couldn't be real, I thought," Lawless said. "No way! I was just out of the academy and had caught a professional poacher? Remember, I was a city kid. I had read about gator poachers in the Glades, seen programs about it on television, but this was different. This was reality.

"In fact, during the immediate instant when the poacher froze in our light, I thought sure the gator tail was just a spare tire. Certainly not a real alligator tail. It had to be our sergeant or lieutenant acting out the part in some kind of realistic training scenario designed to test our alertness and behavior in the field."

Lawless was stunned. He had nailed the poacher who had been ravaging the Glades for weeks. But this was only for a second or two. The wardens ran down to the suspect and cuffed him. That's when Lawless put the man and the black truck together in his mind. There was something familiar about the defiant poacher. Then Lawless remembered. The suspect was the same one he had seen entering the Green Frog earlier that week.

The first words uttered by the stoic captive were chilling. "You're lucky you got the jump on me or I would have killed both of you." There was no emotion, just a coldness that matched that of the reptilian predators who stalked the marsh. Lawless didn't doubt for a minute that the poacher was serious.

There on the levee, the young man talked easily about his tactics and techniques and the art of gator poaching. Years later, after hundreds of poaching arrests, Lawless remembered this brazen poacher as the smartest he'd ever arrested. The suspect seemed pleased to discuss how one did the job right. He led them down to the canal where he had killed the bull gator. The wardens used a line with a snatch hook on the end to pull in the severed front half of the carcass for evidence. There was the spear point of a harpoon protruding from the reptile's head.

"Remember, we never heard a shot fired," Lawless said. "This kid told us how he shined his light until he saw the reflected orange glow of a big gator's eyes and then called him over by imitating the distress grunt of a young gator. He was a pro who knew all the tricks.

"Most of these poachers were born in gator country. A poacher calls a gator in like some people call their pet dog. He imitates the grunting noise a gator makes when distressed or threatened. Most often this will alert the nearest other gator to come towards the sound, searching for another wounded or sick gator for a meal. Gators are cannibalistic and frequently prey on one another. A few years ago one of our wildlife biologists opened up the stomach of a twelve-foot-long dead gator. Inside he found a six-foot gator, neatly chopped into two segments.

"That's what this guy did," Lawless said. "When the gator came towards the bank, the poacher stuck the harpoon into its head. The steel point detached from the harpoon's wooden shaft but remained connected to the thrower by a restraining line secured to a ring at the base of the point. The poacher just pulled in the line and plunged an ice pick into the huge animal's tiny brain. Killed it instantly. In total silence. The guy was a pro."

The wardens hauled off the poacher to Dade County Jail, where U.S. marshals later arrived to take him to federal court on charges of killing a federally protected endangered species within a national park.

Lawless's most vivid recollection of the defendant was totally out of character: This rough-and-tumble denizen of the Green Frog—the cold hunter who would have killed both wardens if given the chance, the man who slew a giant gator with an ice pick in the dark night of the Everglades wilderness—came to court with his mother. She was a well-dressed, conservative-looking lady who had a certain dignity despite the circumstances. The suspect was neatly dressed, sported a fresh haircut, and had a shine on his shoes. Lawless wondered what the boys back at the Green Frog would have thought.

• • •

A good game warden doesn't just depend on luck, although most admit that a little luck plays a key role in most wildlife arrests. Game wardens must be willing to put in the time and effort to cover all the bases—both in the field and when the case goes before the judge.

Lt. Bill Ashley is a good game warden. For many years he worked undercover on a daily basis, cultivating the friendship of various riffraff you might find in places like the Green Frog, the Red Gator, or the Devil's Den. This quiet, tall man looked the part, with his drooping mustache, long hair, faded T-shirt and jeans, and old cowboy boots. Like so many transient laborers, he didn't work regular hours and roamed around in a rusted pickup filled with various tools thrown carelessly about in the back. He was just another good ol' boy.

Outlaws who knew him in those years would have been startled to learn that this rough character was a deacon in the First Baptist Church of Wellington, a former missionary who had worked with the Navajos on their New Mexico reservation near Sante Fe, and a college graduate with a degree in animal husbandry. The outlaw was, in fact, an undercover game warden who sometimes taught Sunday School at his church.

Although born in Alabama, Ashley, 45, grew up in Homestead and Miami, where his father was an oral surgeon. Like so many game wardens, he grew up hunting and fishing, killing his first wild hog at the age of twelve near Immokalee, Florida. At six feet, eight inches, Ashley played defensive end for a semi-pro football team, the Florida Sun, from 1975 through 1977. The 250-pound weight lifter once bench-pressed 450 pounds. He is not a man who is easily intimidated.

One confidential informant Ashley cultivated was a Hell's Angels member who lived a in camper/trailer parked in an area called "The Squares," near the J. W. Corbett Wildlife Management Area near West Palm Beach. The land had been the proposed site for a residential development, but the backers ran out of money after they constructed the road network. Since the site was adjacent to the sixty thousand wilderness acres within Corbett, it wasn't a bad place for a poacher to call home.

The Hell's Angel was one of a few score residing there in a strange collection of battered old trailers, campers, and even canvas tents. There was no water or electricity, and people usually kept to their own business. Perhaps that was the attraction for the biker who seemed content living in an isolated and remote refuge.

"You don't want to know too much about a confidential informant," Ashley said. "You don't ask their motive for coming forward with information. You just use them."

Ashley pulled up to the Angel's camp in his beat-up pickup. Game Warden Ken Parramore followed in his patrol vehicle. The informant came out of the trailer, and the three men talked. The

Angel was right out of the book: a three-hundred-pound mound of
muscle padded with fat and wearing a long goatee, his arms and
visible body parts covered with garish and vulgar tattoos. He was
dressed in leather and hardly a candidate for the cover of
Gentleman's Quarterly.

The Angel told the game wardens that a man who camped about
a mile away had, that very morning, killed a two-foot gator in a
nearby canal—shot him with a rifle. Ashley guessed that the
informant had some sort of grudge against the man or simply
wanted to eliminate the competition in the area.

A few minutes later, Ashley pulled up to the alleged poacher's
trailer, which sat along a canal. That's when a pickup truck, with
several men in the front seat and one riding in the bed, stopped in
a cloud of dust on the other side of the canal.

A bearded man in his forties, wearing only cutoff shorts and no
shoes, jumped out of the truck bed with a shotgun in his hands. He
yelled something at Ashley and then alternatively waded and swam
across the canal. The undercover warden played it cool and didn't
go for his concealed revolver.

The oncoming suspect was angry and probably thought Ashley
was breaking into his trailer. That's when Game Warden Parramore
revealed himself in full uniform. The suspect's demeanor changed
dramatically. They talked. In a few minutes the other two men came
driving up the road in the pickup they had taken over a nearby
bridge.

Ashley and Parramore found a cowboy boot speckled with blood,
a bloody bucket, and a six-inch hunting knife in the truck. They
questioned all three suspects. Each claimed he had nothing to do
with illegally killing a gator. If the trio thought they were free and
clear, they were dead wrong. After the interview, the wardens
searched the area and quickly discovered the carcass of a two-foot
gator.

Ashley took the bloody boot home with him and performed a
simple chemical test developed only a few years earlier. Ashley was
trained in the use of the test kit and was qualified as an expert
witness in court. In a few hours, the reading confirmed that this was
gator blood. A check with the NCIC computer revealed that the
main suspect had a felony record.

Gator poaching is a third-degree felony in Florida. Ashley saw the state's attorney the next morning and got his warrants. After he was found guilty, the defendant—the shotgun-toting man who had come charging across the canal—was sentenced to six months in Hendry County Correctional Institute.

Several months later, a Palm Beach County sheriff's deputy stopped a man at 1 A.M. in a rural area after watching him throw a bag into a canal. He stopped the suspect, thinking he had just disposed of some drugs, but was unable to gather enough evidence to justify an arrest. But he did have the man's identification and address.

Thinking the bag might have contained gator or deer parts, the deputy contacted state Game and Fish. That Sunday Ashley was posted at the back door of the suspect's house while Game Warden Tom Quinn rang the front doorbell.

"That's when this woman bolted out the back door with a pan full of gator meat. She ran right into my grasp," Ashley recalled. "The poor woman was startled to say the least."

It was Ashley's turn to be surprised when, during questioning, the woman said her husband was gone to visit his father in prison. It turned out that the father was the same man Ashley had arrested a few months earlier for gator poaching in the Squares.

The son would have followed his father's path to prison except that the judge only levied a stiff fine because the young man was a first-time offender. Poaching is often a family affair in south Florida, and cases often involve relatives working as a team.

"Like father, like son," Ashley remarked.

● ● ●

White-tailed deer are a favorite target for outlaw hunters. One memorable case involved Game Warden Ken Parramore back in the mid-1980s.

This was a case that was solved over several months through persistence and patience and a desire to nail the outlaws who were regularly poaching deer in an orange grove near the J. W. Corbett Wildlife Management Area in Palm Beach County.

While on routine patrol, Parramore and several of his fellow officers had found sign—boot prints, bent grass, tread imprints, and drag marks—telling them that someone was hauling dead deer out of the grove and loading them in a pickup. Parramore, Warden Jeff

Ardelean, and Lt. Roy Burnsed made it a point during the next several months to check the area frequently. When they found fresh sign, they sat on it, hoping to nab the violators as they came out of the grove with gun and deer in hand.

"We came up empty a bunch," Parramore said. "One of us was out there every few days and during the night as well. We knew these guys were smart because they didn't park a vehicle. Another poacher dropped them off and picked them up at a designated time."

Flights over the area had not picked up telltale beams of light. These poachers were not "fire hunters," who risked detection every time they spotlighted a deer; they were hunting at dawn and dusk when you could still see to shoot and when deer were most active. A single small-caliber rifle shot usually didn't attract much notice.

The wardens noted that the truck tire imprint had a distinctive pattern, a signature which told them that this was the same group of poachers repeatedly raiding the grove for deer. After a heavy rain one afternoon, Parramore went to the grove and quickly found the distinctive tire track in the mud. Footprints led into the area. This was "one-way sign," which meant the violators probably hadn't left yet.

Parramore called for backup. At around 6 P.M., he was joined by Warden Ardelean. They hid their vehicles under camouflaged netting and took up a surveillance position under an orange tree. It was high summer, and the light held for a long time. It was hot and humid, and the air swarmed with mosquitoes.

"They were just fierce that night," Parramore recalled. "We were raking them off our arms. You could reach out and grab a handful right out of the air. They were that thick."

Three hours passed. No truck. No poachers. Then, just as the sun was dropping, they heard footsteps and soon glimpsed the shadows of three men coming down the trail.

"Two of them were carrying the carcass of a six-point buck trussed up by the legs underneath a carrying pole with one man in front and the other in the back like some African safari movie," Parramore remembers. The third man had a rifle in his hands. The suspects crossed the road and hid in the underbrush. The wardens could hear them talking quite distinctly. They were waiting for the pickup.

"Jeff and I figured that if we ran out at them then, they would scatter into the woods like so many quail," Parramore explained. "This wasn't the time to step out. We could hear them talking, complaining that their ride was late. We waited."

Ardelean maintained surveillance while Parramore slowly crept away deeper into the grove, where he could safely use his handheld radio. He alerted Lieutenant Burnsed, who immediately set up a blocking position on the only access road.

The wardens had closed the gate of the trap. Now it was only a matter of a little more patience.

An hour later, yellow headlights came bobbing up and down the dirt road. The pickup of the deer and three poachers took less than a minute. The waiting poachers threw the deer and rifle in the back and sped down the road. Burnsed was waiting. The game warden waved them over to the shoulder, and gave them a cheery good evening. It was routine from there on in. The suspects may have mumbled a few remarks about nosy game wardens, but there was no resistance. A few minutes later, the other wardens drove up. They seized the deer, the rifle, the truck as evidence. The three young male suspects from nearby Loxahatchee were charged with trespassing and deer poaching.

The hours of sitting on sign, slapping mosquitoes, and sweating in the steamy humidity of south Florida had paid off. The wardens went home happy. They had made a good case, and perhaps the subjects would hesitate before they hunted deer out of season again.

At least one could always hope.

• • •

Rick Douglas spent most of his days hunting, legally and illegally. He was a burly, bearded man around fifty-five years old with iron gray in his dark hair. After a twenty-year career in the U.S. Navy, he had moved to Miami, worked as a carpenter for a few years, and then was injured when Hurricane Andrew took the roof off of his house in 1996.

Since then he'd been living on disability and spending most of his time in the woods. That was plain to see. Douglas habitually wore dirty, bloodstained hunting clothes and roamed about in a dilapidated pickup with a rifle or shotgun always prominently displayed on the rack behind the rear window. He was a man with a lot of time on his hands and apparently not a lot of ready cash.

On this day in the fall of 1996, Douglas drove his pickup into the driveway of a modest home in LaBelle, the seat of Hendry County, which lies northwest of the Everglades. He walked into the backyard and entered a small outbuilding where a man he didn't recognize was butchering a deer. The building was outfitted like a slaughter-house, complete with a set of huge freezers.

"Where's Carl?" Douglas asked.

"Not here," the man remarked casually.

"I brought him a hog," Douglas said. "It's out in my truck. Weighs about sixty pounds. Carl told me on the phone he'd give me twenty-five dollars for it."

"Not a problem," the man replied. "Go on and bring it in, and I'll pay you the money."

Douglas came back moments later with the carcass thrown over one shoulder and effortlessly tossed it onto one of the cutting tables.

After the money changed hands, Douglas—a talkative, outgoing man with a ready smile and a joke—engaged the meat-cutter in conversation.

"What else do you guys buy?" Douglas asked.

"Anything."

"Anything?"

"Deer, turkey, ducks, deer, possum, coon. Everything," the man replied casually.

"Deer too?" Douglas asked in surprise.

"Sure."

"How much can I get for a deer?"

"Depends on the size. Anywhere from sixty to seventy-five bucks," the man answered.

"Wonderful!" Douglas replied with a wide grin. "I love to hunt anyway. Now I can make a few dollars at the same time. This will be great."

Douglas told his new friend that he didn't have a regular job, spent most of his days in the woods, and relished the opportunity to make his hunting hobby pay hard cash. They shook hands and parted friends.

The meat-cutter was unaware that the conversation had been taped by the electronic "wire" strapped to Douglas's chest under his hunting shirt. Two other undercover game wardens listened to every word while parked nearby in their inconspicuous civilian truck.

The man calling himself Rick Douglas was Lt. Dick Lawrence, the veteran game warden now assigned to the Investigations Unit. His natural-born acting talent and gift for gab were invaluable in his role as a poacher looking for easy money. His mission was to infiltrate the illegal commercial wildlife operation in LaBelle, collect evidence, and lay the groundwork for a big bust. Since Lawrence had actually served a tour in the Navy and was an experienced and avid hunter, his cover story was a perfect fit.

Now Lawrence had taken the crucial first step toward winning the trust and confidence of the LaBelle poaching ring. It was part of the plan conceived and directed by his supervisor, Capt. Steve Blissett, who headed the ten-man, plainclothes Everglades Investigation Unit. The covert operation had been, as so many times in the past, sparked by a call from a confidential informant.

Blissett was a twenty-five-year veteran who knew the covert business from the ground up. One of his first assignments as a young game warden had been deep undercover in the Ft. Myers area, where he infiltrated a major ring dealing in alligators, deer, and saltwater sport fish. No one had a better appreciation for the risks Lawrence was running as an undercover game warden. Blissett knew that many individuals dealing in illegal wildlife were often violent, frequent drug users or dealers, and willing to make a buck on anything. Most carried weapons and knew how to use them.

"An undercover game warden has to deal with that telephone call in the middle of the night when your target calls you and asks for a meeting in a swamp twenty miles from anywhere. Sometimes this might be at three A.M. It could be just another buy or it could be a setup. That thought is never far from your mind," Blissett said.

"But you've got to go and meet them or you lose face and jeopardize your hard-won credibility as one of the boys. As you drive there in the dark, you keep wondering if they've discovered your true identity. You could be walking right into an ambush. All you can do is stick a little .25-caliber automatic pistol in your back pocket and hope it doesn't come to that."

At the same time, Blissett knew how valuable covert operations were in infiltrating and eliminating the illegal wildlife dealers. The traditional uniformed game warden in the woods might apprehend a single deer poacher in the course of a week-long patrol. But a covert effort could reach up the food chain and nail the wholesaler, who might control thirty to fifty illegal hunters. An organized ring that large can rape a county of its wildlife over several years, illegally killing hundreds of deer and other animals out of season.

Illegal commercialization of wildlife is a threat to the law-abiding sportsmen whose game is stolen, and—if unchecked—poses an even more serious threat to the survival of wildlife populations. History records that unrestricted commercial or market hunting had nearly wiped out a number of species in the late nineteenth century, including the American buffalo, the plume birds of the Everglades, and various waterfowl species so prized as restaurant fare.

Now Blissett had his agent, Lawrence, poised at the door of one of the most extensive poaching rings in south Florida history. Shutting them down, perhaps even putting the ringleaders in jail or hitting them with heavy fines, would be a significant victory for wildlife conservation.

A few days after his first visit to the ring's LaBelle headquarters, Douglas returned with another wild hog. He met the ringleader, Carl Bodhai, a native of Trinidad who greeted his new poacher without a suggestion of suspicion or wariness. The garrulous Douglas quickly won over Bodhai who, the officer sensed, took an immediately liking to him. The ringleader encouraged his new friend to return and bring in more wildlife. That's when he told him about the New York connection.

Douglas was surprised to learn that the LaBelle ring served a number of ethnic restaurants in Brooklyn and other Burroughs of New York City. Bodhai unwittingly revealed to the undercover game warden that he made a trip twice a month to New York City with a trailer full of illegal deer, wild turkey, and gator meat. Each trip, he bragged, netted three thousand dollars.

The properly impressed Douglas whistled in admiration. Cleverly, he then told Bodhai how he'd always wanted to visit Yankee Stadium in New York and see snow on the ground for the first time in his life.

"I get bored a lot," Douglas added. "Anytime you need somebody to drive or keep you company, give me a call. It'll give me something to do."

"Sure," replied the unwary target.

Operation Brooklyn, as it was christened by Captain Blissett, was moving right along. Over the next sixteen months, Lawrence and another undercover game warden, Bill Smith, became close friends with Bodhai and many of his ring members. Sometimes Lawrence brought a deer carcass for sale or sometimes just dropped by to shoot the breeze with his new friends. The game warden learned that some of Bodhai's illegal hunters were taking anywhere from seven to nine deer a night. The impact on the surrounding deer herd had to be devastating.

Captain Blissett later estimated that Bodhai's illegal operation was taking more than three hundred deer every year from rural Hendry County. The ringleader was making an income of fifty-five thousand dollars a year off his illegal enterprise, which involved at least thirty deer poachers. The illegal deer harvest in the county probably equaled or exceeded the legal harvest.

In the days ahead, Blissett's undercover agents learned that the ring had been operating for nearly three years. They estimated more than five hundred deer and fifteen hundred wild hogs had been illegally killed and sold during that period. Profits were high. Bodhai bought deer meat at a one dollar a pound and sold it for five dollars. He paid poachers six dollars for a wild turkey and sold it for twenty dollars. The ringleader's operation was served by at least thirty hunters who typically killed the deer out of season and/or at night using spotlights. Bodhai would fill any order, whether it was ten pounds of alligator meat or a half-dozen wild turkeys, whatever wildlife the customer wanted.

Bodhai and those around him were living outside the law. But they didn't appear dangerous. That wasn't the case with one of the illegal hunters. This was the man Game Warden Lawrence nicknamed "John the Snake." During their frequent bull sessions, this dark, lean man with saturnine features quickly got drunk, and just as quickly turned mean. As a veteran game warden, Lawrence had met his share of dangerous outlaws and instinctively knew a genuine renegade when he saw him. The Snake was a dangerous man. He was volatile and unpredictable, a violent human predator, a man to be watched.

As the Snake got drunker, he bragged about killing two people back in his native Trinidad. You could tell from the dull gleam in his dark eyes that he enjoyed the memory like some men might recall a successful deer or duck hunt. Douglas was convinced this was not booze-inspired bravado. The Snake had the look and the eyes of a killer.

Good Guys and Bad Guys

One day the Snake stared into Rick Douglas's eyes and told the undercover game warden that he could draw, throw his knife, and stick Douglas in the head before he could ever draw his pistol. The remark caught Douglas offguard for a moment. The undercover game warden wondered if the Snake had seen past his cover and knew that he did indeed carry a concealed weapon. Was the Snake sending him a warning? Or was it a test?

"What the hell are you talking about, Johnny?" Douglas replied with a smirk. "I don't have no gun on me! No reason to carry one."

The Snake replied, "I'm just sayin' if you did, I could stick you between the eyes before you could clear the holster. That's all."

Douglas took a deep breath. The crisis was over. He was again just one of the boys.

During the same conversation, the Snake described in great detail how to make bombs using chickpeas soaked in gasoline. The Snake was clearly excited as he described how one of these homemade bombs could destroy a house and set its occupants on fire. Sometimes he appeared almost gleeful, explaining in garish and vivid detail how the individual flaming peas would explode like so many primitive bomblets. "He was a real piece of work, he was," Lawrence said.

The Snake kept drinking. Douglas knew he was a hot-tempered drunk. On several occasions he warned Captain Blissett that the suspect could prove dangerous once they reached the arrest stage. They would have to be careful with the Snake, who was as deadly as a cottonmouth in the Everglades swamp.

Captain Blissett shares the attitude of almost all veteran game wardens that the typical poacher is no Robin Hood who hunts to feed his family. Poachers are in the game for fast, easy money. No other reason. And, for the most part, the game attracts unsavory characters like John the Snake. Most people wouldn't want them for neighbors.

"Life on the suspect's property consisted of nightly parties and was a 'hangout' for young adults," Captain Blissett wrote in his final report on the LaBelle ring. "The undercover officers formed new relationships and were introduced to other avenues of criminal activity.

"Narcotics—including marijuana, crack cocaine, and heroin—were present. Many attending the parties were involved in fencing stolen property, prostitution, and burglary. Fictitious passports and Social

Security cards were readily available for a price," he wrote. "Marriages-for-hire were arranged for illegal immigrants, and, of course, the core of the illegal commercial wildlife business was transacted at these parties. Phone calls would come in nightly requesting orders for wildlife. Suppliers would drop off their animals and request payment. Our undercover officers observed all this take place."

As time went on the two undercover game wardens, Douglas and Smith, were accepted without question as members of the ring. The unsuspecting Bodhai didn't realize that every time his friend Rick Douglas backed up his pickup in the ringleader's driveway to unload wild game, the transaction was taped by a concealed video camera in the truck's tool box.

Bodhai even invited the other undercover warden, Bill Smith, to park his camper-trailer on his property while he looked the area over in preparation for beginning a nursery business. This gave the agent the opportunity to observe the daily routine without incurring suspicion. The fox was living in the henhouse.

A major benchmark in the operation came when Bodhai invited the agents to accompany him on a selling trip to New York City. The undercover agents loaded one freezer on their truck while Bodhai loaded his own customized refrigerated meat truck.

"At first we loaded the deer, wild turkey, and alligator—all the illegal stuff," Douglas said. "Then we piled in the legal game: coons, possums, armadillos, and Muscovy ducks. If a game warden stopped us and looked into the freezers, that's all he could see."

The run to New York City was a calculated risk. Major Randy Hopkins, who oversaw all undercover game warden activities in the state, was concerned. They couldn't provide security for the two officers as they drove through five states. If there was trouble, Douglas and Smith were on their own. Hopkins made his early reputation in covert operations and knew the dangers. He personally asked Lawrence if he thought the New York trip was worth risking.

"I told Major Hopkins that there was little or no danger," Lawrence said. "By this time, Carl Bodhai and I were best buddies. The New York trip was too good to pass up. Then Major Hopkins gave us the go ahead."

They left LaBelle at 8 P.M. Friday and rolled into Brooklyn about the same time Saturday night. All along the way, the two undercover agents took numerous photographs. They acted like tourists on their first trip north. Taking snapshots appeared quite normal so there was no real reason to use hidden cameras.

"We sold meat all through the night once we got there," Douglas said. "We drove all over Brooklyn and Queens, selling to meat markets, beer joints, and ethnic restaurants in various West Indian communities—two thousand pounds in total. All this activity was photographed and would serve as compelling evidence in court."

The ongoing investigation also revealed that Bodhai had buyers in Miami, Ft. Lauderdale, and West Palm Beach. Operation Brooklyn had pulled the rock back and revealed the sordid day-to-day details of the illegal wildlife trade. Captain Blissett knew it was time to plan the bust.

In the pre-dawn hours on Monday, December 8, 1997, a task force of fifty-four game wardens swept into LaBelle. Arrest teams were dispatched to the residences of nine suspects, including Carl Bodhai and his wife, Nadia. The takedown was directed by Captain Blissett and assisted by Capt. Bruce Hamlin, who coordinated the arrest teams. Most teams consisted of four game wardens, two for the front door and two for the back. Additional manpower was utilized in a few cases where resistance was deemed likely. Within two hours, Hamlin's uniformed game wardens and Blissett's investigators had rounded up eight of the suspects without any resistance. The final target was located a few hours later. All were taken to Hendry County Jail and charged with various misdemeanors and felonies.

Carl Bodhai, thirty-nine, was charged with five felony counts relating to the illegal commercialization of wildlife. These are third-degree felonies punishable by up to a five-thousand-dollar fine and/or five years in jail. In total, the nine defendants were charged with fourteen felonies and twenty-six misdemeanors.

Lt. Dick Lawrence (alias Rick Douglas, wildlife poacher) was there that day in full uniform, savoring the satisfaction of a difficult and dangerous job well done. His only regret was that the Snake was not among those arrested. Try as they might, the undercover game wardens had never obtained sufficient hard evidence linking the Snake to the illegal ring.

Little did Lawrence know that all those arrested that day in LaBelle would never serve a day in jail or pay fines appropriate to the illegal profits they had made over three years. The elation experienced on the day of the bust was replaced with bitter disappointment when Operation Brooklyn reached the courts. The county state's attorney office and the presiding judge apparently failed to understand the gravity of the charges or the serious implications of unrestrained commercialization of wildlife. A deal was cut, and the targets of Operation Brooklyn left the court without suffering major consequences.

Carl Bodhai, the ringleader, pleaded no contest to his nineteen charges. The judge found him guilty, fined him a total of $1250, placed him on five years' probation, curtailed his hunting privileges for three years, and ordered him to take a state-sponsored hunter-education course.

The other eight defendants got off with even lighter sentences consisting of probation, curtailment of hunting privileges for a year, and fines running from two hundred to nine hundred dollars. They were also ordered to enroll in a hunter-education course.

After a sixteen-month-long covert operation involving a great expenditure of manpower, time, and taxpayer money, the perpetrators walked off with a slap on the wrist. Operation Brooklyn will be remembered as a successful and well-conceived covert infiltration of a major illegal wildlife ring; it will also symbolize for many game wardens and wildlife conservationists the failure of the judicial system to adequately punish those who rape and exploit our precious wildlife.

This is not an uncommon occurrence. Many judges and prosecutors dismiss wildlife and fish cases as insignificant. Until all the courts and prosecutors understand the seriousness of wildlife violations and the importance of protecting wildlife from the greedy market hunters, the dismal conclusion to Operation Brooklyn will be repeated.

The day of reckoning will come only when the nation's conservationists insist to their public leaders that they will no longer tolerate business as usual for those who defy the fish and game laws. One may only hope that this day will come before the rapacious human predators make wildlife deserts out of our forests and swamps.

Chapter 7:
The Outlaw Life

The government killed my daddy. He died in my arms
with a bullet in the heart. His last words were, 'I love you,
son.' That was in 1932. I was ten years old.
                        —Norman Padgett, poacher

M en lived by different rules and had a fierce pride born of the Florida frontier when Norman Padgett was growing up during the 1920s and 1930s. This was the code Norman's people taught him in the tiny and remote fishing village of Sand Cut on the eastern shore of Lake Okeechobee. His mother's father, J. W. Upthegrove, had come to this country as a hunter in search of bird plumes and gator hides in the late 1800s. He and his two brothers founded Upthegrove Beach on the north side of the lake and eventually became commercial fishermen living off the rich bounty of the seven-hundred-square-mile lake.

The Upthegroves were hardy, stubborn folks who didn't tolerate an insult or ask for a handout. They had made this country and persevered despite the suffocating heat, the droning swarms of mosquitoes, the stinging deer flies, giant gators, deadly water moccasins, and the occasional hurricane.

Today Norman makes a living legally hunting and selling frog legs, turtle meat, and gator meat from his home in West Palm Beach. He is a bearded man with strong features and a powerful handshake. Despite his seventy-six years, he looks much younger, and his knotted forearms suggest great strength. He wears coveralls held up with red suspenders, rubber boots on his feet, and a ten-gallon hat perched on his head. Norman Padgett is a quiet-spoken,

Outlaw Life. *Norman Padgett, 78, grew up in a frontier society now largely consigned to history books. His grandfather made his living hunting and fishing, and Norman followed the same path even when it meant defying the law. (Jim Huffstodt)*

polite man whose rather gentle demeanor stands in stark contrast to the stories one hears of his wild youth.

If you wish to understand why Norman Padgett defied the fish and game laws and won a reputation among certain game wardens as a dangerous man, you must travel back to the Sebastian Bridge on December 1, 1922. John Ashley and several of his famed bank-robbing gang were kneeling handcuffed in a line on the bridge, lit by the glare of kerosene lanterns and surrounded by the armed members of Sheriff Bob Baker's posse. The sheriff had pursued the legendary one-eyed bank and train robber for years. And there on the Sebastian Bridge the mythical career of John Ashley, the King of the Everglades, ended in a fusillade of gunshots.

Norman Padgett was only two when Baker's posse executed John Ashley and the others, but he knows the story well. His favorite aunt, Laura Upthegrove, the older sister of his mother, Lola, had been John's sweetheart or, in the tabloids of the day, the Queen of the Everglades. One of Ashley eyes had been shot out by a gang member after an argument following a botched robbery. Sheriff Baker removed the glass eye after the bandit's death and placed it prominently on his office desk like some kind of gruesome hunting trophy.

"Aunt Laura heard he was bragging about gettin' John's eye," Norman said. "So she went up to his office. Sure enough, the eye was right there. She told the sheriff: 'We're burying John today, and if we don't bury him with his eye, then they're going to be burying you the next day.' They buried John Ashley with his glass eye."

She often told young Norman about John and why he had lived a life of crime after killing a man in self-defense in 1911. The law, however, saw it differently. They called it murder.

"John was huntin' the Glades with an Indian, according to Aunt Laura," Norman recalls. "John didn't trust him. White men didn't trust Indians in those days, and Indians didn't trust white men. That's the way it was back then before the First World War. Anyway, the Indian made the first move, but John killed him first. Should have come into town and told them it was self-defense. Instead, John just stuck the body in a gator hole and came on in. That was the beginnin' of John's troubles.

"That's when he started robbin' banks and livin' the outlaw life," Norman said. "John Ashley didn't have no choice about it. He had to keep on the run and live out in the Glades where they couldn't find him. He wasn't no bad man. The only bad man in the gang was this big fella' from New York. He was a gangster who came down after he heard about John's gang. It was him that killed that colored fella' the gang tied to that tree. Ashley didn't do no killin'. That's what Aunt Laura told me.

"We never liked that business of the King and Queen of the Everglades," Norman said. "About ninety-nine percent of what they wrote about John and Aunt Laura was pure fiction. Aunt Laura was a kind, generous Christian woman."

After John's death, Laura's sister, Lola, Norman's mother, married Joe Tracy, a member of the gang.

"Mother married him through the bars of Raiford Prison when I was a little boy. We often visited my stepfather. I grew to know and like him. He was a soft-spoken, slender, dark-haired man, a cattleman from Osceola County who did wonderful things with leatherwork. Joe Tracy died the day before they were going to let him out of jail."

Norman's natural father, Noah, was a hard-fisted farm boy from Bell, Florida, who came to Lake Okeechobee in search of adventure and a job. He married Lola Upthegrove in 1917 but divorced her seven years later.

"Dad was bad for drinkin' and chasin' women," Norman remembers. "And he didn't back down from no fights. Mother was a big, hearty woman who had a lot of pride. She wasn't goin' to put up with a man slappin' her or hittin' her. So they divorced."

Norman grew up in Sand Cut where most of the neighbors made their living as net fishermen on the lake. He and his mother lived next door to her father, J. W. It was a happy time spent fishing for specs and swimming in the lake. "No danger from big gators back then," he remembers. "It was a public service to kill a gator of any size which came near where people lived. People took care of the problem themselves. Weren't no laws against killin' gators until the 1940s when the Florida Game and Fresh Water Fish Commission was created."

The boy spent vacations with his father, who now worked in West Palm Beach as a construction worker building the sea walls that still stand rusting out amidst the breakers off Palm Beach Island. In his spare time, Noah Padgett was a square-dance caller and often took his son along for the fun.

One night Noah Padgett took his current girlfriend and ten-year-old Norman to a square dance in Riviera Beach. The mayor of the little town of Lantana was there too—a high-ranking Mason, a prominent man, who was accompanied by a scarlet-haired prostitute Norman's father had once dated. At first there was no trouble, the two men "drinkin' from the same bottle." But then the redhead incited an argument. The two men fought with their fists. "Daddy whipped him fair," Norman remembers.

After the dance, Norman, the girlfriend, and his father walked outside to their Ford Model T. His Daddy was crankin' it up when the mayor of Lantana came out of the shadows with a pistol in one hand. He shot Noah Padgett twice through the heart. Norman knelt with his father's head in his lap, the sound of the gun still ringing in his ears.

"I love you, son," Noah Padgett said in a weak trembling voice. He died in the boy's arms.

Norman said he went a "little crazy" and started cussin' and screamin' at the man who had killed his daddy. The murderer pulled out a blackjack and was going to strike the boy when a another man took it away from him.

The trial lasted only two weeks. The jury let the killer go on a plea of self-defense. Norman would harbor for many years a smoldering hatred and dreamed of bloody vengeance and justice for his slain father, who didn't matter to the jury who had freed the Lantana mayor, who had the influence, the connections, and the money for a high-paid lawyer from Miami. The way young Norman saw it—the government killed his daddy and the government let the killer walk free.

Government and laws were for the rich and the influential. That was clear in Norman's mind. The government had not only murdered his father but had executed Aunt Laura's lover in cold blood on the Sebastian Bridge; the government had sent his stepfather, Joe Tracy, to prison for life. A man with any pride or courage would, in this boy's eyes, make his own laws and live by his own rules. All the rest of it was just a way rich men ran the world for their own benefit and pleasure.

Life was hard in the Depression, although the people around the lake always had plenty of fish, gator meat, frog legs, ducks, and

Everglades Lawmen

Frontier Tradition. *This 1897 Everglades hunter, posing with his trophy crocodile, exemplifies the culture that produced the values gator poacher Norman Padgett learned growing up in the 1920s and 1930s. (Florida Classics Library)*

venison. Norman took his "push boat," or Everglades skiff, out in the marsh to fish and hunt. Most country people couldn't afford the new expensive airboats that were just starting to become common sights.

The people of Sand Cut lived off the wilderness and its bounty, supplemented by food programs initiated by President Franklin Roosevelt's New Deal. Sand Cut was a remote and isolated community; only a few cars traveled the toll road to West Palm Beach each week. Young Norman grew up in a rough-and-tumble frontier community where men settled their differences in brutal fights, sometimes won by a kick from a booted foot to a delicate area of the anatomy. That's just the way things were. It was a long way from the sophisticated society of Palm Beach and the rich men of leisure who came to the lake for the bass fishing.

In the early 1940s, Norman began fishing the lake for a livelihood, starting small but soon expanding his business with the help of a loan from a prosperous uncle. "I bought a nice commercial outfit, a comfortable houseboat to live on, and three little motorized fishin' boats, one with a steel hull. Sometimes a man could make a hundred dollars pure profit a day with a haul-seine. That was big money back in those days."

Prosperity ended when the voters of Florida voted a referendum to create the Florida Game and Fresh Water Fish Commission to manage the state's game and fish resources. The old and largely ineffectual county game wardens were replaced by a cadre of professional state game wardens. One of the commission's first major acts was to ban commercial fishing on Lake Okeechobee as a threat to the sport bass fishery.

This bankrupted the youthful Norman Padgett. He saw it as the work of rich commissioners who were more worried about their sport fishing than whether a poor man might make a living off the lake. He was convinced that the angler's assertion that commercial fishing hurt the bass population was dead wrong. "By takin' out the trash fish and specs, the commercial fishermen were making room for sport fish like bass. Those specs would eat baby bass by the hundreds," he claimed.

Again the government had come down hard on Norman and his people. At least that's how the penniless young man saw things. In the years ahead he made his living off the land—hunting gators and deer, fishing for catfish with fish traps, and taking jobs occasionally as a roofer and construction worker. Norman worked hard and his muscles hardened into rock. He drank a little and didn't back away from fights. "I whipped some and got whipped," he recalls. Sometimes he drank liquor to get limbered up for a square dance.

Norman no longer dreamed of killing the mayor of Lantana. He had walked into a "holy roller" church as a teenager and was saved. Killing was wrong. But that didn't make Norman a model citizen. In his own words, he "backslid" to his old ways on a number of occasions. And, when it came to the fish and game laws, he had only a quiet contempt. God had provided the fish, frogs, gators, and deer for men to reap and use, to feed families, and to make a life in hard times. No government, game warden, sport bass angler, or rich Audubon member sitting on the Game and Fish Commission was going to set limits or boundaries on free men. Hell, this was still America, wasn't it?

Everglades Lawmen

Game wardens came to know Norman Padgett and other members of his family quite well. They knew he hunted gators in areas where it was illegal; some believed him to be a dangerous man with a quick temper and quick fists. Some of it was true, Norman admits, but a lot wasn't. He blames a lot of it on a magazine story in the 1950s in which the writer painted a picture of Norman as a daredevil outlaw who terrorized the game wardens and led them on bloodcurdling chases through the Glades. Most was exaggeration, Norman contends, just like the stories about his Aunt Laura Upthegrove, John Ashley, and the rest of the Ashley gang.

But it was true that Norman took a deep satisfaction in outwitting the wardens. Gator hides brought good money, and who cared if it was illegal? This was Everglades country, rich with gators. Norman wasn't about to let the game wardens keep him out. They could just try and catch him. That was all. It was a war between poacher and game warden, sometimes waged with a little laughter on both sides, and sometimes in deadly earnest. Norman Padgett was becoming a legend.

Gator hunting was still legal in Lake Okeechobee through the 1960s, but the rest of Palm Beach County, Broward County, and Dade County passed laws against the practice years earlier. There were big gators in those forbidden areas, and Padgett periodically hunted them. Usually he worked alone in his airboat, but in 1955 or 1956, he partnered up with two other locals and went gator hunting on a swamp buggy into the Everglades of Broward County.

"We'd kill gators all day, then hole up in some willows and skin gators most of the night," he recalled. Padgett was there against his better judgment. "There were mucho gators there, but also a lot better chance of gettin' caught."

They were killing gators in a collection of small ponds with a .22 rifle and then hauling them out with a twenty-foot pole tipped with a snag hook. They were working in broad daylight, had collected about forty or fifty gators, and then heard the sound of an aircraft engine.

The aircraft circled and buzzed them. The game wardens had caught them red-handed. Padgett knew they would radio for others to come in on a swamp buggy to run them down. They piled the hides together and burned the evidence. "I didn't want the wardens to get anything that might be worth some money," he said.

The Outlaw Life

It was just before dark when the poachers ran the buggy into some willows. Soon they heard the roar of another buggy cruising the area. The game wardens were on their trail. They abandoned their own buggy and ran to hide in the tall grass and bushes. The game warden buggy came closer and closer, running back and forth through the bushes searching, and soon the men realized they might get run over and killed if they didn't make themselves known.

"We stood up so they could see us," he said. "And we gave up." One of the arresting wardens was J. O. Brown, a man who had camped in the Glades with Padgett. Both men basically liked and respected one another. Friendship, however, had to be put aside, and Game Warden Brown took Padgett and his accomplices in for attempting to take gators.

They had destroyed the hides but forgot to dispose of the rifle and snag poles. That and a cheap defense attorney did them in.

Waiting for Nightfall. *A gator poacher prepares for a night in the swamp, circa 1954. Alligator hides brought good money to those willing to risk arrest. (Norman Padgett)*

Everglades Lawmen

Norman Padgett served forty days in the Broward County Stockade. It was neither the first nor the last time he would be arrested for breaking game and fish laws.

Some people say that Norman had an attitude when it came to those men in khaki. Certainly, his resentment against certain game wardens—those he believed were hateful, vindictive, or over-bearing—was strong and sometimes overcame his Christian ethics. "I backslid a lot," he admits. "Most of it was pure ignorance on my part."

Stories about how bad he was are mostly talk with little or no basis in fact, Padgett contends. Some of the old game wardens don't agree. They say Padgett's memory has gone bad or he is conveniently forgetting those moments when the devil sat on his shoulder.

"I was not a big brave person ready to just put his life on the line," Padgett said. "I respected life too much."

Game Warden Jimmy Sistrunk was one who chased Padgett through the Glades on many occasions. Unlike some, Jimmy grew to like Padgett, rather admired his audacity, and enjoyed matching wits with this old swamp fox. But he did once tell the author that Norman was a "hell of a man and no one to fool with."

Padgett remembers Sistrunk's first weeks on the job when he approached Norman and his gator poaching partner, requesting that they teach him the fine points of gigging frogs in the marsh from a speeding airboat. They were naturally reluctant to take a game warden along on their alleged frog hunts because, in reality, it was simply camouflage for their gator poaching activities. But one night, they ran into Sistrunk and reluctantly agreed to show him the ropes. Padgett and his partner had cooked up a plan. One would keep the warden busy gigging frogs while the other continued about the profitable business of hunting gators a respectable distance away.

They kept in touch by CB radio. When one would shut down to start skinning gators, he would tell the other one, who was "babysittin'" the warden, that he had stopped to clean the spark plugs.

Norman chuckles remembering that night. "Old Jimmy kept tellin' us we sure had more trouble with spark plugs than anybody he had ever heard of. Jimmy was no fool. He knew exactly what we were up to," he said. "But he couldn't go anywhere without one of us tagging along to make sure he didn't arrest the other."

The man out hunting would quickly skin the gator, dump the blood and meat in the water, and then conceal the valuable hide in various ways. Norman's favorite tactic was to wrap hides from the smaller three- and four-foot gators around his ankles and then slide his big rubber boots over them.

"I could get seven or eight hides in each boot," he claimed. "The bigger hides I wrapped around my body, flesh side out with a hole I cut in each end so I could tie it snug with a string. Depending on the length, I could conceal up to twenty hides under my shirt."

"Sometimes when I rode up to the boat landing, I looked like I was pregnant," he laughed. "The wardens were suspicious, but they didn't have legal probable cause to search me or, in some cases, the nerve."

One incident involving Game Warden Sistrunk and Padgett is one they have often both reminisced about together with nostalgia.

Padgett had set up a tidy camp on an island in the Everglades with a cabin ashore, a nice houseboat moored nearby, and a landscaped yard he kept mowed. He even planted trees to make the place look even nicer.

One time he was down there with a hide buyer from Georgia and two young poachers in training. After a very good night's work, the hide buyer and Norman stashed the gator hides up along the road for pickup after they left camp. Unfortunately, the two boys had gone out without Padgett's knowledge and shot two small gators the night before they were going to break camp. It was too late to take them out to the highway for the pickup; so Padgett decided they'd take them out the front gate.

Unbeknownst to them, Game Wardens Jimmy Sistrunk and Jimmy Thompson had observed the boys killing the gators from a nearby pump station. The wardens stayed concealed, locked the levee gate, and waited for the poachers to come on out with the hides. Norman hid the hides inside a twenty-gallon propane tank he had customized by cutting out a hole in the bottom, and sealing it with a removable wooden plug. He could pack up to one hundred hides in what appeared to be just a regular propane tank.

When Norman drove up to the locked levee gate the next morning, he was suspicious. He grabbed a hacksaw and started sawing open the lock and was nearly finished when the two wardens came driving up fast.

"We want to search the car, Norman," Jimmy Sistrunk said.

"What for?" responded Norman in feigned innocence, well aware that the two hides were inside the propane tank sitting on the floorboards by the front seat.

"We think you're takin' out gator hides," Jimmy replied.

"Well, you go on and look," Norman said. "You won't find nothin'."

The search began, and at one point, Warden Thompson took Norman's keys out of the ignition.

"I told him I wanted those keys back," Norman said. "He knew there would be a scrap if he didn't, so he gave them back. Both of them played fair. They were good guys."

Norman sat back down on the front seat on the passenger's side with his foot on the propane tank. Sistrunk came over and asked to inspect the tank. They discussed it and Norman expressed his reluctance to tear apart a perfectly good piece of equipment on the account of a nosy game warden.

"Jimmy walked away a bit then, to give me some breathin' room," Norman said. "That's when I grabbed the propane tank, jumped out, ran over to the rail of the bridge and threw it into the canal."

To Padgett's surprise, the tank floated. And, without a second thought, he jumped after it, landing with a splash in the deep-water canal.

"I grabbed the tank and pulled out the plug underwater and then pulled out the hides. Jimmy came in almost right on top of me," he said.

"There we were both treadin' water, laughing at each other. Jimmy told me, 'Now, Norman, you always promised me not to put up such a fuss if I caught you fair and square. So hand over those hides you got hidden.'"

Sistrunk hadn't seen Padgett pull the hides out and let the tank sink to the bottom. Norman only smiled and nodded agreement. Then he lifted the wooden stopper out from under the water.

"That's when Jimmy realized he didn't have any evidence," Norman recalled with a glimmer in his blue eyes. "We just laughed together. Old Jimmy could take a joke. He was a good guy, a good game warden."

Norman Padgett was never bitten by any of the hundreds of gators he took from the mid-1940s through the mid-1960s. He was injured only once during an illegal gator hunting expedition in the 1950s, which took him down the Miami Canal into the Everglades.

"We had opened that canal up to airboats and broke out the trail for those who followed," he said. "We set up a nice camp and started roddin' out gators from their caves."

"Rodding" involved taking a ten-foot steel rod and driving it into the soft earth, searching for the direction the gator cave took. With a bit of practice, a man could easily trace the cave all the way back. Gators would often "sull," or sulk, in their caves, and "roddin'" was the best technique to find and kill them. A poacher with the "touch" could tell if he struck the gator itself and would "punch him a time or two" to kill the animal in its den. The poachers would dig down to the cave, snag the gator with a pole hook, and haul it up.

One of the gators they dug out measured nearly twelve feet, a real big bull. Somebody produced an 8 mm home movie camera and started to film Norman and his big catch.

"I was holding the jaws open so he could get a good shot," he said. "But that gator head was slick and greasy, and my grip slipped." The inch-long teeth drove right through one of Norman's hands.

During his poaching years, Norman killed alligators with deer rifles, .22s, shotguns, hatchets, rods, and knives. Between trips to the Glades, he made money as a journeyman plasterer. Killing gators was the more profitable of his trades. One of his brothers was impressed when he learned how much Norman was making on a good day hunting gators illegally. He told Norman that he made as much as some of the best lawyers in the county.

If the gators were under four feet long, Norman killed them with his bare hands. He'd jump on a gator from the airboat, stick him between his legs so he wouldn't roll, turn him upside down across one leg, and break his back. But mostly he shot them with a .22 rifle, aiming for the eyes reflecting red in the beam of the spotlight. Big gators were shot, then chopped across the spine with a hatchet, their bodies hanging over the boat so the blood would run into the marsh. A man wanted to make sure a big gator was truly dead before hooking him with a pole and bringing him to the boat. "Dead" gators had an unpleasant habit of coming to life. Norman would always lay a big gator with his head in the water and the tail in the boat.

"I'd take the hatchet and chop him right across the back legs," he said. "Then I'd take a length of clothes hanger—never went to the woods without it—and would run it through the spinal cord both ways. That took the life out of any gator."

Baiting gators with rotting meat was a fool-proof method, according to Norman: "One hundred percent. No exceptions." He preferred taking a dead heron or coot or rabbit and letting it rot to the point where it would float in the water. In this kind of hunting, Norman used a conventional fishing pole with a treble hook at the end. The hook was jammed into the rotting meat. If a gator appeared, Norman steered the boat straight at him. The reptile would sink at his approach, and then Norman dropped off the floating bait as he passed over. The best strategy was to keep moving right along for a hundred yards or so, then slide the boat behind some tall grass or bushes. The wait was usually no more than fifteen minutes.

"That gator would pop right up and charge that bait," he said. "Swallow it right down whole. Then you just reeled him in, hit 'im with a hatchet, and skinned him."

No two gator poaching expeditions were ever exactly alike. That was one reason he liked it so much. The work was hard, the game wardens watchful, the mosquitoes and deer flies bothersome, but it was still fun. Norman smiles when he remembers one night running the L-28 canal next to the Seminole Everglades Indian Reservation.

His half-brother, Raymond Watson, was his partner that night. They were chugging along in a twelve-foot kicker boat, killing gators as they went and throwing them into the boat. Just another night workin' the Glades. It was a busy, profitable night. The little boat was running deep, overloaded with gators. That's when a five-footer suddenly came to life and decided the most direct route back to the marsh was up and over Norman's brother.

"Crawled right over him," Norman remembers gleefully. "Near scared him to death. Raymond let out a scream and we both started trying to get out of the way. That overloaded boat swamped and went right straight to the bottom."

They spent a good part of the rest of the night dragging out their

Once-Bitten. Norman Padgett spent nearly his entire life hunting, living with, and wrestling gators but was bitten only once by a dead bull. (Jim Huffstodt)

boat, cleaning the engine, and recovering their gators. But it was another good story to add to a growing collection. "Every time we went out it was a new experience," Norman said.

It was a good life but one that carried a price. Norman admits that worrying about the game wardens running up on him made him "chew a lot of Tums" while out the Glades. A man with a big family couldn't afford the heavy fines.

When the U.S. Fish and Wildlife Service declared the American alligator an endangered species in 1965, everything changed. Now hunting gators was a federal offense carrying a heavy fine and jail time. A way of life came to an end.

Oh, Norman Padgett admits to "slipping around" a few times in the years since, but his glory days are now only memories. Over those decades this man harvested more than just gators; he accumulated a thousand stories of runnin' the Glades, a thousand tales of critters and wild-spirited adventures. Many of those recollections concern the partners who shared the risks and the game wardens who dogged their trail. He seems to regard both with equal fondness, with an exception here and there.

The author stopped and shared a cup of coffee one afternoon with this survivor of a lost world—a man who made his living in the wilderness. Perhaps Norman Padgett was a bad man in his youth. Today, he is a pleasant companion and an accomplished storyteller. Gone are the nights when he was a will-o'-the-wisp, a ghost, a phantom that stole through the depths of the Glades in the dark of the night, a brother to the water moccasin and panther.

Norman Padgett is a living artifact from another time and place. His breed, his way of life, his adventures will soon be found only in history books along with the legends and exploits of the other strong-willed men who found life and meaning in the American wilderness.

Chapter 8:
Death Lurks in Dark Waters

At this point, any sense of fear was gone. I just wanted my kid back.

—Gary Weidenhamer, father

Ancient cypress trees, some five centuries old, cast their shadows on the coffee-colored water while canoes glide slowly along the serpentine length of the Loxahatchee River near Jupiter. The voyagers are entranced with the silence and splendor of the surrounding forest of venerable cypress, red maple, dahoon, holly, slash pine, and oak. This is a remnant of Florida's wilderness beginnings, a rich resource protected by its designation as the only federal wild and scenic river within the state.

Seminoles called it the "river of turtles." Once its banks echoed with the sound of musketry when that tribe waged its desperate fight against the United States Army, but today the river valley is a peaceful haven, a place for quiet reflection and blissful serenity. Canoeists paddle and drift down its length, their laughter and bits of conversation floating across the slow-moving water.

They come to see wild Florida, to glimpse a raccoon scurrying through a thicket or hear the sharp rap of a pileated woodpecker drilling into a pine tree. Sometimes the lucky ones catch a fleeting image of a bobcat or gray fox padding silently through the forest. The visitors glide down the twisting water path with a confidence that no harm could come amidst such gentle beauty.

But lurking in the dark waters is grim and horrible death. It waits there, camouflaged and still, biding its time with a patience forged in prehistoric times. The predator feels the vibrations in the water of the passing canoes. The great alligator, stretching eleven feet and weighing four hundred pounds, is the dominant predator on the river. Like all of its kind, it feeds on the small, the weak, the young, the sick, and the old. This cruel monarch of the river waits in hiding for the unwary or the unlucky.

On July 25, 1982, Rick Zobel, an off-duty Palm Beach County sheriff's deputy, paddled his canoe down river in company with his fiancée and his seventy-five-pound German shepherd, Sheba. The nine-year-old dog seemed to enjoy the wilderness journey as much as his human companions. Soon they guided the canoe to shore, slid the bow onto a sandy shelving beach, and got out for a rest. Zobel was sitting in a foot of water right off the bank while Sheba was still in the canoe. The young woman was ashore. That's when tragedy struck with the violence and abruptness of a lightning strike. Without warning, a huge alligator slid over Zobel's legs and seized the dog in its massive jaws. The beast dragged its prey into the water and swiftly swam away.

It had happened in seconds. As the gator glided away, Zobel pulled out his police .38 revolver and emptied the chamber, the bullets splashing water around the dark and giant predator. The staccato reverberation of the revolver shots echoed down the quiet tree-lined river corridor.

"I shot that gator five times, but it had no effect," Zobel later told reporters. The gator was probably well over ten feet long and weighed several hundred pounds. Gators don't grow that large and powerful until they are at least fifteen years old.

Gator trappers searched for the killer without success. The beast had vanished into the brown waters, where he resumed his patient waiting. Zobel was devastated by the loss of his pet. And he feared that any animal big enough and strong enough to eat and swallow a seventy-five-pound dog was a deadly threat to humans—especially children. He knew that hundreds of children canoed the river; many also waded the shallows or swam in the deep holes where they might be easy prey for such a large reptile. Innocent lives were at risk.

Zobel expressed his concerns to officials at J. D. Dickinson State Park near Hobe Sound, which encompasses an eight-mile stretch of the Loxahatchee where Sheba had been devoured. People who knew the river believed that the attacking gator had been Big George, a huge gator of legendary reputation and dimensions.

Despite park warnings to the contrary, many passing canoeists fed Big George with leftover sandwiches or hot dogs. The park rangers made an effort to warn visitors about potentially dangerous gators on the river. They were mostly ignored. Many gator experts believe feeding alligators will accustom them to humans and extinguish their "natural fear" of man. Whether a huge bull gator fears anything is a debatable point. Dick Lawrence, a game warden who has captured more than nine hundred alligators over the last twenty-eight years, told the author that a gator longer than ten feet is the "Lord of His Domain" and not to be trifled with. Big George was that size or bigger; he was the monarch of the river. Tragedy lay waiting in the dark waters of the Loxahatchee.

Big George had consumed all but one paw of Sheba. Park officials initiated an alligator watch that lasted a week. They concluded that Big George had not exhibited aggressive behavior toward the scores of canoeists passing down river through the park. Big George, they judged, was not a serious threat to humans. One park official even remarked that the river was not Disneyland. Wilderness always comes with risks, even though the odds might lull the unexpecting into complacency and leave them vulnerable. There were no guarantees of safety.

"If an alligator could take a seventy-five-pound dog from a canoe, it could just as easily take a child," Zobel told reporters. "Children are in danger! Is this alligator going to attack a child the next time?"

Zobel appealed his case to state lawmakers and the state park administration, and sought public support for removing from the river any and all gators over eight feet long. He was passionate and driven, sounding a warning on television news programs and in newspaper interviews. The Florida Game and Fresh Water Fish Commission, which yearly traps thousands of large and potentially dangerous alligators, deferred the decision to the park division of the Florida Department of Natural Resources. Incredibly, many members of the public expressed their support for keeping Big George alive and in the river. Zobel's efforts failed. The dog killer was left in peace to grow even larger. Deadly peril still lurked in the dark and dangerous waters of the Loxahatchee. Death waited in its silent and invisible depths.

Everglades Lawmen

• • •

Game Warden Richie Obach knew the river and he knew gators. The Loxahatchee River was part of his wilderness beat—his turf. He took special pride in his role as protector of the wilderness waterway. Although in his early fifties, Obach was a strong, active man whose glasses couldn't quite hide the fact that he had been a tough city kid from the New York streets. His love of the outdoors and passion for brown trout and wild streams took root and was nurtured during the summers he spent as a youth at his grand-mother's resort in the Catskill Mountains.

As a young man, he had worked as a seaman aboard a German merchant ship bound for Australia, where he spent two years adventuring. Among other exploits, Obach hooked, fought, and landed a world-record marlin while fishing out of Cairns on Australia's north coast. Those who knew him respected him as a good officer and a man who'd been around. He was a veteran officer and a good tracker, and had learned the secrets of the south Florida wilderness under the tutelage of his boss, Lt. Roy Burnsed, a native outdoors man.

A week or so before the busy Memorial Day weekend of 1993, a female canoeist approached Obach and told him of a very large and "overly friendly gator" that had come dangerously close to her craft while she paddled through the river portion of the park. Obach was concerned. Big gators should shy away from people and canoes, not boldly approach them.

On the next day, Obach and Dickinson State Park Ranger Derek Velez put in their boat for a look at this brazen gator. They encountered the big fellow a few miles up river from Trapper Nelson's cabin. Once the home of an eccentric wilderness recluse, the site was now one of the park's more popular stops for canoeists going down river.

As Obach's boat neared the big gator, the officer imitated the grunting noise of a baby gator to attract the huge creature. The gator was brazen and swam steadily toward the two officers in the nearby boat. He was, in Obach's opinion, exhibiting the behavior of a potentially dangerous predator that could pose a significant threat to humans. Since, in all likelihood, this gator had never been hunted by man, it was not intimidated by their presence.

"I called him and he came right over to the boat," Obach said.

"Then he strayed off a little bit; so I threw a Pepsi can in the water. He came right up to the floating can. I momentarily scared him by revving up my boat motor. Then I put my hands in the water and started splashing. The gator started coming toward the boat again."

Obach had taken a good look at the bold gator, which could easily be identified both by its awesome size and by a distinctive golf ball–sized lump over its left eye. The warden surmised that the gator had probably been struck by a prop, or perhaps injured in a savage struggle with another big bull during mating season. It would be easy to identify this specific animal later when the trapper came to remove it. Based on his observations, Obach believed the bull gator was a danger to people canoeing past him down river. Many canoeists who ran the river called the gator with the lump Big George.

The game warden expressed his fears to Velez, who later reported them to the Dickinson State Park superintendent. Obach later stated that, although he didn't use the word destroyed, he told both men that the gator with the lump over its eye needed to be removed from the river. A state park spokesman later claimed that Obach hadn't said the gator should be removed right away. But that was later and representative of the sophistic hairsplitting used by bureaucrats when something goes terribly wrong.

The game warden and Supt. Scott Donald were friends; the latter drove Obach to the airport shortly thereafter for the officer's vacation trip to his beloved Catskills. At that point, Obach said, he expressed his concern about the fearless gator. He knew that his friend was reluctant to remove the gator from a "wild and scenic river." Like many conservationists, Scott believed that the Loxahatchee was an appropriate place for a big gator. There was a danger, but it was remote, as documented by the historical record. No one had been killed by an alligator on the Loxahatchee within living memory. Scott told his friend he would handle the matter. He would send one of his park biologists to have a look.

Park Biologist Walter Timmerman later went up river twice to look for the inquisitive gator as directed by Superintendent Donald. He did find one with a scar over its left eye, but couldn't get real close. The gator acted "nervous and skittish" and swam away at the approach of the biologist's craft. The biologist estimated its length at around nine feet, much smaller than Big George.

"We've had reports for years of a big gator sunning on the banks near there (Trapper Nelson's), but we have never had any reports of an aggressive alligator of that size," Timmerman said later. There, for the moment, the matter ended. The warning had been investigated without resolution.

Park Superintendent Donald was concerned but not unduly worried or alarmed. Indeed, most alligators are shy and wary of humans. They couldn't be accurately called man-eaters in the strict sense of that definition. Giant Nile crocodiles, which kill hundreds of people in Africa every year, are genuine man-eaters. The American alligator is not. Since 1972, there have been nine fatal gator attacks on humans in Florida. Most victims were children; one was elderly. The attacking gators had been very large, the smallest about eight feet.

• • •

Four canoes manned by parents and children wound their way down river through the sun-dappled forest on Saturday, June 19, 1993. The kids were grade-school age and delighted with the outing, which marked the end of the baseball season. Their team, the Lantana Tigers, had finished with ten wins and four losses. Ten-year-old Bradley Weidenhamer had played a big role in building a winning record. He loved baseball and had real talent as a pitcher and catcher. Teammates called him Santiago after the Miami Marlin's star catcher Benito Santiago. In one game, Bradley struck out the slugger of the league, a youngster who wielded a heavy bat. "Bradley could gun him down," Coach Miguel Estrada said in admiration.

The day trip down the Loxahatchee was a reward for the team, but Bradley was a little disappointed. One day on the river just wasn't enough. He wanted to camp out, as his family did when they went north to canoe the Peace River. His parents, Gary and Donna Weidenhamer of nearby Lake Worth, knew that Bradley was in love with the Loxahatchee wilderness, its beauty, its wild things, its "aloneness."

"If there was a spider, he saw it," his mother later said. "A caterpillar. Anything! He didn't miss anything." Like most mothers, she wasn't as keen as her son about bugs. She did love the canoe trips down river but didn't like it when they saw big alligators. Even as a little girl, she had feared the ugly green reptiles with their mouths studded with teeth. They were inhabitants of a child's worst nightmare.

Death Lurks in Dark Waters

People liked Bradley. He was a good kid from a good, church-oriented family. His father taught chemistry at a local high school. The Weidenhamers had standards, values, and goals. They were churchgoing people. Bradley was bright and perceptive, shown in a number of essays written during his fourth-grade year. The boy wrote of an ideal friend, a fellow adventurer, of how they would climb tall trees "to scare our parents." This perfect best friend, he wrote, would be adept at such important boyhood skills as emitting thundering belches. "Someone you could have belching contests with to see who could be the most grotesque," he wrote. "We always argued over who won the contest."

Close family ties were apparent in his writing, especially in passages about his beloved grandparents. February was his favorite month because that's was when Grandpa and Grandma came to visit. "Grandma makes a lot of chocolate pies and my grandpa likes to go fishing," Bradley wrote. Riding to the First Free Methodist Church in Grandpa's recreational vehicle was a real treat for Bradley. The whole world was an adventure just opening its doors for this curious and active child. This was a typical American boy who liked to skateboard, tease girls, and dig up bugs in the backyard. Bradley loved his family, his friends, his life. He was that kind of kid.

Four families, totaling ten kids and adults, had embarked in four canoes rented at Riverbend Park off Indiantown Road. The trip down river to the state park's picnic center at Trapper Nelson's would take several hours. The day was bright blue. It was hot, but the kids didn't mind. They reveled in their foray into the wilderness, like Huck and Tom escaping from school and all its aggravating rules and restrictions. They were free, exploring a wild country. The sound of their laughter drifted down river while they paddled the winding path of brown water. Bradley's canoe suddenly grounded on a sunken log. The boys splashed into the shallow water and pulled the canoe up over the obstruction. A little ways down stream on the left, at a bend in the river, a small sandbar beckoned, a lovely resting spot for the tired paddlers.

Three or four canoes and about ten people were already there on the beach as the party of ballplayers paddled toward shore. An avid swimmer since he began snorkeling at age three, Bradley slid out of the canoe and joined the other boys playing on a sandbar at the far end of the bend. They frolicked in the shallows and Bradley wrestled with a friend before pushing off a few feet into deeper and darker water.

Bradley was treading water when a canoe carrying Karen and Barry Baker passed between him and his playmates on the sandbar. Barry was at the bow paddling when the huge predator came out of the water, seized Bradley, and lifted the boy out of the water as if in a slow-motion horror movie.

The bull gator slammed the body down into the water, but there was, inexplicably, barely a splash. The boy, witnesses later testified, did not shout or scream. The dark creature swam off and submerged with Bradley's limp body dangling from its powerful jaws.

On the shore, Bradley's mother watched apprehensively as one of the boys walked towards her in wide-eyed uncomprehending fear.

"He didn't even yell or anything," Donna said. "He just walked up and said, 'Bradley's been taken by an alligator.' "

Donna screamed her son's name. Her childhood fears of predatory alligators had taken on a terrible reality.

"For less than a second, Donna and Gary thought maybe this was a joke. Kids are like that," wrote reporter Scott Montgomery who later covered the story for the *Palm Beach Post*. "They both looked to the shore to see whether Bradley was hiding near a tree. But at the same time, the voices were getting louder.

"Someone's been attacked by an alligator! Count your children!"

Perhaps Bradley was hiding in the forest, playing a silly child's game to scare the others.

"Bradley, you better not be hiding!" they yelled.

Witnesses described the scene as a vivid and horrible replay of the movie *Jaws*, during which a distraught mother wanders the beach desperately searching for her child, unable to comprehend what has just happened. It was too horrible.

Karen Barker yelled from across the river, her canoe hovering near where the boy had vanished.

"Right here! The gator's got him right down here!" she shouted.

Karen peered into the dark waters, unable to see anything while the nearby Weidenhamer party splashed through the shallows towards her.

"It was so still and quiet, it was like, 'How could anything so horrible have just happened?' " Karen Barker later told a reporter.

The Barkers paddled ashore and then joined the rescuers in the water. Coach Estrada and Bradley's father were desperately searching for a telltale shadow in the water, some sign that Bradley was still near.

Bradley's father saw a swirl of white in the water—his son's shirt.

Coach Estrada shuddered when he made out the form of Bradley, the boy's head still in the mouth of the huge gator.

"When I first saw him there in the water it scared the hell out of me," Estrada later said. "And, then I thought, 'My God! This is Bradley!' "

Bradley's dad grabbed at the shirt and engaged in a tug-of-war with the beast, which wouldn't release his grip on the boy's head. Then he and Karen Barker grabbed one of Bradley's legs and pulled hard, but the gator's strength was enormous.

Now they grabbed both legs. Karen said, "This time when the alligator pulled back we were going to go under with him; there was no way we were letting go!"

Suddenly the gator's ugly snout broke the surface.

"At this point, any sense of fear was gone," Bradley's father said. "I just wanted my kid back."

Lisa Wilson clubbed the gator's head with the sharp edge of her paddle. Coach Estrada flailed away too. Someone was punching the big reptile in its snout.

"It was an incredible thing and very brave for those people to attack that big gator like they did," Lt. Bill Ashley said, after interviewing the participants. "I don't have the words to describe that kind of desperate and unselfish heroism."

Coach Estrada said, "I think I saw his eyes, and I think I aimed at them. I don't know. But I think that was around the time that the gator let go."

The father lifted the limp, bloodied body in his arms and waded through the shallows toward the beach. There Bradley's mother stood, having watched the struggle take place before her terrified gaze. She gathered the others around her. "Pray for my son," she pleaded.

They wrapped a T-shirt around the boy's head and began CPR. Coach Estrada initially wondered if they could get a rescue chopper in, but there was no cell phone and no place for a chopper to land in the forest.

"You're thirty minutes from anything," someone said. "Get Bradley in a canoe and go!" Help was down river at the Trapper

Everglades Lawmen

Nelson picnic ground. That was their only chance, and a slim one at best.

The boy lay in a pool of bloodied water on the floor of the canoe. His father was at the bow, digging into the water with powerful strokes while Karen Barker piloted from the stern. Coach Estrada, a former medic in the U.S. Navy, sat by Bradley, pumping his chest rhythmically.

Gary Weidenhamer repeatedly asked Estrada how Bradley was doing. The former medic lied and told the father he thought the boy had just drawn a breath. Anything to keep hope alive. In his heart, Bradley's father knew the truth. He had seen the awful puncture wounds left by the gator. Bradley had probably died instantly. But they weren't going to give up. They kept paddling, hoping that by some miracle the boy would live.

Down the narrow, twisting river they came, weaving in among low-hanging tree branches and driving the canoe over the top of sunken tree trunks. They didn't have time to stop and portage around. Not if Bradley was to live.

"At that point the adrenaline kicked in and you're able to do things that you can't otherwise do," Gary Weidenhamer said later.

Coach Estrada said it was the longest thirty minutes of his entire life. The battered rental canoe was taking on water from where the seams had parted from the wear and tear of hundreds of trips down river. "Hang on Bradley! Hang on!" his father yelled. Another canoe had gone ahead with the news of the attack, so when they turned around a bend, they saw a crowd of people at the dock at Trapper Nelson's awaiting them.

Karen yelled at them, "We have an injured boy here! He's been bit by an alligator!"

Someone on the dock said in a rather indifferent tone, "Yeah, we know."

Coach Estrada snapped, "This is serious! We need help!" They lifted the soaked, bloodied body from the canoe. Paramedics took a brief look and then carried the boy off to a nearby clearing to await the rescue chopper.

The chopper arrived in minutes, signaling its approach with the staccato rhythm of its whirling blades. The paramedics placed the boy inside, and the Medevac rose up and departed with its tragic burden.

The sound of the helicopter grew distant and faint, and then silence descended again on the quiet place by the river.

In a few minutes, Bradley was wheeled into the emergency room of Jupiter Hospital. At 2:16 P.M., an attending physician declared Bradley Weidenhamer officially dead. The exuberant boy who loved bugs, baseball, and tree-climbing was gone. All they could do now for the boy was to pray.

Sometime later that afternoon Game Warden Gary Liller and gator trapper Mike Rafferty confronted the killer gator very near where the fatal attack occurred. The bull gator charged through the water. Liller fired his rifle at least twice. At the last instant, Rafferty killed it with a scuba diver's "bang stick"—a bullet-tipped rod that detonates when stabbed into the target animal. It proved as effective against a giant alligator as against an attacking shark.

Biologist Tim Regan did the necropsy that night and found the animal in good health but with an empty stomach. Big George measured eleven feet, six inches and weighed more than four hundred pounds. After weighing the evidence, Lt. Lee Beach concluded in the final report that the incident was definitely "a predatory attack."

Few who paddle the Loxahatchee remember or know of the tragedy that occurred there. They are serene in their complacent enjoyment of wilderness beauty, unaware of the gruesome tragedy once enacted on this dark, tranquil wilderness stream.

• • •

Unimaginable horror loomed out of the deep in the frightening and formidable shape of a twelve-foot bull gator knifing through the water towards its unsuspecting prey—an eleven-year-old boy named Robert "Robbie" Crespo.

The boy and a friend were swimming in the canal at Rivergate Park in the little town of Point St. Lucie. Kids often swam here despite several signs warning of alligators in the area. The swimmers were fond of walking down a wooden boardwalk, jumping into the canal, and then swimming back to a nearby boat landing.

On a brutally hot day, August 6, 1984, Carol Fraser of Chester, New Jersey, was fishing near the boat landing. She was the first to spot the huge predator moving fast towards Robbie. The enormous predator was only a few feet short of its target.

She shouted a warning. Chuck Long, a twelve-year-old who had just emerged from the water, also let out a yell. Robbie apparently thought they were joking at first, but then turned around and saw the approaching menace. Robbie frantically tried out-swimming the oncoming gator. As he neared the landing ramp, Chuck Long held out the end of a fishing rod for him to grab. The boy in the canal flailed in the water trying to out-swim his grim pursuer. He never made it.

The gator's jaws snapped shut on one of Robbie's legs and pulled the terrified boy into the murky depths. Sometime later, the reptile broke the surface in clear view of the spectators gathering near the landing.

"It was terrible. I could see the gator with the boy sticking out of his mouth, and the gator was swimming with him down the river," said witness Mitchell Epstein.

Robbie's mother, Mona Heppeard, and his stepfather lived only a short distance from the park. They both were told of the tragedy by local boys who had run up from the scene.

A neighbor remembered the shock she felt when Robbie's mother came up to her and said: "A little boy just told me a gator ate Robbie. Will you please take care of my baby?"

Sue Smith, a reporter for the *Ft. Pierce/Port St. Lucie Tribune,* was there:

"During the search, the boy's mother and stepfather stood on a grassy plot just outside a large shelter awaiting word of Robbie. Mrs. Heppeard was sobbing and wringing her hands as her husband and police chaplain Howard Kennedy . . . tried to comfort her."

Local police officers quickly arrived and spotted the gator several times moving off into the adjoining north fork of the St. Lucie River. Robbie was obviously dead by now, either from drowning or from his wounds. The officers fired twice at the gator with their sidearms and at least once with a shotgun. They missed.

Game Warden Stony Lee arrived about thirty minutes after the attack. Others were on their way. One of the police officers called Lee over to a boat that had been commandeered for the recovery and explained the situation. Lee learned the gator was several hundred yards away, floating just below the surface near the far river bank. The boy's limp body still dangled from the mouth of the giant predator.

Lee clambered into the boat, and they cruised straight towards the gator.

Formidable Predator. *After a 10-year-old boy was killed in the Loxahatchee River by a giant alligator in the summer of 1993, Lt. Bill Ashley bagged this 11-foot-plus bruiser, deemed a threat to waders and swimmers along the same wilderness stream. (Florida Game and Fish Commission)*

"I was on the bow of the boat," Lee said. "I could see part of the boy. It looked as if the gator had him by the left shoulder. . . . Part of the gator's head was visible. I decided to shoot the gator with my service revolver and aimed at his visible eye.

"I fired one round, striking him . . . low. The gator released the boy and disappeared. I could still see the boy until the mud was stirred up by the thrashing of the gator as it submerged and fled."

Game Warden Dale Knapp appeared about that time in another boat and spent several minutes trying to locate the boy with a pole. Frustrated, Knapp soon removed his gun belt and entered the waist-deep water. He was joined shortly afterwards by Lee. The two men, in utter disregard for their safety, spent fifteen minutes searching for the body.

"It took courage and nerve for those wardens to enter the water, knowing that a wounded twelve-foot gator was probably very near, an animal that had only minutes earlier killed a young boy," commented Captain Jim Ries, the senior game warden at the attack scene. "Those officers showed tremendous bravery in their determination to recover that body for the sake of the family."

Gator trapper Mike Rafferty came cruising up in his boat a few minutes later and told Lee he had a long pole with a hook aboard. He used the hook to sweep through the water just off a drop-off only ten feet from where the gator dropped Robbie. He found the body within a few minutes. Robbie was covered in a blanket and returned to the landing, where a crowd watched and waited.

The search for the killer gator resumed. Rafferty and Lee were in one boat. Sergeant David Wilson and Game Warden Carl Young were in another. A third boat contained deputies from the Martin County Sheriff's Department.

A few minutes after 6 P.M., the gator surfaced only a short distance from his last appearance.

"Knapp fired one round, thinking he hit the gator in the head," noted Game Warden Lee. "The gator submerged again."

A short while later, Game Warden Young returned to the ramp to pick up Captain Jim Ries, a veteran officer, rock-steady, calm, a man of quiet authority. The captain carried a high-powered .270-caliber, bolt-action rifle. The Illinois native had grown up with firearms and was deadly accurate with revolver or rifle. Now the recovery team had the weapon and the marksman capable of killing the giant alligator.

"Let's go see if we can get him," Ries said. The boat roared out to join the hunt.

About twenty minutes later, Wilson and Young started shouting and pointing. "There he is! Right there!" The big gator had surfaced about twenty yards away.

Ries propped one knee up against the bulwark of the boat and laid the rifle across it. The monster's huge, twenty-six-inch head loomed into view within the glass eye of the high-powered rifle scope.

"I fired once and just blew the top of the gator's head right off," Ries said. "The bullet just opened his head right up. There was a lot of blood in the water as we pulled up and secured the carcass."

GFC Wildlife Biologist Tom Stice did the necropsy later that day. The monster measured twelve feet, five inches long and weighed more than three hundred pounds. Every indicator pointed to his advanced age. The big predator was probably a half century old or more.

"I don't believe the old myth that once a gator tastes human blood, he'll kill again," Captain Ries said. "But if it happened once, it might happen again. We wouldn't be acting responsibly if we let a gator swim free after wounding or killing a person. And it gives the biologists an opportunity to study the animal and try and determine if there were any physical reasons that might have prompted the attack."

Game Warden Knapp was present at the necropsy. "The alligator was very old," he said. "His teeth were worn down to nothing and he was quite thin through the trunk. This was probably why he attacked a human. After looking at the skull, we found two places where bullets had hit the skull besides Captain Ries's rifle bullet, which had destroyed the animal," Knapp said. "Officer Lee's bullet apparently broke the bony ridge above the gator's right eye. My bullet was still visible, embedded in the broad bone that connects the upper jaw to the socket."

A little boy was dead, his parents were in anguish, and a community was in fear. Fatal alligator attacks generate worldwide press coverage. The horrific nature of a human being killed by a reptilian predator sends shivers up the spine of any person with any compassion or imagination.

Robbie was gone forever. This was a boy who loved to rise up early in the morning, grab a fishing pole and a bunch of worms, and go fishing on the canal or river. Life was just beginning and its pleasant mysteries unfolding. Young Robbie had a girlfriend for whom he had bought a necklace at a neighbor's garage sale.

That neighbor recalled: "He was such a good boy. Just a good kid. He mowed the lawn and never got into trouble."

Let this be the final epitaph for a little boy who never became a man, never married, never fathered a child, never experienced the full joy of adult life.

Children still swim in Rivergate Park, and gators still prowl the dark waters of the St. Lucie River.

Author's Note: The author elected not to use the real name of the superintendent of J. D. Dickinson State Park at the time of the Bradley Weidenhamer gator attack.

Chapter 9:
Predator and Prey

She screamed. That's all she could do. Blood was pouring down her stomach. It looked like a slow-motion cartoon.
—Jason Kershanick, friend

For as long as he lives, Captain David Stermen of the Everglades region will remember the shock, horror, and trauma written on the faces of the children. They had just witnessed a giant alligator attack four-year-old Erin Glover and drag her into the pond. Stermen was a lieutenant in the GFC's South Region on June 4, 1988, when he had the unpleasant task of interviewing the two nine-year-old boys who had been playing with Erin at the pond's edge when the attack occurred. Jason Kershanick was a friend, Justin Glover her brother.

The little blue-eyed blonde girl they called "Gizmo" was walking near the pond near Englewood, Florida, around dusk on a Saturday evening. She and the boys followed her Labrador puppy Shirley down to the water's edge. Although there were big gators in Hidden Lake, they had never posed a threat. Perhaps the presence of the dog prompted the sudden attack. Nobody can ever know. We know the terrible consequences and can only imagine the horror, pain, and terror of Erin's last few minutes of life.

The ten-foot-six-inch bull gator emerged from the water and savagely bit into the little girl's stomach.

"She screamed," Kershanick told the game wardens. "That's all she could do. Blood was pouring down her stomach. It looked like a slow-motion cartoon."

The three-foot-tall, thirty-one-pound little girl with the sparkling smile of a mischievous imp was not much larger than a boar raccoon, often the prey of large gators. Her brother and his friend could only watch while the terrified child cried for help.

"Then he dropped her and crawled away," Jason remembered. "He got back out of the water again and grabbed her from the back and went into the water." The giant gator swam off with the little girl in its steel-like jaws.

"After it happened, then we ran," Jason said. "It was pretty quick. It seemed like a nightmare, a dream. But then the way she screamed, when I saw the blood after he went in, then I realized it was real."

When the game wardens walked down to the shoreline, they found one of Erin's tiny shoes and noted the large slide mark indicating where the gator had slid back into the water with his prey. The game wardens put a boat in the small pond and patrolled for several hours before the huge gator surfaced with Erin's limp, mangled corpse in its jaws. One of the wardens killed the gator with his .357 Magnum revolver. Stermen was on the shore when they brought the girl back. A beautiful child, really little more than a baby, lay bloodied and muddied like some castaway doll. "It was sickening. Just sickening," Stermen recalled.

That night he was present when the GFC wildlife biologist performed a necropsy on the gator, routine procedure in a fatal attack on a human. Everyone recoiled in horror when the contents of the animal's stomach confirmed that this was the killer reptile.

Little Erin Glover was the sixth victim to die from an alligator since the GFC began keeping reliable records in 1972. Since her death in 1988, three more have shared that grisly fate. Statistics document that fatal attacks are rare. That is, however, little consolation for the families of those who became prey for a cold-blooded reptile not far removed biologically from the dinosaurs.

This menacing dragon from the misty past dwells in the murky depths of our most frightening nightmares. The beast is both fearsome and formidable, floating almost invisible among the lily pads, awaiting opportunity with the infinite patience of the predator.

" . . . the dread of a mauling, horrible death in the jaws of a giant gator is a primal, atavistic fear that neither statistics nor scientific logic can banish," wrote Donald Dale Jackson in his article about the reptilian predator featured in the January 1987 edition of *Smithsonian Magazine*.

Everglades Lawmen

King of the Glades. *A big bull gator basks along a canal bank in the Everglades. Florida game wardens routinely capture these predatory reptiles, which can grow up to 14 feet long. (Florida Game and Fish Commission)*

Wildlife biologists emphasize the fact that the vast majority of gators never attack humans. Indeed, far more people are killed each year from lightning strikes on Florida's golf courses than the total killed by gators since 1972. However, facts can't dispel the primitive fear aroused by the sight of a giant alligator. William Bartram, an English visitor to Florida in the late eighteenth century, was one who felt the chill of terror when confronting the giant reptile. "The horrid noise of their closing jaws, the floods of water and blood rushing out of their mouths, and the clouds of vapor issuing from their wide nostrils were truly frightening," Bartram wrote in his *Travels*, first published in 1791.

Myths abound about gators. Some will tell you that an alligator can outrun a racehorse over a short distance; others will claim they live to be five hundred years old. Other "experts" describe the powerful tail as far more dangerous than the jaws, studded with up to eighty teeth. Of course, there is always someone who swears that the only way to escape from an advancing gator on dry land is to run in zigzags.

Nonsense! And, strangely, the facts about this cold-blooded predator are almost as fantastic. Gators can live up to fifty years or more in captivity. They can, in cold-weather conditions, stay submerged for twenty-four hours. They have lived on this planet for nearly two hundred million years. Bulls can grow up to fourteen feet long and weigh up to six hundred plus pounds. Large gators may only eat once or twice in a year and still gain weight.

Every year during Florida's statewide alligator hunt, trappers take a number of gators in the thirteen- and fourteen-foot range. The state record gator was killed at Lake Apopka in 1956. It measured seventeen feet, five inches. Only a fool would claim that a predator anywhere near that size is not a threat to any human swimming nearby.

Most attacks on people don't result in death. Each year gators make from ten to twenty unprovoked attacks on people. The vast majority of victims fight their way free, although many sustain serious wounds.

South Florida is frequently an area where attacks occur. This is primarily because of the open-water system that links the coastal canals with the gator-rich Everglades. These canals are "alligator highways" that allow the reptiles access to the ponds and lakes that dot the residential areas of West Palm Beach, Ft. Lauderdale, and Miami.

Almost every attack is different and reflects the essential mystery of why alligators will choose a human as its prey. In the following accounts, the varied circumstances of the attacks are linked only by the universal terror experienced by those hunted and attacked by gators.

Robert Stryker was dangling his legs in a flooded rock pit in Ft. Lauderdale on July 18, 1972. He ignored the warnings of nearby construction workers who saw a large gator approaching him. Instead, Stryker went into the water and was swimming when the seven-foot-four-inch gator snapped at his hand. When the swimmer turned to escape, the predator clamped its jaws on one of his legs. That's when Dale Sargent, a laborer on a nearby construction site, grabbed a two-by-four and plunged into the water. Sargent clubbed the gator on the head, drove it off, and then helped the victim back to land.

Everglades Lawmen

The kids in the North Lauderdale neighborhood had names for several of the big gators that swam in "their canal." One was "Big Moe," the other, "Murr." Sometimes the children fed the gators pieces of bread.

On one July day in 1972, Denise Tetlow, ten, was playing down by the canal with her brothers and sisters and friends when they saw "Murr" swim down the canal. At eight feet plus, he was the biggest gator in the area. One boy was wading in the water. Denise and the other children yelled, warning him of the oncoming reptile. The beast came fast, but then turned to the bank and scrambled ashore.

Denise was horrified when the gator grabbed one of her arms in its steel jaws.

"I guess he would have pulled me right into the water but everyone started yelling and screaming," Denise recalled. "He got scared and jumped back in the water and swam away."

The ten-year-old escaped with deep cuts and lacerations—and a terrible memory that will always remain terrifyingly vivid in her mind, a nightmare that really happened, a gruesome fate narrowly avoided.

It was late summer, 1972. Nearby construction workers warned the three little boys not to swim in the manmade lake across the street in Lake Worth. Only a few weeks had passed since the attack on Denise Tetlow. One of the boys "looked scared" and went home. Patrick Parler, twelve, and Jeffrey Horton, eleven, defiantly swam in the little pond.

Joe Harrison was working at a service station nearby when Horton came running up. He was shouting. "My buddy's in trouble!" Harrison and a friend raced to the pond, where they found Patrick wet and bleeding, lying on a roll of plastic construction material.

A large gator, perhaps twelve to fourteen feet long, had attacked him in the water.

"The alligator snapped at me, but he let go, so I just kept swimming away," Patrick said.

He later told a *Miami Herald* reporter: "Jeff got out of the water, and I started to get out when something grabbed hold of my stomach. It was holding onto me. I pushed at it," Patrick said. "I opened his mouth a little bit, and it let go. Then I started out of the water and Jeff helped me get up on land. It was holding onto me."

In the melee, his friend was struck by the flailing tail and suffered a minor injury to his foot. Patrick spent five hours on the surgeon's table. The boy suffered severe puncture wounds to the stomach, back, and right arm. "I hurt all over," the victim later said.

The giant gator was never found despite a long search by game wardens and civilian gator trappers. The swimming hole where the attack took place measured only forty by one hundred yards. "The kids had apparently already seen the alligators and knew they were there, but they went in anyway," said Sheriff's Deputy Robert Ortiz. Perhaps they believed they were safe from gator attacks there in the middle of town. They were wrong.

Capt. Eddie Wheeler was convinced that the bite wounds on the six-year-old boy were consistent with that of an alligator attack but couldn't be absolutely sure. No one had witnessed the attack on Robert Farina Jr. when he swam in the Plantation canal on the late afternoon of August 18, 1988.

The little boy told investigators he was standing by the seawall when fire ants began biting his legs. He jumped into the canal to escape and—only seconds later—was pulled underwater by what the boy described as a "big fish." Robert broke free and started swimming away. The "fish" swam up over the boy and bit his head. He again broke free.

"After the second bite the young boy stated that the 'fish' was splashing next to him while he swam but never bit again," Captain Wheeler wrote in the official report. "The young boy never saw the alligator, only seeing a large tail splash next to him."

This tough little tyke swam more than three hundred feet until he reached a place where he could climb out of the canal. Game Wardens Ken Avinon and Bruce Cooper later killed a seven-foot gator lurking in that section of the canal. A necropsy by biologist Tom Stice failed to confirm if it had attacked the boy.

The woman on the phone was hysterical. She kept shouting that there was a big alligator bumping its snout up against her ground-level kitchen window trying to break in so he could attack her two small dogs.

Radio Dispatcher Liz Williams got the call at three o'clock one morning in 1996. Williams tried to calm the woman, telling her that gators were normally not aggressive. The woman and her dogs should be perfectly safe.

That's when the caller screamed and dropped the phone. The gator, all nine feet of it, had just smashed the window and slithered into the woman's kitchen.

Williams kept shouting for the woman to return to the phone. "Then there was a loud shot, and I could hear a lot of movement," Williams said later. "After that, the woman finally came back on the phone. Still a bit frantic, she advised that we should send someone out immediately."

The woman explained that her husband had appeared from the bedroom with his .357 Magnum revolver and shot the gator dead. The incident, along with the tape-recorded scream, was later featured on the syndicated television show *American Journal*.

Hundreds of thousands of tourists visit Everglades National Park in south Florida without incident. They come, admire the brilliant plumage of the wading birds, perhaps glimpse a deer from their car, and almost always get a close-up look at an alligator.

But this June day in 1996 was different, dramatically and deadly different, for seven-year-old Alexandre Teixeira, a Brazilian boy on vacation in the park with his family. They rented bicycles for a trip down the Shark Valley Tour Road, which penetrates nine miles into the Glades.

Suddenly, Alexandre lost his balance. He fell from the bike into the shallow water of the nearby canal where, almost instantaneously, a large gator snapped its jaws shut on his chest. The unbelievable was unfolding before the eyes of his horrified family.

"I took the mouth in my hands," Helio Teixeira, the boy's father, said later. "I tried to open it, but it was impossible. So I tried just to keep it from moving."

Patrick May of the *Miami Herald* reported the graphic details of what followed:

"Suddenly, the unimaginable happened: Teixeira felt the gator dragging his seven-year-old son . . . below the waterline. 'He went under. Just one time. That was our worst moment,' said Teixeira.

"He stayed with the gator as it resurfaced, his son snared by long rows of teeth, in pain and too petrified to even utter a sound. The

father and the gator remained locked in this bizarre standoff—
neither man nor beast willing to release its grip.

"Teixeira's wife, Maria, vaulted into the water without hesitating.

'I put my hand inside the gator's mouth,' Maria said. 'I wanted to
try and open it so it would let go of my son. I felt the alligator press
down one time on Alexandre, then suddenly release its jaw. And his
mouth opened. The alligator bit my hand and tried to pull me in.
Then, it let me go, too.'"

Alexandre suffered a punctured lung and severe lacerations. He
lived, thanks to the bravery of his parents.

"It's just instinct," the father said later. "You don't think. You just
act."

Why did these alligators attack? What was the trigger? The question cannot be answered with any certainty and may remain unan-
swerable. Wildlife biology is an inexact science, and no empirical
research has revealed the key. People rub shoulders with alligators
every day in south Florida. Nothing happens in thousands of
human-gator encounters. Then, a tragedy.

The following list covers alligator attacks in Florida as of February 15, 1999.

Year	No. of Attacks	Year	No. of Attacks
1948–1959	3	1985	3
1960–1971	0	1986	13
1972	5	1987*	9
1973*	3	1988*	9
1974	4	1989	13
1975	4	1990	18
1976	2	1991	17
1977*	14	1992	10
1978	5	1993*	18
1979	2	1994	21
1980	4	1995	19
1981	5	1996	13
1982	6	1997*	8
1983	6	1998	9
1984*	5	**TOTAL**	**248**

* Includes nine confirmed deaths since 1972, before which accurate
statistics were not kept.

Everglades Lawmen

Some biologists believe feeding a gator will result in the reptile's losing its natural fear of humans. Some believe the attacks on humans are simply mistakes. Some think nearby dogs attract the alligator to the human owner. One biologist even suggests that the alligator mistakes a man in the water for another alligator.

These are, at best, nothing more than educated guesses. Perhaps the most logical and credible conclusion was reached in a study of two nonfatal alligator attacks that occurred in the 1970s.

The article titled "Two Incidents of Alligator Attacks on Humans in Florida" by T. C. Hines and K. D. Keenlyne appeared in the November 25, 1977 edition of *Copeia,* the professional journal published by the American Society of Ichthyologists and Herpetologists. This remarkable study carries an undeniable authority because the junior author, Kent Keenlyne, was himself the victim of a vicious attack by a large alligator while checking turtle traps on the Oklawaha River on October 22, 1975.

The thirty-four-year-old biologist with the Florida Game and Fresh Water Fish Commission had placed the traps in a small lagoon near some half-sunken logs where the turtles would bask in the sun. He pulled into the lagoon in his small johnboat powered by a ten-horsepower engine. It was around 1 P.M.

Resetting the traps required Keenlyne to wade through the waist-deep water. Keenlyne removed several turtles from two traps and was in the process of resetting the second trap when the nightmare exploded from the water.

"The attack came when he turned toward the boat. He was first aware of the alligator's presence when it knocked him from his feet, apparently with a quick lateral movement of its head. As Keenlyne's feet were knocked from under him, he fell near the alligator, was struck a second time and caught by the arm and shoulder. The alligator then proceeded to shake Keenlyne," the report reads.

"Keenlyne grabbed the alligator's nose with his free left hand and pushed; as a result of their combined movements, the muscle was torn out, allowing Keenlyne to free himself. He stood up and struck the alligator as hard as he could with both hands, shouting loudly at the same time. The alligator struck again with a sideways head slash, but Keenlyne partially warded off the blow with his hands. The alligator disappeared under the water and Keenlyne quickly climbed into the boat and did not see the alligator again."

Predator and Prey

Based on the teeth marks in Keenlyne's flesh, it was later determined that the attacking gator was more than eleven feet long and undoubtedly a bull. The victim suffered multiple lacerations on the right arm and shoulder, tooth punctures in the right arm and back, and a severed tendon in the right shoulder.

The unprovoked nature of the three repeated attacks directly contradicts the prevailing theory that the alligator is a timid creature with a natural fear of man that only attacks by mistake or when provoked. The Keenlyne attack was clearly a predatory one and no accident. Keenlyne's turtle traps were not baited. Apparently no one had fed this gator. And the noise of the approaching boat should have spooked the big predator.

The other attack cited in the Hines-Keenlyne paper involved Thomas Chickene, a forty-five-year-old man who was swimming in a rock pit in Saddle Creek Park near Lakeland on June 16, 1975. The nature and specifics of the attack were documented in a report compiled by Game Warden Don Arnold and Wildlife Biologist Frank Montalbano.

Like Keenlyne, this individual was an adult male in good physical condition. He was described as a "strong swimmer" and a weight lifter at a local gym. Again the attack scenario did not reflect the conventional wisdom about why and who an alligator will deliberately attack. The study stated:

"While swimming under water he (Chickene) bumped into what he thought was a log. As he surfaced, a 'large' alligator seized Chickene by the chest and pulled him under. He was able to surface two times with the alligator still holding on. As Chickene was pulled down for the third time, he pushed his hand down the alligator's throat causing the animal to release its grip, but it grabbed Chickene's wrist before he could surface or fully free himself.

"He eventually was able to wrench his wrist loose and, upon surfacing, found that three men were in the water trying to assist him. The men had been attracted by Mrs. Chickene's screams as she watched from the bank. The men saw the alligator swim away. Chickene stated that the animal did not submerge after he escaped, but crawled out on the bank and bellowed once."

A game warden killed the eleven-foot gator an hour later. The victim suffered an open fracture to the sternum, fractured collar bone, fractured right scapula, fractured ribs, and multiple deep lacerations to the neck, chin, chest, and back.

Again the attacking gator had launched his assault without provocation and without evidence of having been fed by people, and continued the attack despite vigorous resistance by a strong, healthy adult male. He desisted only when the three rescuers made their appearance and later even bellowed his defiance from the shoreline.

This does not mean that alligator attacks are not rare. They are. It does strongly suggest that the larger gators, those more than ten feet long, may not have a natural fear of man. A generation ago large gators were shot on sight as a public service. Today in many Florida residential areas, they grow up in a protected environment and may never learn to fear man.

The report concluded:

"Never before in modern-day Florida has the alligator been so free from human persecution by hunting, and never before have so many large alligators lived in such close contact with humans. Although only a handful of attacks—most of them minor—occur each year. The potential for serious accidents is growing as greater numbers of alligators grow larger. The problem is accentuated even more as these large alligators are exposed even more frequently to tolerant humans as the human population grows.

"Perhaps the widespread notion that the alligator is naturally afraid of man also needs closer scrutiny. Experience in Florida has demonstrated that the alligator can quickly lose whatever 'natural fear' it has of man and may become a dangerous animal. There is no reason to believe that humans would not be a suitable size prey for a large alligator, and the two cases presented suggest that large alligators will attack humans with the intent to eat them."

Nine people have died horrible deaths by predatory alligator attacks since 1972. Four were children. One was a teenager. One was a seventy-year-old woman. The others were adults. The last victim, three-year-old Adam Trevor Binford, was attacked by an eleven-foot bull gator while the little boy was picking flowers off lily pads in Lake Ashley in Volusia County on March 21, 1997.

Nightmare and grim reality merge in present-day Florida. One can be certain only that more victims will die in the coming years. It is only a question of who, when, and where.

Chapter 10:
Gator Man

There's an alligator in my back yard! Alligator in my swimming pool! Alligator blocking the driveway! Alligator on the golf course! That was every day!
　　　　　　　　　　　　—Game Warden Dick Lawrence

Passengers gazing out the jetliner's windows as the aircraft made its landing approach at Palm Beach International Airport were stunned. Below on the tarmac was a lone man wrestling a giant alligator that must have been twelve feet long.

"Welcome to south Florida," was the pilot's announcement over the plane's intercom. "And keep an eye on those alligators."

The giant, five-hundred-pound, twelve-foot gator, whose awesome bulk endangered landing aircraft at West Palm Beach's airport, was only one of more than nine hundred alligators captured by Lt. Dick Lawrence during his twenty-eight year career.

His first gator was a seven-footer caught in a North Miami lake in 1970. Lawrence noted the event in his day book and continued the practice over the next three decades. At last count, he had recorded 921 gator captures.

Incredibly, the "gator man" was bitten only once. "That was my fault, not the alligator's," he admits. "I was sitting on top of a five-footer and slammed the jaw shut on my right thumb. Still have a little scar as a memento."

Lawrence believes strongly that the alligator has a much worse reputation than it deserves. Although he respects gators of any size, he contends that their ferocity and aggressiveness have been highly exaggerated over the years.

"If alligators were that mean, I would have been bitten nine hundred twenty-one times, not just once," he said. "Most of the gators I tangled with had only one thought in mind—to get away. Dangerous gators are found much more frequently in Hollywood films than in Florida's lakes, marshes, and canals."

Lawrence scoffs at accounts in which gators lie in ambush for people, leap out of the water, and drag them to their deaths. Such stories are fueled by fear and vivid imaginations, in his opinion. Actual attacks, he contends, are usually accidental or provoked.

"Don't get me wrong," he elaborated. "I would never swim in a pond where there are large alligators, especially not in the early morning or dusk when they normally feed. Once you're in the water, you're on the gator's turf, baby!"

Once every several years a scuba diver collecting golf balls from a pond on a south Florida course will be bitten by a gator. Lawrence attributes this to the gator's territoriality. "He'll defend his territory against other gators. A diver underwater probably looks like another gator. It's a simple case of mistaken identity."

The Minnesota native had been a game warden for about a month when Lt. Tom Shirley told him to go capture a gator that had been eating ducks in a residential pond in north Miami. The fact that the new game warden had never even seen a gator outside a zoo, much less captured one, apparently didn't concern his supervisor.

Back then in 1970, game wardens in south Florida spent most of their time from about March through September removing what were called "nuisance gators" from south Florida residential neighborhoods from West Palm to Miami.

"They were endangered species, protected by state and federal law back then," Lawrence said. "You couldn't just kill them. You had to capture them alive, transport them forty miles out into the Everglades, and let them go. We were hauling gators from morning till night in those days."

Despite his inexperience, Lawrence was willing. After all, he had discussed the basic capture technique with other game wardens. In most cases, they employed a rod and reel with a lead-weighted "snag hook" on the end of the line. The idea was to snag the gator with the big treble hook, pull the animal ashore, leap on him, slam the jaws shut with your hands, and then tape the snout closed. Nothing could be simpler or more fraught with danger.

"Didn't sound too hard, I thought," Dick said. "Hell, it sounded like an adventure to me. These alligators really intrigued me. So, what the hell!"

There was a small crowd of curious adults and children awaiting Lawrence when he arrived at Sky Lake in his green patrol vehicle.

"Of course, they hadn't the vaguest idea that I had never captured an alligator in my life," he said. "I was the man in the green uniform, the professional. And I didn't enlighten them either."

Lawrence quickly spotted the gator. He stalked his target, moving slowly and quietly along the shoreline and got within twenty yards of the animal slowly cruising on the water's surface.

Lawrence cast his line and missed completely. The weighted hook splashed ten feet beyond the target. He would miss a lot that day. Maybe fifty or sixty casts without a hit.

"I chased that gator around that hundred-acre lake all day with a crowd at my heels," he said. "I just didn't have my casting technique down right at that point. But finally I hit pay dirt.

"When I yanked on the rod, there was a watery explosion, a huge splash like somebody had just taken a belly flop into the pond. That gator churned around in the water like a big mix-master.

"The rod bent double," he said. "It was like fighting a swordfish or marlin. My muscles were flexed. I was yelling like a madman. You can't believe the adrenaline flow. The reel screamed as the gator took line. Total excitement!

"Half the neighborhood is following me around that lake like I'm the Pied Piper," he said. "By then I'm in my T-shirt, had kicked my shoes off, and am sweating like you can't believe. Hadn't the slightest idea where I'd put my gun belt and wallet. Didn't care. The gator was all that mattered.

"People are cheering me on," he said. "Others are snapping pictures. One guy is filming it on his home movie camera. Some are even cheering for the gator. It's a real show. You just can't imagine. What a circus!"

After ten minutes or so, Lawrence had worked the gator to within a few feet of shore. He handed off the pole to a bystander and grabbed a catch pole. This four-foot hollow metal pole has a wire that runs through the tubular handle and forms a loop at the end that can be placed over the gator's head and pulled tight.

Lawrence waded out into the water up to his knees, placed the wire noose over the gator's head, and lassoed him. Before he could pull in the slack, the gator started rolling towards shore, tangling himself up in the wire and forcing Lawrence to back away.

"He finally bumped into a log and stopped," he said. "That's when I jumped on him with a role of electric tape in my mouth, slammed his jaws shut, and wrapped the mouth shut. He just laid there. It was like he knew he'd been beaten, knew it was time to give up."

Now the warden finds himself surrounded by the excited crowd, the center of attention, the hero of the hour. "I'm on a complete ego trip at this point," he said. "I'm sky-diving, baby. People are shaking my hand. Some are even applauding. My hands are trembling like I had just caught a world-record marlin."

Lawrence threw the gator over his shoulder, tossed him in the trunk of his patrol car, and transported him out to the Glades for release. At the marsh's edge, Lawrence untaped him, leaped back, and the gator lay motionless. Later, Dick learned this was typical gator behavior after the stress of capture and riding in the trunk of a car. He prodded the gator with a pole. No response. Eventually, the animal leisurely slid into the water.

"This was a mistake," he said. "I just didn't realize at the time I was putting that gator in danger. Its body temperature had gone up in that hot trunk. The shock of suddenly going into the cooler water could have killed him. Later on, I let the gator take his own sweet time about going back in the water."

Throughout the 1970s Lawrence captured anywhere from two to six gators a day during the busy mating and nesting season. That's when the temperatures were hot and the animals were on the move, seeking mates, hunting nest sites, and looking for prey. Late March through early August was the peak period.

"Sometimes I'd have the trunk completely full of gators and start throwing them in the back seat," he said. "They couldn't do much, with their jaws taped shut and their feet tied back. They could slither though; they would always jam their faces up against the side windows of the car, or a small one might climb up on the shelf under the rear window.

"I remember stopping at a light in Miami and seeing all these people staring at this game warden with a car full of live gators," he said. "They couldn't believe it. "Being a real comedian at heart, I would roll down the window and yell, 'Hey, I've got some real ugly kids, don't I?' "

After nearly thirty decades of capturing almost a thousand gators, Lawrence knows this creature better than many wildlife biologists fresh from college. He knows how they move, knows where they hide, and knows what they think. Lawrence has a hands-on Ph.D. in "gatorology."

People believe the strangest things about gators. Lawrence is always amazed at the individuals who believe, without a doubt, that the gator's tail is his most fearsome weapon, that it can break a man's leg with one powerful swipe.

"It's myth and exaggeration," he said. "A big gator might give you a good whack, but he won't break your arm or leg. The danger is in those powerful jaws with those eighty sharp teeth that can crunch up a big freshwater turtle like so much popcorn. Think what it does to a human arm.

"The tail is the gator's means of locomotion," he said. "He drives himself through the water with powerful tail strokes. The tail is just one big muscle that acts like a propeller on a ship. And believe me, they can move silently through the water. They often approach their prey underwater, unseen, and without hardly a ripple on the surface."

Dick has seen gators use their long tails to sweep small game to within striking range of those cruel jaws.

"The gator will lay up along the shore with its body curled in a half-circle, tail facing head," he said. "The strike zone is inside that half-circle. If a gallinule, duck, dog, coon, or possum ventures too close, the gator slaps it with its tail. Pops the critter right in its mouth. I've seen it happen many times. But a lot of people won't believe that."

Alligators strike fear in many people, but Lawrence became less and less concerned as his capture skills increased. His casual bravado and increasing confidence are certainly not shared by other law enforcement officers, as documented by one memorable incident in the Miami area.

"Metro-Dade Police called and told us they had a big gator

Bare Hands and Guts. *Game Warden Dick Lawrence hauls in an eight-foot alligator during the early 1970s, one of hundreds he's captured in a career approaching the three-decade mark. (Florida Game and Fish Commission)*

surrounded in a parking lot at the Midway Mall and needed assistance," Dick recalled. "I'd been in that very area about a month before and had caught an eight-footer with a bob-tail and with one leg missing. Probably bit off by another gator. Anyway, I drove out there and found quite a sight.

"This was about midnight. The parking lot was deserted except for three Metro-Dade police units surrounding this gator. They had all their police cruiser emergency lights on, each officer sitting up on the hood of his vehicle pointing his shotgun at the poor gator.

" 'What's the trouble, guys?' " I asked. "One said, 'No gator is going to make a lunch out of me, pal. We'll shoot him first.' "

" 'Put your shotguns down,' " I told them. " 'This is no problem.' That's when I saw right off that this was the bob-tailed, three-legged gator I'd caught about a month back, and only a few hundred yards away from the mall. The bull had swum thirty miles back in from the Everglades where I'd released him."

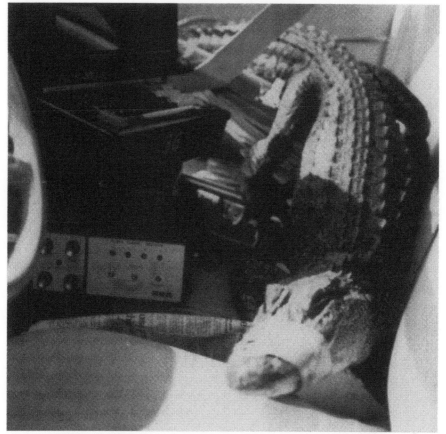

On the Road Again. *Game Warden Dick Lawrence recalls driving through crowded Miami streets in the 1970s with five or six captured alligators slithering around his patrol car. The big reptiles were transported to the Everglades and released. (Capt. David Stermen)*

Lawrence got out his steel lasso and slid it over the reptile's neck, jumped him, and clamped his hands around the jaws. That's when the gator started rolling. Lawrence hung on while the deputies jacked shells into their riot guns.

" 'Don't shoot! Don't shoot!' " I yelled. "Hell, I was a lot more afraid of getting shot by mistake than getting hurt by the gator. Well, anyway, I got the gator under control and had him taped and tied and in my trunk in ten minutes.

His fears weren't groundless. Panicky deputies later shot and wounded a gator trapper's assistant in Ft. Myers when the animal snapped his jaws shut on the man's arm. The victim survived but was badly hurt.

Everglades Lawmen

Through the years Lawrence perfected his gator capture technique and expanded on his knowledge of the animal's behavior and life history. By 1978, he had captured more than six hundred gators. It was routine. A piece of cake. That was until the day he got the telephone call from the manager at Palm Beach International Airport about a huge gator sunning himself on the tarmac.

Many people knew about the airport gator. He had been there for decades, swimming in the nearby canal that was linked to an underground system of drainage culverts under the landing strip. That was his home and his refuge. He liked to crawl up onto the tarmac and warm himself day or night. In fact, he was spending more and more time out there on the landing field.

"Airport management was concerned the gator was a possible safety hazard," Lawrence said. "They had several complaints from pilots who saw this big beast laying across their path when they landed or took off. If an airliner hit an animal this big—four or five hundred pounds—with its landing gear, there's no telling what might happen. You could have a major airline tragedy. It was obviously time to move the gator."

Lawrence and Warden Bob Banister arrived at the field the next morning. They met a large contingent of airport personnel. It was a major production with a half dozen service and emergency vehicles parked at the edge of the field. The gator was down at the end of the strip taking his daily sun bath.

He was big, real big. Twelve foot, six inches! Maybe seven hundred pounds or more! As Lawrence approached, the reptile slithered off the field down into the canal. He soon entered one of the culverts under the airfield. The culverts were about five feet in diameter and filled with about a foot of water.

While the airport workers stood fascinated, Lawrence hefted a long pole, about ten feet long and tipped at the end with a barbed shark hook. He then waded into the canal, splashed up to the culvert entrance, and peered inside. The gator lurked in the shadows—a dark and menacing bulk with a huge head.

For several hours Lawrence probed with the pole, trying to snag the gator. It was useless. The gator was wary and stayed well away from the culvert entrance. Going inside the culvert after the beast was not a viable option, even for a man as audacious as Lawrence. Too dangerous. No room to maneuver. There had to be another way.

Lawrence told the airport manager that the gator was too spooked, that he would come back tomorrow. That night a local newspaper ran a banner headline reading: "Airport Gator 1, Game Warden 0." Lawrence found it funny, but it also motivated him to go back and nail that bad boy.

The next day was another study in frustration. The gator quickly entered the culvert system and would periodically vanish for long periods.

"He knew those culverts very well," Lawrence said. "Hell, he could go under the airport and emerge on the other side if he wanted. You could look down through the drainage grates and sometimes glimpse that huge head about six feet down. Then he would disappear again."

That night the newspaper ran another headline: "Airport Gator 2, Game Warden 0." This really got Lawrence's competitive juices flowing. There was no gator in Florida, in his mind, that was going to beat him at this game, culverts or no culverts!

On the third day, they found the gator in the culvert. You could see the awesome reptile through the iron grate in what was basically a "junction box" where four culverts intersected. Lawrence had an airport backhoe wrap a chain around the huge grate and pull it off. Lawrence told Banister and an airport employee to lower him down into the concrete box. He stood in about a foot of water. He squinted into one of the culvert openings and saw the gator about twenty feet down the long tunnel. Its size registered with a jolt. "This gator was big. This was the mother lode, baby," he said.

The gator was still too far back to hook with the pole. Lawrence quickly improvised. He asked the airport people for several lengths of three-quarter-inch plastic pipe. They brought it a few minutes later, each section about eight feet long.

Lawrence took his shark hook and tied it on a line, which he fed through the pliable pipe. He jammed it into the hole, then glued on another section, and then another. Now the pipe with the hook at the end was poised right above the gator's monstrous head. With a jerk of the line, Lawrence dropped the snag hook into place. They pulled out the pipe until Lawrence could grab the line. He pulled with all his considerable strength and felt the four-pronged hook bite into the gator's hide.

"That bull gator went absolutely bonkers!" he said. "There was a huge splash and he let out a bellow that echoed and magnified inside the culvert. It sounded like there was some damn dinosaur down there.

"The gator gets all twisted around and starts banging that big head up against the side of the metal culvert," he said. "That sound reverberates down the tunnel. It sounds like cannons going off. And water is pouring out of the culvert and over my feet.

Bannister was standing right beside him as Lawrence worked the gator closer. The giant might appear any moment, and Lawrence ordered the men above to lift Bannister out. "Now you get out of here, Bob," he yelled. "There's not room for the two of us and the gator down here."

A minute later his crew lifted out Lawrence as the gator emerged from the culvert tail-first. Its bulk quickly filled up the four-by-four concrete box. Lawrence and several others tried pulling the monster up, but the gator got all twisted and jammed in the constricted space.

Lawrence feared his line would break. He had to get a heavier line on the gator. There was only one way.

"You guys are going to have to grab my ankles and lower me head-first down into the box so I can get a wire noose around his neck," Lawrence told the stunned bystanders.

They reluctantly lowered him down until his face was only a foot away from the gator's awesome head, which was pressed up against the concrete wall. Lawrence used a small wooden stick, about a foot long, and worked it in between the gator's head and the wall.

"The fear is all gone now," he said. "There is no fear. You don't even think about what could happen. It's just you and the gator. Nothing else exists. Nothing!"

Lawrence pried the head back an inch or two with one hand, then took the noose with the other hand and laid it on top of the stick. He worked the stick down the head and neck and around the huge jaws; the noose slid down behind it. Those terrible teeth were only inches away from his hand.

"I pulled the stick away," Dick said. "The gator just stayed there, not moving, the head still a few inches from the wall. Then he just slowly laid his head back against the concrete. I had him then."

Lawrence signaled those above to pull him on up. Now they had the gator secured with a noose attached to a heavy line. They could pull him up without fear of breaking the line and losing the gator.

"We brought in the backhoe and attached the line to it," he said. "The operator just used the hoe like a crane to lift that bull gator right out of there and laid it down on the tarmac."

The jets roared overhead as they landed or took off. Lawrence was oblivious to everything as he prepared to tape the gator's jaws shut.

Later he learned that a National Airlines pilot, landing at that point, told his passengers from the North to look out the right windows. They glanced down and saw Lawrence leap onto the back of a giant gator. "Welcome to south Florida, folks," the pilot told his amazed passengers.

Lawrence wrapped both of his taut, muscled arms around the gator's snout and pulled back with a grunt. Bannister quickly stepped in and taped the jaws together. For a moment, Lawrence feared the gator would roll, but it didn't.

The exhausted game warden jumped free and admired his work. A half dozen men loaded the monster into the trunk of his patrol vehicle. "There was nothing but gator in there, baby," he said. Before he could leave to take the animal out to the Loxahatchee National Wildlife Refuge for release, the airport staff insisted he drive by the office so the secretaries could see.

Lawrence obliged and a crowd of office workers surrounded the vehicle, curious to look at the famous airport gator who had evaded capture for three days. They clapped and cheered when Lawrence finally drove off.

That night the newspaper ran a different headline: "Game Warden Wins in Final Round. Gator Loses on Points."

Ironically enough, it was a run-of-the-mill seven-footer on a routine complaint that almost cost Lawrence his life. About a year after capturing the airport gator, he was sitting in the West Palm Beach Everglades Regional Office when a complaint came in from a nearby residential area off Cresthaven Boulevard.

Rather than assign the job to one of the civilian gator trappers who worked under his direction, Sergeant Lawrence ran out of the office with his gator rod in his hand, eager for a respite from the tedium and drudgery of office work. He was definitely a hands-on administrator who still relished testing his strength and cunning against gators.

Everglades Lawmen

A five-minute drive brought him to a thirty-acre lake surrounded by single-family homes, no different from a thousand other south Florida communities. A seven-foot gator had been "eating the baby ducks," and certain residents wanted him out of there. Just a routine, everyday nuisance gator complaint, or so Lawrence thought.

"I nailed him on the first cast," he said. "Pretty soon a bunch of kids and parents gathered; some thought I had hooked a big fish. There was really nothing to it. No big deal at all. I had taken hundreds of gators, many a lot bigger than this guy."

Lawrence played the gator for a few minutes until his quarry swam into a thick patch of duckweed. The warden was afraid that the rough edges of the weeds would fray his thirty-pound test line and allow the gator to escape.

" 'Hey, kids,' " I said. " 'Does anybody have a small rowboat around her I could use?' " They nodded yes and raced off to a nearby home. About ten minutes later here come several adults hauling an eight-foot boat."

After handing the pole to one of the adults, Lawrence stripped for action. He slipped off his shoes, his uniform shirt with all the heavy brass, his wallet, and gunbelt.

The crowd had grown by now, which stimulated Lawrence's innate showmanship. He was standing up in the boat now, reeling in his quarry. To the onlookers' delight, he was singing: "Oh, I'm the old man of the sea! The old man of the sea! I go after the big 'feesh' because I'm the old man of the sea!"

When he got within a few feet of the duckweed, the gator bolted and swam underwater right across the bow of his boat. "I could see the gator's murky outline about four feet down. That's when I sat down, slipped the pole under one leg, and grabbed my snag line and hook with the other. This was a heavier line with a four-pronged shark hook at the end."

Lawrence lowered the hook slowly and placed it right under the head, then jerked hard with both hands. "That gator went crazy," he said. "It was some commotion, let me tell you."

The warden popped a roll of tape in his mouth and then used both hands to haul up his catch. The gator broke surface head-first, its body suspended tail-down in the water.

"Bang! He hit his head against the side of the boat," Lawrence said. "The back of his head was right against the boat. I dropped the snag line and quickly grabbed his jaws with both hands.

"He's quit doing anything at this point, just hanging there suspended," he said. "So I decide to haul him in the boat; braced my feet against the gunnel, stood up, and reared back. Damn, if that boat didn't tip upside down. Here I go, backwards into the water with my hands around a seven-foot gator. The pole and the snag line are all tangled up with us. We go right to the bottom, about eight feet down.

"No way am I about to let that gator loose underwater," he said. "When you're in the water, you're in his world, baby. I held on tight and kicked off the spongy bottom and broke surface, gulped some air, and then sank back down again.

"At this point I realized that the shark hook had snagged my trousers," he said. "Now I was scared. Not only might the gator bite me if I let go, he might drag me down and drown me."

In his desperation, Lawrence freed one hand and twisted around so he had the gator's jaws clamped shut with a forearm. He used his free hand to hold tight by twisting it into his T-shirt.

"I paddled to the surface," he said. "Once on top, I could swim using one arm. I would take about four or five strokes before sinking back down. The shoreline was about forty yards away. I could hear police sirens. Somebody had called for help when they saw me go in the water.

Lawrence finally touched bottom and stood up. He removed the soggy tape from where he'd been holding it in his mouth and started wrapping the gator's jaws.

A sheriff's deputy who knew the game warden called out, "You okay, Lawrence? We thought the damn gator ate your ass."

" 'Yeah, yeah,' I answered. I sort of shrugged like it was no big deal. See, I was back to being a big shot again. But I knew myself that it had been a damn close call. I learned that day that no nuisance gator call is ever necessarily routine."

If the author ever doubted that anything can happen in south Florida, that was forever erased by his participation in Lawrence's most bizarre and unlikely adventure on June 6, 1988.

Capturing an alligator is a game warden's rite of initiation. And I had passed the test several times in company with Dick and Captain Lee Kramer, a colorful civilian gator trapper from Delray Beach. We

Everglades Lawmen

All in a Day's Work. *Capt. David Stermen demonstrates the correct way to grip a gator's jaw during a training session at the Florida game warden academy, circa 1996. As a young officer, Stermen single-handedly captured a 12-foot bull. (Florida Game and Fish Commission)*

---

had chased gators all around an affluent Boca Raton neighborhood for the better part of one day.

Now don't get me wrong. I'm no hero. Dick and Lee did the really dangerous stuff, but I did lend a hand here and there, even got in the water at one point in an attempt to capture a ten-footer with a big snag hook. But that was nothing compared to what was to come.

As the Everglades public information officer, I had made arrangements for a television crew to go along on one of our "routine" nuisance gator calls. They were filming a piece for a children's television show.

The video crew followed us in their van as we headed for the location of a recent complaint. That's when the radio crackled, and one of the most memorable days in my rather sedate and safe life commenced.

Dick and I laughed when we first heard the report. The

dispatcher said a caller from a Royal Palm Beach neighborhood had reported an eleven-foot, three-hundred-pound crocodile lying across his sidewalk in front of the front door.

We laughed because we knew better. Callers often exaggerate. Many ten-foot gators turn out to be three feet or less when the game warden arrives. Furthermore, there were no American crocodiles in Palm Beach County. Hadn't been any within living memory. In fact, there were only a few hundred of the endangered animals left, and they were far south in Everglades National Park, at the federal crocodile refuge in Key Largo, and at Miami's Turkey Point Nuclear Power Plant.

Despite our skepticism, Dick decided to respond to the "crocodile" complaint rather than the original call. Who knew? It might be fun. It was raining heavily when we pulled up in front of the Royal Palm Beach residence.

There was no crocodile or gator across the sidewalk. Nothing. Perhaps it was all a prank? I thought for a moment until my eye caught movement along a chain-link fence.

"Jesus Christ, Dick! Look at that monster!" I told Lawrence. Both of us were incredulous. Neither of us could believe it. It was an Australian saltwater croc, although the dimensions differed from the complainant's estimates. The damn thing was even bigger! He must have weighed more than 450 pounds. He was gigantic.

Oh, I knew it was an Australian saltwater croc. No doubt in my mind. Only the week before, I had been reading *Sports Afield* magazine aboard a jet airliner on my return to Florida from Chicago, near where I grew up. The cover story was about great man-eating crocs of the world. Right on the cover, in living, horrifying color, was a shot of one of the deadliest—the Australian saltwater croc, which makes its home in the southwestern Pacific.

This was no shy American alligator. This was an aggressive, dangerous predator known to kill and eat people on an all-too-frequent basis. I had turned and remarked to the passenger in the seat next to me: "Thank God, I won't ever have to deal with a brute like that. I work for Florida Game and Fish, and alligators are more than scary enough for my tastes."

Now a week later, I found myself only a few yards from that very beast. All the grim and grisly stories about the species, so graphically reported in *Sports Afield*, flashed through my memory. At that moment I could see the video people in the van behind us gesturing and pointing in excitement. They too had seen our all-too-real nightmare croc.

We got out in the driving rain and went to the car trunk. Dick eventually fished out a rather unimpressive roll of what looked like clothesline. Actually, in my fevered imagination, it looked more like a string of yarn or even thread. We were going to capture "Godzilla Jr." with a roll of yarn?

If anything, Dick Lawrence was confident. He assured me that we could get the job done. Now I knew how those Civil War soldiers felt when they wrote home admitting that they didn't run in battle only because of what their comrades might think. Even for a timid bookworm like me, there was really no choice. If I had only taken out that extra life insurance.

As we approached, the monster scurried along the fence line and hid behind some plastic garbage cans. Dick moved in slowly until he was right next to the cans and tossed his noose at the croc's massive head.

That beast came up hissing and lunged over the top of the cans, snapping his jaws together with the metallic sound of a bear trap being sprung. Dick and I leaped backwards. The speed and ferocity of the lunge was inspiring, to say the least.

Dick pulled in his line and tried again. Same result. Same frightening snap of the jaws lined with glinting teeth. Even with its jaws closed, you could see huge teeth protruding several inches. Even a man with a poor imagination could visualize what teeth like that could do to a vulnerable human body. And remember, I have a very creative imagination.

Now Dick's tactics changed. He gave me the lasso and picked up some sticks off the ground. At our approach, the croc opened its jaws and hissed, displaying that cruel garden of deadly teeth. But when Dick tossed a stick at him, the croc clamped his jaws shut, giving me the opportunity to lasso him. I missed. We tried again. I missed again. Dick took back the lasso, and I started tossing the sticks. The croc lunged at us several times and we scurried backwards to relative safety.

All of this was played out in the pouring rain while the cameraman videotaped us. The director, a rather effeminate man with a lilting English accent, danced around in joy like a ballet dancer on speed. He kept repeating: "Oh, this footage is just precious. Oh, how precious. Just precious."

I wonder if the spectacle of the croc eating Dick or me would also be regarded as "precious footage." Somehow I had the feeling that it would be. Anything for ratings, as they say. But I won't be too critical. I'm sure the network would send flowers to the hospital or funeral parlor. They have feelings too, you know.

Suddenly, Dick had the croc collared. Both of us were on the rope when the big reptile raced down along the fence line. We pulled hard and slowed him a little. This animal was incredibly strong. We were perhaps ten feet from his menacing jaws.

I thought, How in the hell did I ever end up here with the rain pouring down in my face, holding onto a rope with a giant croc on the other end? I'd been in similar situations before, like the time the Viet Cong blew up my tank on Highway One near Duc Pho in 1967, or during the riots protesting the Kent State shootings when I was a student at Southern Illinois University. Had felt the same way back then, too.

Real fear returned when the croc, in its frustration, bit into the wire-mesh fence, snapping the wire with a loud twang-twang-twang. Then the incredible happened. This eleven-foot behemoth literally crawled up the five-foot-tall fence, pulled about half its bulk over the top, and would have gotten completely over if Dick and I hadn't dug in our heels and pulled with all our might.

The croc fell back with a loud thump and then started twisting around and snapped its jaws. I breathed more easily when he settled down a few minutes later. Like all big cold-blooded reptiles, he had great strength and speed but no endurance. He appeared spent. Thank God!

Lt. Charlie Dennis appeared at that moment, and we soon got another line on the beast. At one point—how, I don't know—somebody dropped the other line for just a few seconds. The croc came to life and trundled right for me. I ran backwards faster than some Olympic qualifiers and only stopped when the others grabbed the loose line. I believe Lt. Dennis made one of his famed sarcastic remarks about this time. He seemed rather amused by the spectacle.

That's when the owner showed up. He calmly informed us that the croc was his personal pet. Had the proper papers, kept it in a cage behind his home a few blocks away. Called the croc "Rusty" and seemed concerned that we had been so rough with his cute little playmate.

Five of us strained every muscle to slide Rusty into the back of the owner's pickup. When the truck rumbled off in the rain, I turned to Dick Lawrence and said, "That's the last time I go out on a nuisance gator call with you, buddy."

There is a happy ending to the tale. After some negotiating, the owner admitted that a residential neighborhood wasn't the proper place for a man-eating croc that measured eleven feet long. Rusty was sent away to a facility where he could live out his life without the danger of escaping and perhaps killing or mangling some unsuspecting child.

To be honest, I was rather proud of the small part I had played in the drama. My ego was quickly deflated, however, upon returning to the office, where Major Jim Ries listened to our epic of bold adventure. Clearly, he was not impressed with our exploit.

"You two guys are nuts," he said calmly. "No way should you have taken any chances with an animal that big and dangerous. If I'd been there, I would have shot it dead with my revolver."

Should you doubt the authenticity of the story, there is a video record of the incident which was featured in a *National Geographic* special titled "Miami Wild." Unfortunately, the cameraman was loading another cassette when the croc started climbing the wire fence. Now that footage would truly have been "precious."

I hope I never have to capture another croc or gator. Like my three-year stint in the U.S. Army, it was a valuable learning experience but one I wouldn't want to repeat. But if I had to confront another giant man-eater, there's only one man I'd want by my side: Lieutenant Dick Lawrence, the Gator Man.

Chapter 11:
Poacher's Secret Lair

Roy Burnsed was a native south Floridian who had hunted these woods since he was a boy. For all I know he probably did a little deer poaching along the way himself before he became a game warden. I do know he was good and knew the woods. Roy taught me more than anybody in my life about the woods, the wildlife, and tracking. He didn't teach me just to look, but to really see.

—Game Warden Rich Obach

Canoeists leisurely drifting down the Loxahatchee River didn't notice anything unusual about the small johnboat puttering near the mangroves within J. D. Dickinson State Park near Jupiter. They probably assumed that the three men in the boat were fishermen out for a day's sport, or just friends sharing a beer and the beauty of the surrounding woodlands.

They would have been wrong. These men were deer poachers on their way to a secret camp they had constructed in the heart of the state park, where hunting was prohibited year-round. They slowed their boat at a familiar landmark and waited until they were alone on the river.

This thick, seemingly impenetrable wall of mangrove bushes had an opening, one they had cut with machetes long ago. Two of the men went to the front of the boat and lifted out the dead mangrove so the boat could nose through a narrow avenue up a small tributary creek. They replaced the dead mangrove "door" before they proceeded upstream. The unnamed stream weaved through cypress swamp. The sublime silence was broken only by the occasional bird song or the scrambling of a squirrel through the tree branches. It was wild and unpeopled—a hunter's country.

The going was slow. Several times they came to deadfalls where huge tree trunks had fallen across the narrow stream. They were not surprised. They had created many of the obstacles to discourage anyone who might accidentally discover the mangrove door into their private hunting preserve. Sometimes they hauled the boat up and over the log or portaged around it. They ignored the swarming mosquito clouds, a mere nuisance for serious men intent on killing the big cypress swamp deer that roamed this wilderness. They were trophy hunters who wanted things easy. They were not hunters. Not sportsmen. Not wildlife conservationists. They were game thieves and poachers.

They were nearing their destination. Soon they throttled down the engine and the boat slid into the shore. Around them was an encircling wall of wilderness. They could have been one hundred miles from anywhere. In fact, they were little more than a mile from park headquarters. Their very audacity gave them a certain security, even though they had come to poach deer in what was supposedly a game sanctuary.

Calmly and without hurry they unloaded their bows, the small-caliber rifle, the crossbow with the scope, the arrows and the ammunition, the bottled water, the food, and the other essentials. They had come to stay awhile. The men walked a few yards away from the creek, which they knew often concealed a huge bull gator. The monster of the swamp had, on at least once occasion, chased one of them up the tree. That was good, in their minds; it was one more deterrent to unwanted visitors and nosy park rangers.

They smiled to each other as they looked at their poachers' lair, a snug cabin, about twelve by twelve, and perfectly camouflaged with layers of palmetto fronds stapled to the outside. The plywood walls had been painted a washed-out gray and brown that blended with the terrain. The structure had been designed to vanish into the surrounding landscape; its angular dimensions were obscured and distorted by the layer of vegetation. A man could stand twenty feet away and see nothing.

Inside were all the comforts of home. The interior was dry and snug even during the torrential south Florida rains. There were three bunks, one above the other, a table, chairs, a sink, a fan, an electric light with a homemade shade of tinfoil that directed the glow down onto the table. A breeze wafted through the screened windows on all sides. There was a sump pump outside that drew water from the creek for a primitive shower and for the sink. Power was provided by a powerful marine battery. It was a camper's dream, a poacher's refuge.

They came here often, talked of it to others not at all or rarely. Not even their wives knew of its existence or location. When they took these camping trips, they always said they were going to north Florida or the Panhandle. Secrecy was paramount if they were to preserve their hunting monopoly here where the big swamp deer roamed. Perhaps they played cards that night or shared hunting stories. One of them might have thumbed through the hunting magazines filled with tips on how to bag big Sunshine State trophy bucks. The poachers were at home and at peace. They had been coming here for a very long time and saw no reason why it couldn't continue indefinitely. The park rangers rarely, if ever, came into this thicket of pine, cypress marsh, and palmetto.

They sought only the big bucks with perfect racks. They hunted both in the night and the day. Reflector tacks stuck into the surrounding trees allowed them to move about easily in the night. They had several tree stands up in the tall pines and usually used the crossbow or conventional bow. The 5mm Remington rifle was useful at times too. Its sharp little bark couldn't be heard far through the dense undergrowth.

One poacher was removing several tree stands on a Sunday afternoon in the fall of 1985. He paused, heard the crackle of palmetto and the soft drone of human conversation in the distance. People were coming! The poacher lay flat and motionless in the underbrush as the strangers came nearer. They stopped and talked only a few yards away, unaware of his presence. He couldn't see their faces and deliberately avoided direct eye contact, a dead giveaway if you're hiding in the woods.

The visitors walked around the area for some time, looking and seeking something, before merging into the wilderness tangle. The poacher stayed quiet and motionless, waiting until the noise of their passage faded completely away. Then he hurried back to the cabin. It had been a close call, a very close call.

The intruders had been Lt. Roy Burnsed and Game Warden

Everglades Lawmen

Richie Obach. They had been called by the park manager, Capt. Scott Donald, after the latter had received a tip that hunting was taking place in the park.

This had led to an initial reconnaissance of the area by Obach, the park manager, and the tipster—a rugged, bearded man who moved easily through the woods and had a record of poaching in north Florida. He showed the officers five tree stands positioned high in the tall pines, thirty to forty feet in the air. As with most confidential informants, the man's motivation was not an issue. The officers saw him only as a tool to apprehend others who were breaking the game laws.

The party plunged into the wild country. This was an area of tall pines and saw palmettos that tore at their clothing. A great part of this Florida jungle was wet and mucky marsh, knee-deep in places. Obach called the area the Loxahatchee River Swamp. Few ever explored this wild place where they were no trails, paths, or camp-sites. It was wilderness, untouched and—to many—forbidding.

"It was almost inaccessible," Obach recalled. "You had to beat your way through very heavy saw palmetto or go through the swamp itself and wade through the muck and water and take your chances with any water moccasins or gators that might be in the area."

When the investigators found the tree stands, Captain Donald expressed skepticism. He thought the stands were probably placed there by wildlife photographers. Obach disagreed. He pointed out that there was no place for them to mount a camera tripod. To his eye, the stands looked like they were well suited to deer hunters, not cameramen.

Obach staked out the stands for several days in a row, entering the area surreptitiously and long before dawn. He also came in the evening. No luck. The woods were quiet and empty except for the melody of songbirds and the whisper of wind in the pine branches.

One Sunday afternoon he brought the boss to see the site. Lt. Roy Burnsed was a native Floridian who had grown up in the woods and swamps. He was a robust man in his mid-thirties who had biceps as hard as an old cypress trunk and who spoke in a deep drawl redo-lent of Florida cowboy and Cracker roots. Poachers didn't like Burnsed, but they respected him. Few ever challenged his commands. They knew he had a fearsome temper and was ready to back up his words with fists. Roy admitted that he had a tendency to "bow up" when someone gave him back talk.

Burnsed had taught many of his woodcraft skills to Obach, another one of those oddball Yankees who had come to south Florida for adventure and challenge. "Nobody taught me more about the woods than Roy," Obach said many times. "Every trip to the woods with Roy was a learning experience. He just didn't teach me to look but to really see. There's a big difference between the two."

Obach was a willing and adept pupil. He had won Burnsed's grudging respect as one of the "few tough Yankees" the Floridian had ever met. That toughness was forged on the streets of Brooklyn, where Obach had run along the edges of the law as a leather-jacketed hood in the 1950s. But he had another side. Childhood summers were spent at his grandmother's lodge in the Catskills. It was there that he developed a love of the quiet woods and the streams where trout rose at the temptation of a fly cast with skill and accuracy.

Like many game wardens, Obach had led an interesting life before joining the game and fish department. An article in the men's adventure magazine, *Argosy,* led the twenty-four-year-old postal worker to work his way Down Under as a seaman aboard a German freighter called the *Cap Ortegal.* The tough street kid from New York learned to paint, chip rust, and do whatever else the crusty German boatswain mate demanded. Few crew members spoke any more than a few words of English, but the boatswain mate was eloquent in attitude and gesture. He didn't like the wise kid from New York. Both men were stubborn and brash.

Crossing the equator was memorable. Lowly "Pollywogs" had to earn King Neptune's respect, as had each of the older sailors in his youth. These were rough men who liked their fun the same way. Obach remembers the German sailors blindfolding him and tying his hands. Then they stuffed rotten fish down the New York kid's throat until he vomited; they shaved part of his skull and beat him with rubber hoses. They chained Obach to a chair and smeared his body with paint, grease, and oil. The burly sailors lifted the bewildered, still-blindfolded pollywog up and dumped the Yank into a saltwater-filled dunk tank they had rigged on the cargo deck.

"Why, I actually thought these crazy German sailors had thrown me into the ocean," Obach recalled. "I thought I was going to drown. Then they pulled me out and shouted, 'How many beers?' I told them, 'One.' Back I went underwater. They pulled me up again. I was coughing up salt water, sick as a dog. 'How many beers?' they shouted. 'Five!' I said. They lowered me underwater again. The next time, I shouted, 'Ten! Ten beers!' "

The thirty-day journey to Sydney was a lesson in hard work, hardship, and long hours. The German sailors were not members of the YMCA or the Salvation Army. They were men of the world, at home with the whores of Shanghai and Sydney as well as the street-walkers of Hamburg and Kiel. Obach learned a lot about life aboard the Cap Ortegal but was glad to walk down the gangway at voyage's end. An interesting and vast land lay before him with the promise of love, adventure, and new horizons.

For two years, Obach roamed the outback. During one phase, he helped build a railroad through the North Queensland rain forest, one thousand miles north of Sydney. He loved the camaraderie of the friendly Australian blokes who gathered each evening around the campfire. There were endless rounds of Foster's beer and senti-mental songs bellowed out against the curtain of wilderness sky painted with silver stars. That was hard work but nothing compared to cutting sugar cane. The absolute worst was hauling bags of cement in a cement factory where the dust billowed up like so much smoke from hell, and sweat poured down your bare chest in rivulets through the chalky white dust.

On the north coast of Australia, in the town of Cairns, Obach met a fellow American. He was from Ft. Lauderdale, stubbornly trying to start a sport fishing charter business in this then-unknown corner of the world. George Bransford knew there were huge marlin out there in the cobalt blue water and believed rich men from all over the globe would come to Cairns for the opportunity to catch one. Obach signed on as a deck hand, but there were many days afloat when they had no customers. Bransford encouraged his new mate to sit in the fighting chair and troll. There would be no better advertisement than sailing back into Cairns harbor with a world-class marlin in tow.

One memorable day the young American adventurer hooked a true monster of the deep, the kind of fish memorialized in the terse prose of Hemingway's classic, *The Old Man and the Sea*. It was an epic contest, a three-hour, sweat-soaked, muscle-aching struggle of man against fish. This was both adventure and ordeal, both physical suffering and exaltation, a classic tale of a young man testing his hardened muscle and sinew and his strong will against a king of the ocean depths. Obach won his trial of combat. They sailed back into harbor with the monster: thirty feet, ten inches long. The marlin was weighed on railroad scales before an appreciative crowd of Aussies. Strangers kept shoving beers into the young American's hand and slamming him on the back with the jovial roughness of men from the outback. Obach was a happy kid. His catch was a world record: 1,060 pounds.

There were other adventures. He did finally hunt crocodiles as the *Argosy* magazine story had described and sold them to Japanese tourists for seventy-five dollars a hide. And then there was a stint as a roustabout on a west Australia sheep station. They shot kangaroos for sport and meat. "It was tough, but you were so hungry you didn't care," the American remembered. Obach was still a wild kid and got involved in a "punch up" in a hotel pub where somebody pulled a knife. He was arrested, broke out of his hotel room "jail cell," and headed for Sydney.

That was the strange and colorful life that preceded his joining the game and fish department as a game warden in south Florida. Old timers, even the dyed-gray-in-the-wool Southern boys, somehow sensed in Obach a kindred spirit. He didn't know much about south Florida, alligators, snakes, and such, but he was game and wasn't afraid. The dark Florida woods and skulking deer poachers didn't intimidate the former hood from the city. He would do fine, just fine.

For the next decade and more, Obach learned his craft, tested his wits against game violators, and became comfortable in the cypress swamps and piney woods of south Florida. This was, although he didn't know it, all preparation for his greatest challenge. That really began the day he took Lieutenant Burnsed out to look at the tree stands in J. D. Dickinson State Park.

A few days later, Burnsed went up in the GFC helicopter and hovered over the area, searching for something out of the ordinary, something that didn't quite belong in the wilderness picture below. Then he saw it—a ribbon of bright, artificial green. Burnsed marked the general location, taking special note of a very tall pine tree that towered over its neighbors. He would return for a closer look, this time on the ground. Few knew the woods like Burnsed. He moved slowly as he studied the ground, always watching, always listening, in tune with his wilderness surroundings. The way the tall grass lay, a palm frond bent backwards, a smudged track in the muck, they all held a message for someone with the patience to read and understand.

He was about a half mile from where they had found the illegal tree stands when the green and brown maze directly in front of him took on an unnatural character. Burnsed stopped and studied. Gradually, his eyes detected the angular lines of a man-made structure less than twenty feet away. He moved closer. The outlines of a cleverly camouflaged cabin came into focus.

The game warden opened the cabin door carefully and looked into the interior. Inside he carefully examined the contents, noting certain items that told him of the cabin's reason for existence. He found a bottle of buck deer lure on a shelf, a bow case, several hunting arrows concealed in the rafters, and a set of rattling horns used to attract rutting bucks. This wasn't some hermit's hideaway. This was a poacher's camp, boldly planted in the heart of the state park.

Burnsed admired the care and skill that had gone into the construction of the cabin. It was snug, clean, and comfortable. The game warden took special note of how the structure was held together with wood screws. He assumed the structure had been built at another location, dismantled, and then reassembled on site. The walls could be joined with the screws, probably to avoid the alarm bell of the sound of hammer on nail.

The easiest course of action was to burn the cabin and eradicate its secrets. The details of its finding and purpose would be included in the weekly report and ultimately buried in some file cabinet in Tallahassee.

Burnsed had other plans. He wanted to find and arrest the men who had built this cabin and used it as a base camp for illegal hunting within the park. The very boldness and ingenuity of the poachers demanded a similar response. The cabin's existence and purpose was a defiant challenge to the game laws. Its builders must be punished.

The key was to apprehend the individuals when they were actually using the cabin for deer poaching purposes. The game wardens must time the bust so the poachers would be caught with hard evidence linking them to illegal hunting. Curiosity came into play too. The cabin raised many questions that only its builders could ever answer absolutely. How had they gotten the cabin components to the site, surrounded as it was by a nearly impenetrable wall of marsh and woods? That was a puzzle Burnsed pondered as he walked the area carefully looking for other sign.

He walked down to the creek and figured that was the highway upon which they carried the construction materials. The next day, Burnsed and Obach paddled the Loxahatchee River looking for access to the small creek. They drifted for several hours along the barricade of mangroves. For a while it didn't seem like Burnsed's theory would survive the afternoon. Perhaps the poachers had airlifted the materials by chopper? It was possible. But the painstaking search, frustrated at times by several false trails into the interior, finally paid off. Burnsed noticed that certain mangrove roots had been cut with a saw or a machete, allowing them to be removed like a natural trap door. The narrow portal allowed a canoe or small boat to move up the creek into the park.

Obach gave the secret camp its name. He described all the cabin's creature comforts to Burnsed as "gingerbread." From then on, it would be known as "Gingerbread Camp" and would become the main focus of Obach's efforts for the next year. Every week, he would slowly work his way through to the cabin, coming in the hard way so he could conceal his patrol vehicle away from prying eyes. Sometimes Burnsed took over the surveillance and once crawled up on a huge rattlesnake, which he killed quickly and quietly with a tree branch. But Obach carried the brunt of the surveillance effort.

Game Warden Obach took no chances. He glued strips of outdoor carpeting to the soles of his tennis shoes so he wouldn't leave obvious sign. When he worked his way through the under-brush, he always went around spider webs for the same reason. He came and went in silence and secrecy. On one occasion in the marsh he had a close-up view of a cottonmouth and sometimes wondered if the creek concealed any large gators. He would learn about the aggressive bull that lurked there only much later, long after his forays into the wilderness.

Everglades Lawmen

"I didn't know what kind of people we were dealing with here," Obach said. "The possibility of set guns or other booby traps in the woods or in the cabin was always in the back of my mind. I carried the rod tip of a fishing pole with me at all times and swept the areas as I walked.

"These were clever poachers. The only thing consistent was their inconsistency. They had to be aware that it would be impossible to charge them with anything except trespass unless we could catch them with their hunting tools and equipment.

"I was very impressed that they rarely left a track behind them," he said. "They left everything as natural as they could and avoided even the narrow, winding game trails. I followed the same principles on my scouts so they wouldn't be spooked by a track or other human sign."

The turning point came on November 15, 1986. Obach crept close to the cabin and spotted a small boat pulled up on the shore. He approached very quietly and carefully. He peered into the boat and saw two crossbow bolts lying on the deck. He also took a few seconds to write down the boat's hull registration numbers. Later that day, he learned the boat was the property of Douglas Brooker from Jupiter. The picture was beginning to crystallize. Time was running out for the outlaws of Gingerbread Camp.

"Lieutenant Burnsed decided we were going to hit them after midnight the next morning," Obach recalled. "We got there around one A.M. There was Burnsed, Jeff Ardelean, Carl Young, Ken Parramore, and myself. We wanted to have a lot of people to surround the cabin and make an impression of overwhelming force. We didn't want anybody running off into the woods in the dark."

They agreed that Obach, who knew the country best, would make one final scout to confirm that the poachers were still in the cabin. It was a relatively cool evening with few insects, but Obach felt himself sweating under the cumbersome bulletproof vest. Before he left, he checked his shirt pocket for the cigars he had bought to celebrate the bust. The only light he carried was a little penlight with a red beam that couldn't be picked up farther away than a few yards.

"I was leery about using the light unless I absolutely had to," he said. "The swamp is different at night, and it took me awhile to make my way to the cabin. I remember being very wary of water moccasins. It wasn't an easy task."

As Obach entered the swamp, he heard the hoot of a great horned owl and then the throaty response of a barred owl echoing in the darkness. "It was quite eerie," he said. "Spooky, really."

He waded the creek slowly and quietly. The water came up to his waist, and he wondered if there were gators nearby. The boat was still there. They had timed it just right. Obach moved a distance away from the cabin and whispered in his handheld radio to Burnsed: "They're here. Come on in."

The minutes dragged, but finally the dark shapes of the other four wardens materialized across the creek. They cautiously forded the stream and joined Obach. After a few whispered words, the officers surrounded the cabin.

"We had one man on each of three walls, ready to shine his flashlight through the screen," Obach said. "Our two strongest guys, Burnsed and Ardelean, were at the front and ready to break down the door."

When the two burly wardens put their shoulders to the door, the others snapped on their lights.

"Game wardens! Law enforcement! Police!" they shouted. "Don't touch any knives! Don't look for a gun! We have the cabin surrounded!"

The apparent ringleader, Booker, sat bolt upright in the top bunk and cracked his skull on the rafter above. Later he told the investigating officers that he had thought it was all some strange dream.

"As we frisked them down, we could tell they were rattled," Obach said. "They were out of focus. Didn't know what was going on."

They kept asking the officers what the problem was. Right from the start they claimed to be hikers who had stumbled on the cabin and were simply spending the night. The story seemed rehearsed and contrived.

After searching the cabin and the nearby underbrush, Obach's initial elation gradually gave way to worry. "The shock started to hit me," he said. "We had found no firearms, no arrows, no bows. Nothing! There was no evidence to tie them to deer poaching."

The game wardens clambered on top of the cabin roof next. Nothing! Then one warden crawled under the cabin. Nothing there either! The darkness was beginning to fade, and the suspects still kept asking what the problem was.

Obach suddenly thought that it was part of a plan. The poachers had come into camp this first night without their guns and bows simply to "test the water." They wanted to determine if the wardens were watching their camp. Their presence that night in the cabin was bait, a ploy to draw the law out into the open.

"I was walking around shining my light when I saw it—a welcome sight, a never-to-be-forgotten find," Obach related.

In the garish yellow glow of his flashlight, he saw the camouflaged stock of a cross bow mounted with a 4x scope. He picked it up carefully by the bow string. By Florida law, a crossbow was considered a firearm.

"Roy! We got 'em," Obach said loudly. "Look at this!"

Burnsed came over, smiled and then said: "Okay, now we've got to find out who this belongs to."

Each suspect denied owning the crossbow. The game wardens bluffed and claimed they could see fingerprints on the crossbow despite the glare and poor light provided by flashlights. The inference was clear. The scientific boys in white coats at the crime lab would certainly have no problems. Come clean now and cooperate, or we'll hit you with the book. It was a classic police bluff. But would it work with these shrewd and clever lawbreakers?

One suspect grudgingly admitted the crossbow "might" be his.

"Is it or isn't it?" Burnsed asked.

"It's mine."

Daylight brought more finds including a Remington 5mm rifle, crossbow bolts, arrows, and bows—all hidden around the cabin in palmetto bushes and brush. Inside the cabin, the game wardens discovered several deer hunting magazines. One article was titled "Florida's Best Trophy Hunting—Tricks that Take Sunshine Cypress Bucks."

"These guys weren't meat hunting," Obach insists. "They were only after the giants."

They also never admitted to deer poaching and never revealed the secret of how they had constructed Gingerbread Camp. Much later, Obach heard they had brought the big pieces in by helicopter, but that was never confirmed.

The suspects pleaded guilty in Martin County Circuit Court on March 23, 1987, to armed trespass and possession of a gun in a refuge. The defendants included Douglas J. Brooker, Timothy J. Henning, and David C. Blakeman—all from nearby Jupiter. Judge Pfeiffer Trowbridge sentenced them to four years probation and four years loss of hunting and fishing privileges, and fined each man fifteen hundred dollars. The court ordered the confiscation of the boat, engine, a long bow, the rifle, the crossbow, and other items.

The tough Yankee from New York City and the Florida boy had solved the mystery of Gingerbread Camp. Their diligence, determination, and doggedness had overcome frustrations and obstacles, disappointments, and temporary defeats.

The men who built and used Gingerbread Camp regarded Jonathan Dickinson State Park as their private hunting preserve. Game Wardens Obach and Burnsed reminded them that the park was for the people, not poachers.

• • •

Game wardens spend their days and nights conjuring up new methods and strategies to catch the game violator, the wildlife outlaw, the one who disdains the fish and game laws. The tactics and tools of the game warden grow ever more sophisticated and effective.

Take, for instance, the "swamp track," a snuffling monster that gives warning of its coming long before it actually appears by the squeak, squeal, and mutter of its engine and metal tracks. The mechanical creature climbs its way up out of the cypress swamp, then looms into view. The occupants ride atop a steel platform taller than a tall man. This specialized vehicle easily transverses difficult and flooded terrain as the game warden patrols a hostile environment.

The typical track is home-built, fashioned from an old truck engine and cast-off parts, and put together with a good deal of imagination and the kind of mechanical ingenuity not taught at engineering school. The operator steers from atop the deck with a conventional steering wheel attached to a long rod descending into the maw of the machine. There are no brakes, and the ponderous people-mover weighs several tons.

Hunters and game wardens both drive tracks in certain designated areas of the Glades at certain times of the year. This stripped-down version of an army tank can negotiate just about any terrain.

Everglades Lawmen

The game wardens ride atop these metal monsters and sail out into the sea of wilderness.

The swamp buggy is another invaluable tool for south Florida game wardens. This is similar in design to a track, except it runs on huge tractor tires. Swamp buggies vary in size and design. Many of the originals were rather small affairs made from WWII surplus jeeps. They can plow their way through the thickets and ford deep streams that would swallow whole a conventional jeep or other off-road vehicle. The swamp buggy is a magic carpet into the Glades used by law enforcement, sportsmen, and lawbreakers.

Machines sometimes evoke an unexpected sentimentality in men. Lt. Greg Taminosian, or "Tami," is such a case. He's a burly, sometimes gruff character who has a Southern twang and always packs a thick chaw of tobacco in his cheek. His ancestry is Armenian, but he is, for all intents and appearances, a typical Cracker game warden. Like many game wardens, he was a talented athlete. He played baseball in the American minors and for a professional Dutch team in Europe.

The Big Cypress National Wildlife Preserve, all 565,000 acres of it, has been Tami's playground for many years. This is rugged country, nearly inaccessible in places except for those with the proper equipment and a ration of pure grit. Tami's swamp buggy has taken him on many missions—rescuing lost hikers or hunters, jumping deer and turkey poachers, and providing assistance to stranded sportsmen. He and his men are the law out here in the wild and remote corners of the huge swamp and forest.

Sometimes the duty hasn't been pleasant. On a number of occasions, Tami found lost hunters or hikers after they had spent a frigid night in the swamp. The temperature doesn't go down much below thirty degrees in south Florida, even in midwinter, but it is a wet and penetrating cold. Tami remembers running up on the naked corpses of those who had not come prepared. They had succumbed to hypothermia, which deceives the mind into thinking that the body is hot rather than cold. The deluded victims run through the woods, stripping off every item of clothing in a desperate effort to cool off. Eventually, they stagger and fall. Some never arise again.

The lucky ones hang on until they see Tami's swamp buggy, "The General," come lurching and dipping across the horizon, a noisy and mud-smeared angel of mercy. The rescuer is a sometimes

Tall in the Saddle. *These Everglades game wardens could see for miles from their elevated platform atop a home-built track designed expressly for the sawgrass marsh. At the wheel is George Eddy. One game warden even once dedicated a poem to a veteran swamp buggy nicknamed "The General." (Florida Game and Fish Commission)*

profane and often incensed Armenian, a legend among game wardens for his cranky temperament and colorful, but always imaginative, vocabulary. It doesn't matter. To those lost in the Big Cypress, this dark, mustached bear of a man is as beautiful as the latest *Playboy* centerfold.

Few would suspect Tami has a sweeter, sentimental side, but he does. This same rugged character was once moved to write a prose poem dedicated to his swamp buggy. This dilapidated machine from

Swamp Buggy Boogie. *The late Richard Long guides his swamp buggy through flooded terrain at the J. W. Corbett wilderness area near West Palm Beach, circa 1975. (Florida Game and Fish Commission)*

1948 had served several generations of game wardens before Tami put on the uniform and gunbelt in 1976. But we can safely assume that the Armenian Cracker was the first who ever expressed his affection poetically for a cantankerous chunk of steel.

"Countless axles, broken springs, sheared U-joints, and an array of other obstacles befell the 'General,' " Tami wrote after twenty years of bumping and swaying on top of this iron steed. When the old buggy stalled or stuck fast in the mud, Tami and the other game wardens in the Cypress never used its given name. They utilized a vivid and eloquent dictionary of oaths and curses that would have done justice to a frontier mule skinner.

Tami wrote that other times he would plead with his machine, mouthing such endearments as "honey" and "baby." But when the machine failed to respond, when the tires kept spinning in the mud hole, or the engine wouldn't turn over, the sweet nothings were soon replaced by #@*!!!###*#&*#!!!. Or words to that effect.

"Evidently 'General' did not mind the physical and verbal abuse because every November, after a coat of paint and set of plugs and several yards of bailing wire, it was ready to go again," Tami wrote. "And go it did for many seasons, carrying young officers to their duties year after year and then witnessing those young officers retire with a little gray in their hair and a storehouse of stories about their adventures aboard the 'General.'

"Men and machines share a common fate: one day both men and machines must quit. And, after nearly fifty years, the 'General' quit for the last time. A landfill is hardly a fitting resting place for such a noble buggy. It deserves a coat of paint, new decals, and display site at the Game and Fish Headquarters."

But the old-timers like Tami will never forget the old rust bucket that carried them safely though the wilderness in all kinds of weather, day and night, for nearly a half century. He wrote: "In the days ahead when the only swamp buggies are those in old men's tales, someone will remember the 'General' and 'honey' and 'baby' and '!!!##**#*#*!.' "

• • •

On dark nights, the fire hunters steal into the woods. They shine the headlights of their vehicles or a beam from a handheld spotlight into the dark tangle of palmetto and pine, yellow fingers of light searching out the deer. It is a technique first practiced early in the nineteenth century, when pioneers used metal reflectors to direct the bright glare of a torch or pan of glowing coals toward the startled animals.

Wild animals are mesmerized by a beam of light. Deer actually seem to pose, standing motionless for long seconds, long enough for a poacher to unlimber his scoped deer rifle and send a bullet into its brain or heart. Nailing these "gun and light" violators is meat and potatoes for wilderness game wardens. They spend thousands of hours each year rolling along the back roads, headlights out, looking for that telltale beam of light and listening for the sharp report of a high-powered rifle.

High overhead in the night sky aerial game wardens are also on

Secret Camp. *Framed by a poacher's telescope-equipped crossbow, Officer Richie Obach examines a camouflaged cabin, the base for a ring of deer poachers in 1986. (Lt. Jeff Ardelean)*

patrol, skilled pilots like Lt. Jim Truitt, Lt. Bill Clayborn, and Lt. Danny Angles. These expert fliers and fully certified game wardens spend long hours aloft in a GFC Cessna single-engine aircraft or helicopter. They are skilled and practiced, their eyes seeking out in the dark void below the telltale yellow beacon of light. Some nights there is nothing but deep black satin below dotted with the yellow light of isolated cabins and the headlights streaming down the main roads. But on other nights, the fire hunters—also called jack lighters and spot lighters—give away their location and purpose to the game wardens in the sky.

It takes skill and practice to fine-tune the coordination of aerial surveillance with ground units. The pilot must fix the position and direct the wardens on the ground to where he last saw the telltale gleam of light. You might liken it to a fox hunt conducted in the wilderness and at night over a playing field of millions of acres of swamp and forest. This aerial arm of the game warden is an effective and intimidating law enforcement tool. Most of the flying is done at night and at low altitude. Aircraft crashes have claimed two game warden pilots, ominous documentation of the risks inherent in this type of flying.

Down in the Everglades region, the GFC also maintains a Bell helicopter for rescues and other unusual missions. The mission of the wardens in the sky is to carry out law enforcement surveillance at night or during the day, assist in search-and-rescue missions in the wilderness, and ferry game and fish wildlife biologists as they undertake aerial surveys of deer, wading birds, eagles, or other species.

• • •

About a hundred yards off the road in rural St. Lucie County, a six-point buck white-tailed deer stood picture-perfect against the backdrop of pine woodland. Every so often the deer would turn its head to survey the surrounding countryside. All the while its tail swished away the pestering flies and other insects.

Several cars slowed down, and one driver honked his horn, but the deer didn't bolt. The magnificent buck simply stood there in the sun of a beautiful summer day in 1995. Several minutes later a pickup slowed down when the driver spotted the unsuspecting deer. He drove a few hundred yards down the road and turned around and came to a stop right across from the still-grazing deer. He stared at it intently for several seconds.

Then the driver checked his mirror repeatedly and swiveled his head, looking up and down the road making sure there were no other cars coming. He quickly reached under the seat and pulled out a rifle gun case, unzipped it, slid a scoped deer rifle out, loaded the rifle, and aimed through the open window at the unwary deer.

Shooting deer from a road is illegal in Florida, and it was out of season too, but the temptation was overwhelming. In fact, this particular stretch of rural highway was known as a favorite spot for road hunters who liked to bag their deer the easy way. The rifle barked and the .270 bullet struck the deer in the chest. Hair flew in the air, but the deer miraculously remained on its feet, slowly turned its head, and continued flicking its tail. Incredulous, the shooter jacked another cartridge into the chamber and shot again. The grazing deer didn't move. Could he have missed both times? And why didn't the deer bolt for the nearby wood line? The poacher shot twice more before Game Wardens Ben Johnson and Cathy Jackson came out of concealment.

The bewildered poacher was had. He was the first violator in the Everglades region duped by the latest weapon in the game warden's arsenal: Robo-deer. Capt. Andy Love and Lt. David Wilson were pleased with the day's work. Their new toy had proven its worth.

After citing the poacher, the wardens walked out to the grazing deer, which had now stopped its movements. One officer lifted the head off the body, and the other easily lifted the body. They headed back to their nearby patrol vehicle carrying the dismantled robotic deer, whose appearance and behavior had so tempted those driving by on that isolated country lane.

Robo-deer is a lifelike mannequin covered with an actual deer hide and antlered head. A small electrical motor concealed in the deer's neck powers the tail and head. Game Warden Fred Cagle had stayed hidden nearby and operated the deer with a radio-control device. He could move the head and tail at will. Actually, the technology involved is pretty simple, very similar to that used by model airplane enthusiasts for decades. The effect is startlingly lifelike.

Game wardens have used dummy deer and even cardboard silhouettes for years, usually at night. But this moving, perfectly life-like deer is far more productive and enticing for roaming deer poachers. And its incredibly lifelike appearance makes it equally effective even in bright daylight.

Shikar Safari Club International donated a small herd of Robo-deer and a Robo–black bear to the Florida game wardens. Each life-sized deer costs approximately one thousand dollars. Occasionally, a poacher's bullet strikes the electric motor in the neck, which must then be replaced. Otherwise the decoys stand punishment well.

"Word spread quickly that we were using these moving robot deer, and that was another positive benefit to the program," Maj. Jim Ries said. "We wanted those poachers to wonder whether that deer in the field was real or a decoy. This deterrent factor undoubtedly saved many real deer from a poacher's bullet.

"We eventually hosted a major press conference attended by representatives of the major print and television media in south Florida to give them a demonstration of the new technology," Ries said. "At the same time we made available video taken surreptitiously during actual Robo-deer operations. The story went all over the state."

Dozens of deer poachers have been fooled in the years since Robo-deer made its debut in south Florida. The game-greedy outlaws just can't resist taking a shot at such an inviting target. Not everything is what it seems, not even in the quiet woods and swamps of south Florida.

Chapter 12:
Trials, Tribulations, and True Tales

Standing there on the levee you could never believe that a giant jet aircraft had crashed into the marsh. The Everglades had swallowed that aircraft whole. You didn't see any evidence of the crash until the airboat reached the actual impact point. It was the most devastating and desolate sight . . .

—Game Warden John Reed

Hell fell out of the sky that day of May 11, 1996. Only a few solitary fishermen in their bass boats viewed the aircraft's death spiral. The giant jetliner plummeted down out of the sparkling blue Florida sky and merged into the green, brown, and gold wilderness marsh below. Some of the first on the scene were local game wardens skimming above the water in their airboats. Very soon they knew the truth. There were no survivors. There was hardly any visible wreckage. From the levee, a few hundred yards from the point of impact, a person couldn't even tell that a giant airliner had perished there only a few hours earlier. There was no need for a rescue operation. There was only the grisly task of exhuming the twisted wreckage and the body fragments from the swamp, where alligators and wading birds went about their routine as they had for thousands of years before man came to south Florida.

Lt. John Reed had seen death many times, often in its most grotesque and stomach-churning manifestations—cars obliterated after head-on crashes and small aircraft and helicopters whose metal bones still littered the inner recesses of the Glades. But Reed had

Death in the Glades. *Tom Shirley (right) and another game warden used this surplus army track to reach the scene of a 1963 Everglades jetliner crash. Two other airplane crashes occurred in 1972 and 1996. Game wardens played a key role in all three rescue-and-recovery efforts. (Florida Game and Fish Commission)*

never seen anything like the wreck of Valu-Jet Flight 592. He guided one of the airboats to the crash site the next day after the tragedy, ferrying in the chief crash investigator from Washington.

Four airboats went out that day, and one by one they slowed to a stop at the center of the impact point. The shallow water lapped about their hulls, making little slapping noises. It was quiet here and peaceful, but all around them floated the ghastly human debris of the crash. The air smelled of aviation fuel and the stench of decay and death.

This quiet patch of Everglades was a wilderness graveyard for 109 men, women, and children. Their remnants floated and bobbed in the ebbing wakes of the now stationary airboats. There were no intact bodies, only chunks, parts, pieces, strips of skin, fragments of legs and arms. Few, if any, of the game wardens present had seen horror of this magnitude. Reed later said, "It was something no one could ever, ever, ever imagine."

Everglades Lawmen

His airboat rocked slightly while the gentle wind blew along the water's surface. The boats were surrounded by a sea of clothing, bits of bodies, and skeins of human skin. Luggage and the vague shapes of aircraft parts and debris were almost all sunk deep into the turbid marsh, shadows in the gloom.

"I was sitting there in my airboat in a numb state of shock trying to comprehend what must have happened when Flight five ninety-two exploded on impact," Reed said. "All around were submerged pieces of the aircraft. Here and there you saw a hand or an arm floating in the water. I remember seeing a lot of chopped-off legs with the tennis shoes still tied to the feet. It was hard, especially for our younger officers who never had been exposed to anything remotely like this."

Of all the nightmarish images, the sight of a woman's severed hand floating near the airboat left its indelible imprint. Like most men, Reed appreciated the beauty and grace of a pretty woman. And for him, the polished, manicured nails of a woman's hand symbolized feminine allure and delicate beauty.

"I looked down at that hand and thought about this woman painting her fingernails the morning of the flight, saying goodbye to her friends and family, boarding the aircraft, laughing, smiling. I started to visualize a face to go with the hand, the sound of her voice. That was dangerous, not the way to deal with the aftermath of tragedy. Right away I stopped myself. 'You can't do this!' I told myself. 'You can't think of this as belonging to an individual or you'll go crazy.' I couldn't think that because it would have torn my guts out," he said.

His mind still reeling, Reed suddenly glimpsed an open Bible lying on top of the sawgrass. He saw it as God's answer to his unspoken prayer. He drew strength from the sight of a Bible, which had been clasped in the hands of a person fated to meet his judgment day in the wilderness marsh.

"From that point on, I was able to deal emotionally and psychologically with this terrible tragedy," Reed recalled.

Game Warden Roy Martinez was one of the first on the scene. For him, this was déjà vu. The nightmarish and haunting overtones echoed back decades to his first days as an officer in the Everglades. As he stared into the marsh, his thoughts returned to December 29, 1972, when Eastern Flight 401 had gone down in the Everglades only a few miles away. The memories were vivid and disturbing.

Dead, burned, and dismembered children and the body of a young pregnant woman branded their images into the mind of the father-to-be that terrible day so soon after the Christmas holiday. But, unlike Valu-Jet Flight 592, there were survivors—ninety-two individuals walked out of the swamp, leaving behind the bodies of ninety-six victims. Martinez will never forget the sight of a group huddled together in misery on the canal levee, singing Christmas hymns in celebration and thanks for their incredible good fortune. During the Valu-Jet recovery, Martinez thought of them and the other survivors of Eastern Flight 401. But there were no survivors this time, not even complete bodies, just human debris rotting in the sawgrass marsh.

Miami Herald reporter Cyril Zaneski wrote a piece describing the Everglades as a daunting adversary for the recovery teams, who, he said, didn't exactly know how and where to begin.

"Workers trying to retrieve bodies and jet debris buried in the murky depths of the great marsh found themselves repelled Sunday by the same primitive obstacles that challenged the most daring explorers at the turn-of-the-century: Razor-edged grass, quicksand-like mud—and hungry alligators."

For many weeks the game wardens with their airboats transported investigators and recovery specialists into the remote crash site. Flight 592 had gone down on May 11, 1996, after improperly stored oxygen bottles in the cargo bay sparked a fire. The aircraft came down about three hundred yards east of the L-67 Levee, about eleven miles north of the Tamiami Trail.

The tragedy took the lives of five crewmen and 104 passengers, a cross-section of America: two brothers who had attended another brother's college graduation, the winner of the Mrs. U.S.A. Petite Beauty Contest, a University of Miami football star, a Georgia family returning from their annual Caribbean cruise. Now they were entombed in the silent swamp.

Game wardens played a crucial role in the recovery effort. Usually eight airboats were maintained on-site. These airboats recovered a great portion of the human remains and nearly seventy percent of the aircraft wreckage. The recovered wreckage was reassembled in a hangar at nearby Tamiami Airport, where investigators looked for clues to the cause of the aerial tragedy.

Everglades Lawmen

Grim Duty. *Recovering the wreckage and remains of victims of the 1996 Valu-Jet Everglades crash was physically grueling and emotionally draining for game wardens on the scene, (from left) Roy Martinez, Monty Hinkle, and Bill Burns. (Capt. David Stermen)*

Conditions were brutal. Because of the biohazard on-site, the officers had to wear cumbersome and sweltering protective suits. Recovering this wreck from the heart of the wilderness would stand as one of the most daunting and complicated operations ever mounted by the National Transportation Safety Board (NTSB), the Federal Aeronautics Administration (FAA), and the other varied state and federal agencies that participated.

Even now the crash area is off-limits to the public out of respect to the families of the victims. Lt. Jerry Lord, who was there at the site from day one, still drives his airboat out to the wreck site on a melancholy and forlorn duty. The swamp loosens its grip occasionally on clothing and other personal items, which slowly break loose from the muck and float to the surface. It might be a man's wallet, a purse, an article of clothing, a shoe—all bitter reminders of the horror and the pain of that terrible accident. Lord is always looking for identification so that these items might be returned to the rela-

Paying Tribute. *Game wardens lay a memorial wreath in the marsh containing the wreckage of Valu-Jet Flight 592. No one survived the 1996 crash. Game wardens played a key role in the long and tedious recovery operation in the Everglades wilderness. (Warden Tom Haworth)*

tives. In other cases, they are disposed of in a respectful and proper manner.

Though time has passed since Valu-Jet Flight 592 dove into the desolate wilderness, for Lord and the other game wardens who still patrol the site and occasionally recover personal items, the mourning has never quite ended.

• • •

A great wind came howling ashore in the early morning hours of August 24, 1992. Hurricane Andrew carved a swath of destruction and devastation through south Florida. Thousands were rendered homeless or sheltered in the pathetic wreckage. There was no electrical power. No running water. Great blocks of trailer homes had been flattened as if at the center of a nuclear explosion. All that was left were concrete trailer pads, a few pieces of furniture, or a solitary refrigerator rising up like some bone-white tombstone above the plain of destruction.

A team of fifty game wardens was mobilized within hours and was dispatched to the hardest hit communities of Cutler Ridge, Kendall, and Homestead. Their mission was to uphold order, suppress looting, direct traffic, and assist survivors in any way possible. Hundreds of other law enforcement officers from various agencies were there too, as well as the National Guard and the Federal Emergency Management Agency (FEMA).

"It was still raining and blowing when we got there in the late afternoon," Lt. Bill Ashley remembers. "This was where I grew up, but everything was changed. The street signs were down, many of the more visible landmarks were gone, and the streets were littered with glass, nails, and debris. Power lines were down all over and presumably live. It was like a scene from Beirut during the civil war of the nineteen seventies."

Ashley saw little looting in his particular area of assignment, although massive looting was reported elsewhere. The wardens were instructed to avoid making arrests except for major felonies or violent crimes. "If you just turn on your blue lights, and the looter drops that television, you have done your job," Maj. Jim Ries told his men. Ashley stopped one man who was emerging from the wreckage of a convenience store with a bulging trash bag over one shoulder.

"The guy told me he was collecting food for his family," Ashley said. "I ordered him to open it up. The bag was full of cartons of cigarettes. I guess that was his idea of food. He was an older guy, not the type you'd expect to be a looter. Actually, I was really surprised at how well people treated each other during the hurricane aftermath. It brought out the best in ninety-nine percent of the people. They treated one another with compassion and caring."

That first evening, a semi-trailer came rolling up into the parking lot of a mall where Ashley and his men were headquartered. The truck was stuffed with canned foods for the survivors. Ashley and his wardens quickly set up a line so distribution could be carried out orderly and fairly. For hours they handed out cans of beans, beef stew, spaghetti, and tuna fish. When darkness fell the crowd disappeared, fearing they would be arrested for curfew violation. Ashley told those still there to spread the word: "I'm the man enforcing the curfew and there won't be any arrests until we distribute all the food." Within twenty or thirty minutes, the line reappeared.

By 10 P.M., the huge semi-trailer was empty. That's when a forlorn little girl in a pretty dress came out of the dark and shyly asked, "Where are the cookies?"

"Honey, I'm sorry, but we gave them all away. We gave everything away," Ashley replied.

The girl, a brown-haired tyke, around six or seven with a sweet Shirley Temple face, turned sadly away.

"This kid had been through a lot," Ashley said. "Her safe little world had been shattered. You were supposed to have cookies. Kids in America aren't supposed to go without."

An instant later, Ashley remembered the cooler he had packed many hours before. There was a bag of cookies there. He ran to the back of his patrol vehicle, grabbed the bag, and shouted at the little girl as she was walking away.

"Come back! I've got your cookies!"

Ashley remembers the incandescent joy on the youngster's face. She was "smiling and ecstatic." One piece of her little world had been restored. Sadness, anxiety, and doubts were banished for at least a little while. Sometimes even the small gift of a bag of cookies can make all the difference to a little girl whose world lies in ruin all around her.

• • •

When the two men went down on their knees to lap water from the muddy puddle in the dirt road, Sgt. Al Hofmeister knew they were probably the convicts who had escaped the day before from the Glades Correctional Institution near Belle Glade.

Hofmeister watched the suspicious men with his binoculars. They were at least a half mile away. His patrol vehicle was parked off the levee road out of their line of sight. His suspicions grew. What were two men doing out in the middle of the Everglades without headgear, a vehicle, or fishing poles? The game warden was wary. One of the escaped cons was serving a life sentence for the murder and robbery of a man on a Pompano Beach golf course. The other escapee was serving a twenty-five-year term for robbing an elderly woman at gunpoint.

Hofmeister could see that neither one had a long gun, but it was possible that one or both had a sidearm stolen from some unsuspecting fishermen or hiker. These were desperate and dangerous men. The veteran game warden took his time thinking out his plan, determined to capture the two cons.

This area of the Everglades in which the fugitives were wandering was the Brown's Farm Wildlife Management Area, a 4,460-acre tangle of myrtle trees and thick undergrowth. The prison was nearly fifty miles north of here. The escapees had certainly had a rugged time. No food. No water. No headgear. No real plan.

Hofmeister took his twelve-gauge riot gun from the rack in his vehicle, checked to see if it was loaded, and then called radio dispatch for backup. A few seconds later, he was stalking slowly through the underbrush toward the distant men. Sweat ran down his face and back. It was brutally hot, and he could feel his heart beating rapidly under the damp uniform shirt.

Long minutes later, he had closed to within seventy feet, hidden behind some bushes. He eased the safety off the shotgun and was preparing to show himself. At that very moment a police car came rumbling up the dirt road, spouting a dusty rooster's tail in its wake. The convicts melted into the surrounding wilderness. It was nearly 8 P.M., and darkness was near. The fleeing criminals still had a chance, but the odds were growing slim as various police units, K-9 teams, and helicopters arrived on the scene.

Soon a K-9 dog with the Palm Beach County Sheriff's Office started whining and barking in the direction of the nearby canal. His trainer, however, refused to let the dog loose. The police chopper overhead had reported the canal was swarming with dozens of large gators. A dog swimming in that water at night wouldn't last more than a minute.

The sheriff's chopper roamed slowly up and down the length of the canal, illuminating the dark waters with its powerful search-light. At times the thundering chopper hovered only twenty feet above the water while the pilot and observer peered into the murky depths for sign of the fugitives.

Hofmeister was standing on the levee bank with fellow Game Wardens Richard Dubberly and Ken Avinon. That's when the chopper pilot saw the silhouettes of two men lying on their backs in the mucky shallow with only their faces above water. Several large gators lurked only feet away from the unsuspecting escapees. The pilot quickly alerted his fellow officers on the ground. Three game wardens and a sheriff's deputy splashed into the canal, dragged the convicts from the water, searched them, and cuffed them. The faces of the escaped cons were grotesquely swollen from mosquito bites. They were deeply fatigued, their desperate eyes showing strain and fear.

One may suspect that three hot meals a day and a clean prison bed didn't seem so bad after all, compared to the gator- and mosquito-infested swamp.

• • •

It must have sounded like thunder when big Bill Ashley pounded on the door of the Riviera Beach crack house with the handle of the ax he held in one of his huge hands.

"Wildlife officer! Police! I've got a search warrant. Open up or we're coming though this door."

Nearby, a snarling pit bull chewed at the end of a catch pole as Lt. Charlie Dennis tried to capture him. Several feet away, Sgt. Ken Parramore stood tense and ready, the loaded twelve-gauge riot gun at the half-port.

The nondescript house was deep in a crime-ridden black neighborhood of Riviera Beach, the kind of place where one doesn't normally see a game warden, much less nearly twenty of them, about to bust the local crack dealer. From within came the sounds of flushing toilets. The suspects were dumping bags of coke and vials of pills in a desperate attempt to destroy evidence. The pounding on the door grew louder and more insistent.

A young man opened the door and quickly subdued the dog. The entry team went in fast and secured those inside, making them sit down on a couch with their hands behind their heads. Another entry team, led by Lt. Roger Brown, entered from the rear. When Brown encountered Ashley he blurted out, "Hey, the backyard is full of pit bulls!" The confidential informant had failed to tell them that. But, oddly enough, the fighting dogs had simply ignored Brown's officers as they came climbing into the backyard.

Inside, the game wardens moved fast looking for drugs, guns, stolen property, and, above all else, endangered sea turtle eggs. This was what had brought the strike team of wardens to an inner city neighborhood. The local crack dealer, the informant had said, often traded dope for the eggs of endangered and threatened loggerheads that came to nest in the sands of south Florida's beaches from May through October. Some south Florida residents from the islands of the Caribbean believe erroneously that these rich turtle eggs act as a powerful aphrodisiac. Turtle egg poachers were getting two to three dollars an egg on the street. This illegal trade was, and still remains, a potent threat to the survival of several sea turtle species.

The dope dealer was an important buyer and seller of eggs. Intelligence gathered by the plainclothes investigators, Lt. Bill Ashley and Lt. Roger Brown, had established that fact. In a matter of days, working closely with Capt. Eddie Wheeler, they put together the plan to put this dealer out of business.

They knew the chief suspect was a convicted felon, dealt in stolen property, fought his pit bulls to the death for entertainment and profit, and had dozens of weapons in the house, including—it was said—a machine gun and even grenades. Busting this crack house could get somebody hurt or even killed. It was a sobering prospect.

The dealer, Fred L. Frederick, forty-seven, was gone when the heat came down on July 21, 1988. His eighteen-year-old-son, a thirty-eight year-old woman, and her two grade school–aged boys were the only ones inside. They put up no resistance and cooperated with the game wardens. No one got hurt, suspect or warden. That was a big relief for those who had planned this potentially dangerous raid so far removed from the typical duties of a game warden.

Other wardens clad in bulletproof vests and cradling their shot-guns in their arms stood out in the dark in a circle around the house. Captain Wheeler directed the perimeter security, which was there to discourage any neighborhood residents from interfering with the operation. It was that kind of place.

"We believed a strong show of force would overawe the occupants of the house and minimize the chance of resistance," Lieutenant Ashley said later. "There is no point in taking any chances in this kind of situation."

The house search soon produced results. "Everything started to happen at once," Ashley said. "We found the MAC-11 machine gun with silencer in the dealer's bedroom. Other contraband began showing up—stacks of VCRs, dope, stolen guns, a video of an illegal dog fight. That's when Frederick, the chief suspect, came walking into the house."

Heavily Armed. *Undercover Game Warden Bill Ashley brandishes an illegal Mac-11 machine gun with silencer and an automatic pistol, two of 26 weapons seized during a raid on the home of a Florida crack dealer who also traded in endangered sea turtle eggs. (Jim Huffstodt)*

After discussing the situation with Ashley, Frederick told his son to go get a bag of turtle eggs hidden in a closet. The youngster came back with a plastic sack containing 107 loggerhead turtle eggs. Frederick had been selling them for fifteen dollars a dozen.

The search ultimately uncovered twenty-six weapons—revolvers, automatic pistols, rifles, and an illegal sawed-off shotgun. The wardens also found thirty-one pounds of marijuana, a stolen all-terrain cycle, two safes jammed with twenty-one thousand dollars in cash and savings bonds, expensive watches, gold chains, twenty ten-dollar cocaine rocks, a cocaine wafer big enough to produce a hundred rocks, a small amount of cocaine, and various drug paraphernalia.

Fred Leroy Frederick was taken to jail and charged with unlawful possession of marine turtle eggs, possession of cocaine with intent to distribute, possession of marijuana with intent to distribute, and possession of firearms by a convicted felon. Later, a Federal weapons charge for possession of a machine gun was added to the list.

The defendant posted three thousand dollars' bail and went home, where, Ashley said, he continued to carry out his varied criminal activities while awaiting trial. Frederick eventually served a year in prison for his blatant disregard for the laws of the state of Florida and the federal government.

It would be nice to report that, since the crack house raid, no one poaches sea turtle eggs along south Florida's beaches. Unfortunately, this is not the case. And all because of a patently false myth about the aphrodisiac qualities of sea turtle eggs.

"This stupid myth is behind the illegal trade in sea turtle eggs," Maj. Jim Ries said. "These magnificent turtles, some of whom weigh three hundred pounds, could vanish if we don't continue the crackdown on the poaching of their eggs."

•   •   •

Those who know Game Warden Tom Haworth appreciate his wry, often self-deprecating sense of humor and marvel at his propensity to find himself in the most outlandish situations. During one period it seemed that Haworth was invariably involved when horrified citizens called about spotting huge boa constrictors in their neighborhoods. The officer was ideally suited for this assignment since he'd worked for a time on the staff of the Miami Metro-Zoo.

In the course of a few weeks, Tom captured three of these escaped "pets," one of which measured sixteen feet long. Those exploits were featured in media reports and won Tom the unofficial title of the "Snake King." On another occasion, he was the investigating officer on a complaint alleging a neighbor was cooking owls on a backyard barbecue grill. Sure enough, when Tom arrived at the location, he discovered a man cheerfully grilling parts of several protected and threatened burrowing owls.

Like most game wardens, Tom is an interesting fellow. The

Warden on the Water. *Game Warden Tom Haworth patrols Lake
Clarke in 1999. (Jim Huffstodt)*

Miami native studied wildlife biology in Colorado and distin-
guished himself as a professional kick boxer before getting involved
in conservation law enforcement. Even though he's not a large or
tall man, Tom's athletic ability and self-defense skills would make
him a formidable opponent for any combative wildlife poacher. He
fits the description of Florida game wardens as defined by retired
Col. Bob Brantley, who said they get the job done even if it means
wrestling in the mud.

In the author's opinion, Tom's most memorable humorous
escapade was like a chapter from one of Edgar Rice Burroughs'
classic Tarzan books. The episode took place in the Lennar Groves
in Palm Beach County, a favorite spot for local deer poachers. Tom
and his fellow wardens made a series of poaching arrests during one
period, and then nothing. The bad guys had, it appeared, spotted
where the wardens were hiding their patrol vehicle before entering
the grove. If they saw that "calling card," they postponed their

Powerful Python. *When residents of a West Palm Beach neighborhood discovered a snake skin 16 feet long, they called for help. The
skin belonged to this huge python, captured by Officer Tom Haworth
and several bystanders. Not native to Florida, this snake was probably a pet released by its owner. The snake went to Lion Country
Safari in Palm Beach County. (Warden Tom Haworth)*

illegal deer hunting.

Tom was determined to find a new way into the groves, which
would allow him to conceal his vehicle in a different location. He
drove around the grove and approached its back door.
Unfortunately, an intervening canal prevented him from simply
walking into the area. There was no bridge or catwalk. And the canal
was too wide to jump.

That's when Tom's attention focused on a tree along the canal
where some children had evidently rigged a rope swing. This inno-
vative game warden was instantly struck with a marvelous idea.
Perhaps he could swing across the fifteen-foot water barrier, drop on
the opposite bank, and enter the grove without alerting any
poachers to his presence. Childhood memories of Tarzan swinging
from his jungle vine surely passed through Tom's mind as he
contemplated the possibilities.

At that moment, a man suddenly emerged from the undergrowth
on the far side of the canal. This individual was dressed in camouflage and carried a hunting bow. The eyes of the deer poacher and
the game warden locked across the intervening moat. There was no

hesitation on Tom's part; he gripped the rope swing with both hands and sailed across the watery divide.

The athletic game warden made a perfect three-point landing only a few feet away from the startled suspect. With his character-istic aplomb, Tom proceeded to cite the man for illegal trespass while projecting an air of nonchalance as if swinging on a rope across a canal was just everyday routine when arresting deer poachers. To say that the illegal archery hunter was stunned by this sudden appearance of a game warden is certainly an understate-ment.

Tom's mistake was deciding to leave the way he had come. While the deer poacher watched, the game warden casually gripped the rope and swung back in the other direction. The return trip, however, turned out to be a different and damper story thanks to a fatal miscalculation. Our acrobatic game warden had failed to notice that the other bank was significantly higher than the grove side.

The game warden's swing didn't clear the other side. He collided into the far bank, lost his grip, and tumbled down into the ten-foot-deep canal. All this took place in full view of the poacher who, we may safely assume, took a certain satisfaction in the warden's watery fate. On the bright side, the canal contained no voracious Nile croc-odiles as in the Tarzan movies. Lucky for Tom!

His fellow game wardens know that Tom's humorous misadven-tures aren't a fair representation of his twelve-year career. He doesn't talk about it much, but Tom saved the lives of three people in different life-threatening emergencies. Two of the potential fatalities were medical situations in which his first-aid, first-responder training was crucial to the victims' survival. On another occasion, Tom rescued a teenager at a hunt camp who shot up in flames after foolishly throwing gasoline on a burning fire. Game Warden Tom Haworth was officially honored by the GFC for his prompt and skilled intervention in these three potentially fatal instances.

• • •

It seemed like we had run fifty miles through the pitch-black Ocala National Forest in central Florida. The author, an admittedly sedentary armchair adventurer, was paying dearly for his inatten-tion to regular physical exercise.

Most embarrassing of all, I was staggering and stumbling behind

Everglades Lawmen

Capt. Eddie Wheeler, a game warden nearly fifteen years my senior, who was giving me a lesson in endurance and game warden grit. This Florida boy, at the age of nearly sixty, was weaving his way through the shadowy forest undergrowth like a startled deer. Far behind, I puffed along like a wheezing steam locomotive, tripping over unseen tree roots and tumbling to the ground several times. Doesn't this old game warden ever get tired? I wondered.

I knew that in a few minutes the dogs would be on our trail. No, this wasn't a jail break, but rather a training exercise for the game warden's newest tool—the K-9. Wheeler and I had been assigned the task of "laying trail" so the nose-sensitive dogs could show their stuff. And, believe me, we tried our best, moving quickly, crossing water several times, skipping across stony ground, and—it seemed to me—bullying our way through the roughest terrain. We knew that twenty-five minutes after our start, the dogs and their trainers would commence a search to test the success of our efforts at evasion.

We knew that Game Warden Leonard Bailey from the Everglades would soon be scrambling through the woods behind Wise Guy, his intensively trained black Labrador retriever. It was the fall of 1990, and the first class of K-9 dogs and their trainers was nearing completion of a rigorous three-month training course. The K-9s, all donated by concerned conservationists, included four black Labs, four yellow Labs, and a Chesapeake retriever.

These were not attack dogs. The game warden's dog is selected for his keen nose, not for the sharpness of his canines or an aggressive personality. The K-9's mission is to track down poachers; rescue lost sportsmen; detect hidden game such as duck, quail, and deer; and locate other evidence such as castaway firearms. In a pilot program, two dogs showed potential with a ninety-three percent tracking success rate. Of seventy-four wildlife conservation cases, the dogs were instrumental in obtaining twenty-six arrests.

During the afternoon before our midnight run, Captain Wheeler, Maj. Jim Ries, Capt. Andy Love, and I—all from the Everglades—had witnessed an impressive demonstration of the dogs' capabilities. Game Warden Chip Leavine orchestrated the presentation, which went flawlessly. Most impressive was how the K-9s quickly detected game animals hidden in secret compartments and unlikely corners of a pickup truck. The dogs took less than a minute to lead their handlers to the concealed evidence.

Even so, I was confident that Captain Wheeler and I had given the dogs a real challenge later that evening after we finally came to a halt in a clump of pine trees. It took several minutes to get my breath, and then I remarked that surely our evasive tactics and overland route would pose considerable problems for the pursuing dogs.

I was dead wrong. In less than ten minutes, far less time than we had spent running, we heard the rustle of leaves and the telltale pant of a Labrador approaching in the darkness. Soon we were being nudged and licked by a friendly Labrador whose doggy grin seemed to mock all our strenuous efforts at eluding capture. It was apparent to us that man's best friend was also going to be the poacher's worst nightmare.

"These K-Nines are living, breathing conservation law enforcement tools," Game Warden Leavine told me afterwards. "They can be as important as a game warden's gun, vehicle, or boat. And they will save valuable time in the field. A K-Nine can search a vehicle or boat in a fraction of the time it takes a human game warden."

• • •

Drawing on the faint light of the stars and the moon, the night-vision scope provided a fuzzy green panorama of beach and pounding surf. Game Warden Ken Parramore peered through the lens and observed the hump of a giant loggerhead sea turtle emerge from the shallows and slowly swim and then crawl up onto the sandy plain. This was one of hundreds of endangered and threatened sea turtles that came ashore to lay their eggs every nesting season in south Florida following a sea journey of thousands of miles.

The game warden watched in fascination as the two-hundred-pound-plus female scooped out its nest with its broad, paddlelike feet. The process took only minutes, and then the huge turtle positioned herself over the hole to begin laying eggs. Once the egg-laying commenced, Parramore could approach and watch the forty or so slime-covered, soft-shelled eggs fill up the nest. Once finished, the sea turtle carefully filled in the hole with broad sweeps of her paddle feet, then crawled back into the surging waves. The massive hump slowly submerged in the dark waters until it vanished into the immensity of the Atlantic Ocean.

On this hot and humid night in the summer of 1989, Parramore

Everglades Lawmen

Eyes in the Night. *Sgt. Ken Parramore explains how a U. S. Army "starlight" scope helped him arrest a chronic poacher who was pilfering hundreds of eggs from the nests of endangered sea turtles along south Florida's Atlantic beaches. (Jim Huffstodt)*

was—for the fiftieth time that nesting season—waiting in conceal-ment amidst the sea grape atop the dune running parallel to the deserted McArthur Beach lying just north of West Palm Beach. It was well after midnight, and the air was thick with pestering mosquitoes and sand gnats. The previous summer, Parramore and Game Warden Ross Welborn caught several sea turtle egg poachers leaving the park with more than a thousand eggs, looted from ten or more nests. That had been the biggest single confiscation of sea turtle eggs ever made.

On the vast majority of nights, however, Parramore's lonely vigil on the beach resulted in nothing more than a collection of insect bites. The monotony was broken by an occasional glimpse through the night-scope of lovers writhing in passion among the shadows. Beach patrol was usually a tedious, thankless task but still an impor-tant one. Poachers regularly raided the nests, scooped up the eggs, and sold them on the street. The myth of the eggs providing sexual vigor is a contributing factor in the gradual decline of several sea turtle species nesting along south Florida's beaches.

But on this particular night, Parramore's patience was rewarded. The outline of a man appeared in his night-scope viewfinder. The stranger moved slowly and cautiously, stopping to stare up and down the beach every few minutes. He carried a bag in one hand and carefully examined the sandy beach looking for the crawl marks left by a nesting sea turtle. At one point, the man left the beach, climbed the dune, and scouted the area from that vantage point before returning to his task.

Parramore remained silent and in concealment, biding his time, his heart thumping with the excitement known only to hunters. He watched as the man knelt down in the sand and began digging. A minute or so later he bent over and reached into the uncovered nest with one arm, removing the valuable eggs one by one and placing them inside a leather bag. Then he filled the nest back in, stood up, threw the bag over one shoulder, and began walking down the beach.

The watching game warden was about thirty yards away on the dune, moving carefully on a parallel track to the poacher, waiting for the opportune moment to make the arrest. "When it came time to take him down, I needed to be as close as possible," Parramore remembers. And for nearly a mile, he shadowed the stranger, who was now walking at the edge of the ocean, skirting the waves sliding up and back again along the white beach.

They had left the desolate stretch where the stranger had uncovered the turtle eggs and had entered a developed area where a wall of multistory condominiums flanked the ocean. Parramore slid up to a boardwalk and placed the night-vision scope down for safekeeping. He was about as close to the target suspect as he could get.

Parramore bolted out of the shadows, running hard and shouting: "Freeze! Game Warden! You're under arrest!" The startled man threw the bag of eggs into the churning surf and took off running down the length of the beach. The game warden paused to wade into the water, grabbed the leather bag, and threw it up on dry land. Then he resumed his pursuit, splashing along the edge of the incoming waves. When he closed the gap, the fugitive waded straight out into the ocean, quickly moving out until he was neck deep.

"If you want me, come and get me!" he yelled, taunting Parramore.

The poacher refused the game warden's repeated orders to return to land. He began moving slowly off parallel to the beach. "Now we had a standoff," Parramore thought at the time.

At one point, Parramore waded into the water up to his gunbelt but backed off. He concluded that wrestling with the suspect in the water wasn't the best strategy. The distant figure continued to wade and sometimes swim down along the edge of the shoreline, keeping up a string of taunts, daring the game warden to come and get him.

"Come out right now!" Parramore shouted back. "You're under arrest for poaching sea turtle eggs. Don't make it harder on yourself."

The man shouted back, "I'll come out when Allah tells me it's okay to come out, not before. Besides, you didn't see nothin'. You didn't see me do it. You're lying!"

These exchanges went on for a half hour or more. Parramore kept the man in the water illuminated in the beam of his flashlight. He knew the fugitive had to leave the water sooner or later, and the waves were steadily getting bigger and more frequent. The poacher's head briefly disappeared several times under the churning surf.

Parramore shined his flashlight on the windows of a nearby condo and shouted for help, identifying himself as a law enforcement officer in need of immediate assistance. Finally, a figure appeared on a tenth-floor balcony. Parramore pointed his flashlight at his own chest, illuminating his badge and other insignia. "Call the police! I need help!" he shouted. The man on the balcony disappeared behind the sliding doors.

Ten minutes later, a Riviera Beach police officer came jogging down the beach. After Parramore filled him in on the situation, the officer started yelling at the poacher to come out just as the game warden had been doing for nearly forty-five minutes.

"And then for some unknown reason, the guy just starts marching up out of the water," Parramore said. "Both of us tackled him in the sand and took him down. We got handcuffs on him immediately. He didn't really fight. There were no more choices open to him at that point."

The two officers quickly learned that the suspect in their custody was Alvin "Popcorn" Keel of West Palm Beach, a coke addict who

Protecting the Resource. *Sgt. Ken Parramore (right) and Warden Ross Welbourn admire a young, protected loggerhead sea turtle at the Marinelife Center in Juno Beach. Both men were involved in several historic cases that discouraged the profitable, illegal trade in sea turtle eggs. (Jim Huffstodt)*

used the money earned selling sea turtle eggs to fund his drug habit. Parramore later walked back down the beach, retrieved the leather ski-shoe bag, and found 125 loggerhead sea turtle eggs inside, in addition to a crack pipe.

Keel was taken to jail, charged with poaching endangered/threatened sea turtle eggs, given a court date, and released as a first-time offender. Several weeks later, Parramore was reading the local newspaper when he recognized a picture of Keel. The accompanying story claimed Keel had been caught by Palm Beach Island police riding on his bicycle away from the beach carrying a bag filled with 348 sea turtle eggs. The man in the mug shot, however, was identified not as Alvin Keel but as Robert Henderson.

The Palm Beach Island Police had also released Keel, alias Henderson, unaware of his previous arrest on the same charge. Lt. Bill Ashley, a plainclothes investigator, was soon on Keel's trail. The fugitive was found one morning sweeping the walk in front of an apartment house. The arrest was made quickly and without resistance. Ashley, Parramore, and Game Warden Jeff Ardelean took the accused felon to Palm Beach County Jail, where he was booked.

A follow-up investigation quickly revealed that Keel had been arrested four times that summer for sea turtle egg poaching by four different law enforcement agencies. The suspect had given false names in three cases and gone right on with his nightly beach visits. His four arrests resulted in the confiscation of 583 eggs. Parramore and Ashley were convinced Keel had been collecting the eggs on orders from a dealer. There was no telling how many hundreds of eggs Keel had poached during the four-month nesting season. The impact on the sea turtles, Parramore believed, had been significant. Court records also documented that Keel had been arrested on the same charge as far back as 1980.

Keel ended up serving two years in jail for his illegal harvesting of sea turtle eggs. The lesson, however, didn't take. Keel was arrested in the summer of 1998 for taking sea turtle eggs on a Palm Beach County beach. His case is an example of how drug addiction not only negatively impacts human society but also can contribute to the decline of endangered and threatened sea turtles.

• • •

Waiting and watching in the shadowy forest tested a man's patience. At least an hour had gone by without incident. Game Warden Tim Miller fought the doubts haunting his mind and stayed hidden in the tangle of trees at the edge of the Fort Drum Wildlife Management Area. Somewhere out there was Miller's quarry: a human predator of illegal prey, a professional wild game poacher.

This twenty-thousand-acre tract, located fifteen miles west of Vero Beach, boasted some of the best wild turkey hunting on public land in the whole state. Most hunters followed the rules and applied for the yearly computerized lottery. The handful of hunting slots ensured that those lucky few who won the lottery would enjoy a quality hunt in a pristine area not overrun with swarms of other sportsmen. Too many other public areas resembled crowded parks with an army of hunters stumbling through the wild swamp, marsh, and forest.

And then there were always a few greedy outlaws whose

contempt for the rules and fair play was exceeded only by their ingenuity and woodcraft in raiding Fort Drum whenever the mood struck them. On this spring night, Game Warden Miller was waiting for just such a game thief.

Actually Miller, a well–set up man in his late thirties, had been hunting this faceless outlaw for the last four years. Like any good game warden, Miller was patient, persevering, and attentive to details. He had the eyes of a hunter.

This epic chase started back in 1995 while Miller nosed around the palmettos covering the ground within a thick growth of maple, bay, and a few willow. The spot was about three hundred yards away from the border of the Fort Drum Wildlife Management Area and even closer to the busy four-lane Florida Turnpike. Fort Drum is a wonderful place to hunt deer and wild turkey in Indian River County.

The eighteen-year veteran game warden judged this a good place for a drop-off. A poacher could exit a vehicle and quickly disappear into the undergrowth. It would only be a short trek from there to penetrate the game-rich Fort Drum, a quality hunting area rich in wild turkey, deer, and hog, not to mention the wide variety and thriving populations of everything from giant alligators and burrowing owls to barred owls and badgers. A man or woman entering this wilderness was figuratively stepping back in time to the wonder and magnificence of wilderness Florida. That's why hunters were willing to face high odds in the computerized draw, pay a fifty-dollar fee if drawn, and wait for years if necessary for the privilege to hunt Fort Drum.

Those law-abiding hunters despised the game thieves who looted the area in contempt of every principle of sportsmanship and, if unchecked, would in their uncontrolled greed strip the wilderness of wild game. The plume hunters and the market hunters of long ago were gone, but these modern outlaws were their spiritual descendants. Selfishness, arrogance, and a colossal short-sighted-ness were qualities shared by all who defied the game laws.

Miller understood the ethical majority of hunters and why they loathed these night raiders. Like many game wardens, he had grown up in the swamps, marshes, and woodlands of Florida and had learned over the years the ways of wild animals and their habitats. Hunting was in his blood, a heritage he is passing on to his own children. Tim and his wife had long hunted the wild turkey, the Osceola so sought by serious hunters, calling in the wary birds in the dim dawn, lying concealed in the palmettos in camouflage, faces blackened like commandos. Miller understood the idea and philosophy of the lottery, limited access, and the importance of preserving truly wild areas where hunters could pursue their sport.

Not long before, Tim's teenage daughter had shot her first wild turkey, a proud moment for her parents, who vicariously shared their child's thrill and remembered more keenly their own first successful hunt for Old Tom. That's a big part of the reason that Tim Miller wears the green uniform. Deep down, this explains his obsession in tracking down and arresting those who threaten his sport, his heritage, his passion. And that's why he waited patiently in the darkness on that quiet night, the murmur of the forest broken only occasionally by the drone of passing traffic on the Florida Turnpike.

On that day in 1995 when Game Warden Miller walked through the palmettos, he was studying the ground intently and moving with the quiet grace of the hunter. Something in his gut told him that this would be a perfect place for illegal entry into Fort Drum. Miller's suspicions soon bore fruit when he uncovered a clutch of plastic milk jugs hidden under the palmettos. The jugs had been slit open by a sharp knife. That told the game warden that a poacher had filled the jugs with water, frozen them, and carried them into the woods to preserve any fresh game he had just poached. It was a familiar pattern.

Every year after, Officer Miller frequently returned to the site. On a half dozen occasions he found empty, slit-open milk jugs but nothing else. Sometimes he set up surveillance on-site, waiting for the mystery poacher to appear. No visitors came except for the mosquitoes and "no-see-ums" that make south Florida uncomfortable for the city slicker. Miller conservatively estimates he checked the area at least a hundred times over four years and staked out the site dozens of times to no avail. Then one November day, Miller's luck changed dramatically for the better. It was about 4:30 P.M. when the prowling warden found an ice chest very near the pile of old jugs.

The poacher had attempted to hide the cooler with a green top under a few ferns. Alongside the cooler was a military-style backpack filled with the poacher's street clothes. The cooler was empty, but Miller was now convinced that the poacher was within Fort Drum. He might be returning at that very minute. The game warden set up surveillance about two hundred yards away. The cooler was out of sight, but the position gave Miller a good view of the road. He figured it would be easier to spot the pickup vehicle when it returned to retrieve the poacher. Most poachers were dropped off by a partner and then retrieved at an agreed rendezvous time. That was the typical pattern. The game warden had concealed himself in a spot with a good view of the road, assuming it would be much easier to make the bust when the vehicle pulled over for the pickup. Events were soon to prove that this poacher didn't fit the pattern and was a lone wolf with an apparently long history of evading detection.

Darkness came to the woods while the yellow glare of car headlights passed by on the nearby Florida Turnpike. Two hours of patient waiting and nothing. Miller was worried. Perhaps he had somehow missed the pickup. That seemed highly unlikely, and Miller began questioning his assumptions about this unconventional game outlaw. The warden returned quietly to the location of the cooler.

The cooler, he noted with surprise, had been moved closer to the turnpike. The street clothes were gone and replaced with camouflaged hunting clothes. The officer peered into the cooler and discovered at least one wild turkey breast. The poacher had been back, might even be prowling the dark woods only a few feet away. That brief glimpse into the cooler was enough for now. There would be time enough later to make a more thorough inventory of its contents once the poacher had been apprehended.

Miller took up another position about ten feet from the cooler. He didn't have to wait long. Around 7:30 P.M., a pickup truck slowed down on the turnpike and pulled over onto the shoulder a few yards away. A man got out from behind the wheel and walked to the tailgate, pretended to urinate, looked both ways, and then pulled down the gate.

The poacher moved quickly, grabbed the cooler, and was lifting it up to the gate when Miller came out of the darkness at a full run, shouting, "Game Warden! You're under arrest!" Taking no chances, he took the suspect to the ground and quickly snapped on the cuffs.

No other game warden was available then so Miller radioed the

Everglades Lawmen

Florida Highway Patrol for assistance. A female officer soon arrived and later took the defendant to county jail. Miller now had the opportunity to fully inventory the cooler's contents: three turkey breasts, three beards, and two sets of spurs—a total of about fifteen pounds of meat.

Around 8:30 P.M., Game Warden Billy Welbourne rolled up to offer his assistance. A third officer, soon to play an important role in the search that followed, was K-9 Jake, a two-year-old German short-haired pointer owned and trained by Miller specifically for wildlife conservation law enforcement and search-and-rescue.

Miller is one of nine game wardens in the state who work with dogs. The four-footed wardens, with their sensitive and educated noses, have proven their worth time and again. K-9 Odie, Miller's first dog, had been a loyal and effective partner. Together, they had made some excellent game cases. But Odie was gone, the victim of Rocky Mountain spotted fever, although his memory lived on vividly in Miller's mind.

K-9 Jake was learning fast and showed every promise of becoming as fine a dog as his predecessor. While Miller took Jake back to the cooler to backtrack the poacher, Welbourne walked along the shoulder of the road until his flashlight cone picked up a tire track in the mud. He worked his way down the road about a half mile and the sign eventually led him to where the poacher had hidden his vehicle in a dried-up creek bed under a bridge. The tire track was the clincher.

The two game wardens reunited. Miller's interest rose when Welbourne told him about the vehicle. Five years before, Miller had arrested a man for trespass and littering who had hidden his truck under the same bridge. All very interesting. The puzzle pieces began to fall into place.

Now it was K-9 Jake's time to shine. The game wardens and the free-roaming dog swept through the woods until they came to the fence marking the border of the Fort Drum Wildlife Management Area. The officers could see fresh tracks in the soft earth on the other side of the fence. They crossed into the area. Miller put Jake on the track and the increasing excitement of the dog indicated he was on to something. It took the dog only a few minutes before he led the game wardens into a patch of palmettos, where they found a Marlin .22 Magnum with scope inside a plastic bag. It was a little after midnight.

Partners on the Prowl. *Game Warden Tim Miller and his canine partner, Jake, scour a thick clump of palmettos searching for sign of a wild turkey poacher. Dogs like Jake are trained to identify various game, search out hidden guns, and track fleeing poachers. The dogs are also valuable in wilderness search-and-rescue missions. (Jim Huffstodt)*

Everglades Lawmen

Jake's sensitive nose had not only uncovered an important piece of evidence but also linked it with the cooler, the footprints, and other physical evidence. After four years, Miller was convinced that he had finally come to the end of the road that had begun with the initial discovery of the cast-away milk jugs. Everything was now crystal clear. The poacher had operated alone. There was no pickup, no accomplice. He dropped off his rifle, cooler, backpack, and hunting clothes first, then doubled back down the turnpike and hid the vehicle under the bridge. He then walked the half mile back to the drop-off. Passing motorists would just see a man in everyday work clothes without a rifle or camouflage jacket, evidently just another hitchhiker or stranded motorist.

It was easy to wait until traffic thinned out and then melt into the woods. The poacher changed into his hunting clothes, grabbed his rifle, and started hunting. He would return with the wild game, place it in the ice-filled cooler, change back into civvies, and walk back to the truck.

"This guy was a pro," Miller said. "I'm sure that he'd gone through this routine many times. You have to wonder how much game he took out of Fort Drum over the years? And he might have been poaching deer as well as wild turkey. A skilled poacher such as this individual could make a real negative impact over time.

"The sad part is that he was stealing game from the legitimate hunters who were willing to enter the drawing, lucky enough to win, and willing to pay for a quality hunt," he said. "Those fees support an ongoing wildlife management program designed to preserve this wonderful hunting opportunity for future sportsmen. The poacher is a game thief who robs the honest hunter who follows the rules. That's the sad part."

Fort Drum is a place worth protecting. Florida Game and Fish Magazine named it one of the five best public wild turkey hunting spots in Florida.

The defendant was charged with three counts of illegal possession of wild turkey taken on a wildlife management area. The accused, a man from nearby Melbourne, Florida, later pleaded guilty in county court. The judge fined him $625 and suspended hunting privileges for three years, all thanks to a stubborn game warden who kept coming back for four years after discovering a pile of ripped-open milk jugs hidden under a palmetto bush. Maybe the honest hunters will have the Fort Drum woods to themselves for a while, compliments of Game Warden Tim Miller's patience and K-9 Jake's golden nose.

• • •

Galloping madly down the center of the hard road through south Florida orange grove country, the dappled gray mare with the empty saddle startled the drivers of several oncoming cars. Several vehicles weaved or drove off along the shoulder to narrowly avoid colliding with the panic-stricken animal.

Game Warden David Wilson quickly recovered his astonishment and pulled his Bronco off the road. Lt. Wilson had seen a lot in his thirty-one years of chasing outlaw hunters through the groves, swamps, and pine woods, but nothing like this. A big man, over six feet tall, Wilson speaks in a soft and gentle voice that most people wouldn't associate with an officer who had come through some tight places, both in the Florida woods and, before that, back in 1966–67 in the war that ravaged Vietnam jungles.

Wilson reacted a split-second after spotting the runaway horse. He slammed on his brakes, pulled off onto the shoulder, and leaped out of his big green Bronco. The horse thundered right at him, but the officer missed in his desperate attempt to grab the reins. The gray blur rushed on by down the rural road on the western edge of Vero Beach in Indian River County.

A woman in jeans and a work shirt had also pulled over, and she also tried snatching the horse's reins without success. She walked up to the game warden and told him not to worry about the animal, as she operated a nearby stable and could easily capture the runaway horse. However, she was concerned about the missing rider and hoped Wilson could locate the woman quickly.

During the last six months, the stable manager had seen a slender woman riding the big gray, always accompanied by several dogs. The missing rider could well be seriously hurt somewhere, maybe helpless and in shock. Wilson nodded agreement and climbed back into his vehicle. That's when Wilson saw the big black-and-tan German shepherd sitting on its haunches along the roadside, staring directly and intently at him.

"Those dark eyes were dead on me," Wilson said later. "And as soon as he knew he had my attention, the dog turned around and ran north along the road, not looking back, running fast along the shoulder."

Was it one of the missing rider's dogs? Wilson didn't know. The stable manager had not mentioned the breed or described the animals to him. But something in his gut spoke to the veteran game warden, something that told him to trust his instincts and follow the dog, which might lead him to the unknown rider.

"Right dog? Wrong dog? I didn't know," Wilson said. "I just couldn't ignore that hunch, that feeling deep inside that this was one of the missing woman's dogs."

Wilson followed in his Bronco about a hundred yards behind the running dog. The shepherd stayed on the hard road for about a half mile and then turned down an isolated dirt road surrounded by orange groves and a border of cabbage palm trees, palmetto bushes, and thick underbrush. The dog loped along for several hundred yards and then vanished into the vegetation. Wilson pulled up, scrambled out of his vehicle, and quickly picked up the dog's tracks in the soft earth. As a game warden and avid hunter, Wilson was skilled at tracking men or animals, his eyes quick to read a scrape in the dirt or a bend of the grass.

About a hundred yards off the dirt road, Wilson climbed over a big log and saw the woman lying on one side in a grassy, shallow swale. Beside her sat the black-and-tan shepherd with another rusty brown dog most Crackers would call a cur or cow dog. The woman was apparently unable to move, perhaps even paralyzed. As Wilson came closer, all he could see in his mind was a picture of one of his two beloved daughters lying helpless this same way. His girls, just like this stranger, were horse lovers and often worried their father when they loped off astride their spirited mounts.

"Ma'am, are you hurt?" Wilson called out.

"Yes, I'm hurt bad," the stranger answered. "I can't move. Send for an ambulance."

Earlier that morning Linda Mikesh, a forty-three-year-old accountant and University of Florida graduate, had saddled her three-year-old horse, Tikka, a blend of Andalusian and Thoroughbred she kept at the Circle M Stable on the western edge of Vero Beach. Morning rides atop the gentle mare escorted by her two dogs were a joy for this outdoor woman who found relaxation, a sense of freedom, and a closeness to God while riding in the

Florida sunshine.

Animals had always been her friends, her family really, ever since her grandfather had set her atop the back of an old horse back up on the farm in North Dakota, where she was born. The family moved to Florida during her high school years and she never left, making her living there but traveling frequently.

Trail rides were always part of her vacations. Linda rode along the golden beaches of Big Sur in California and the winding trails of Central Park in New York City. She was always happier with horses and dogs. And, finally, while living in Miami, she decided to buy her own horse and move further north into Indian River County, where she could indulge her love of animals and nature.

Linda had a girlish quality and exuberance, a warm outgoing personality seen in her laughing green eyes and bright friendly smile. Her age was not apparent, as Linda possessed the appealing air of a spirited waif. Her brown hair with faint blonde streaks was short and casual. She was comfortable in cut-off jeans and a work shirt and had a passionate enthusiasm for her animal friends, salt-water fishing off the Florida coast, and quiet rides in the country.

A cautious and sensible woman, Linda would never have considered riding alone if she had not been accompanied by her two-year-old German shepherd, Bubba—her friend, companion, and bodyguard. Bubba weighed about eighty pounds, and intelligence seemed to gleam in his deep, light-brown eyes. This formidable animal was a rather laid-back sort and quite sensitive. A sharp comment from Linda would send him moping to a corner, where he showed his hurt feelings with a mournful and downcast stare.

Bubba almost didn't get past puppyhood. He suffered from the deadly parvovirus, and Linda had the difficult choice of putting him down or investing in a long and expensive treatment. She chose the latter and never regretted one dollar of the investment. Bubba slept at her bedside, accompanied her everywhere, and brightened every aspect of the daily routine, especially when romping at the side of her horse, Tikka, on almost daily rides. Linda, like most animal lovers, didn't agree with the cynics who attribute the loyalty of dogs to nothing more than instinct coupled with the need to be fed. No one could tell Linda that Bubba didn't love her and would give his life in her defense. "Bubba is at least half human," she contended.

That morning they took their walk around 6:30 A.M. and then

drove to the riding stable where her other dog waited. Rusty, a rugged brown mix of several unidentified breeds including pit bull, weighed about fifty pounds. A year before, Linda had found him homeless and hungry on the doorstep of her mother's home.

"That poor dog has been sitting outside the gate for the last fourteen hours," Linda's mother had said.

Soon after, the tenderhearted pair relented and let the lonely wanderer inside the gate for his first meal in who knew how long. A few days later, Rusty was in Linda's car bound for the Circle M Stable, where he became a very happy "barn dog." Every day he joined Linda, Tikka, and Bubba on their daily ride through the orange groves. Linda enjoyed the outdoor beauty and didn't consider the possibility of an accident or sudden death on such a lovely Florida day, the blinding blue sky etched with the drifting mounds of snowy clouds, an orange sun still low in the east.

"True, you never know what might happen when you ride alone," Linda said. "Things do happen out there. There are risks you take. Somehow I knew that Bubba would help me if something bad happened. In my heart, I knew that he would never abandon me. Never had any doubts. If he did leave me, he would return with help. That was a feeling I had almost from the beginning."

Nothing occurred out of the ordinary until Linda's horse encountered a shallow grassy swale filled with several inches of water. Tikka balked. "She has always been wary of water," Linda said. "Invariably, she tries to jump any water barrier rather than walk through it."

On this bright morning, Linda concluded this was a perfect opportunity to school her reluctant horse to overcome its irrational fear. This was a mistake soon made apparent with almost tragic and irreversible results. Linda urged the horse forward despite Tikka's hesitancy. The gray mare jumped, and her back hooves slid out from under her on the slippery wet grass. Linda tried leaping from the saddle. An instant later, she was on the ground, raising her hands in a futile but instinctive gesture to ward off the descending twelve-hundred-pound bulk of her horse. Then blackness.

"Bubba was licking my face when I regained consciousness," she said. "Tikka was a few yards away eating grass. Rusty was sitting patiently nearby. The dogs just kept looking at me as if puzzled why I didn't just get up. I tried to move, but I couldn't."

There was no pain, only a band of numbness that stretched across her waist. Linda was determined not to panic and reassured herself that there was still feeling in her legs and feet. She was propped up on her side and suddenly glimpsed a blur of a car going by on the dirt road not fifty yards away.

She tried waving one arm and yelling. It was useless. The car passengers had the windows sealed and the air conditioner running full blast. They never heard the cry for help and couldn't see the prone figure screened by palmetto bushes and other thick vegetation. Two more cars came by a few minutes apart. No one stopped.

Linda shouted at Bubba and gestured toward the road. "Go get help, Bubba," she pleaded repeatedly without result. But then Tikka started slowly walking towards the road, apparently intent on returning to the stable. Bubba hesitated, looked at his injured mistress, and then trotted in the wake of the departing horse. Linda was confident that rescue would not be long in coming.

The woman tried several more times to move but was helpless. Fear wasn't a factor, she insisted. A rational and calm individual, the injured rider simply accepted that nothing could be done until Bubba returned with help, and she never doubted that. Not once, not even for a moment.

Fifteen minutes after Bubba left, Linda was overjoyed when Wilson's green official vehicle with the blue dome light of law enforcement pulled up along the shoulder of the dirt road. Almost simultaneously, Bubba came bounding out of the bushes, eyes glinting with excitement and joy. Wilson immediately used his handheld radio and called for help. He stood near Linda and kept up a steady patter of talk to distract her from her situation and its possible implications. Every few minutes he would walk back to the road and look for the ambulance and then return to her side.

About thirty minutes later the ambulance crunched the gravel as it ground to a stop. Two medics carrying a board quickly made their way to Linda's side. They lifted her on the board; Linda's face contorted in pain.

"She screamed like a Comanche Indian," Wilson said. "It really hurt me to see her in such pain. I just couldn't take it. Tears came to my eyes. I had to turn away. I could see in my mind one of my daughters having to endure such excruciating pain."

Once strapped on the board, Linda's pain lessened, and the

Happy Ending. *Lt. David Wilson visits Linda Mikesh, whom he rescued after her German shepherd led him to where she lay, isolated and helpless, after being injured in a horseback riding accident. (Jim Huffstodt)*

medics and Wilson carried her to the waiting ambulance. Then the medics pulled out a collapsible gurney and laid the victim on it before sliding into the ambulance. Before they shut the door, Linda saw a strange woman walking towards her leading Tikka by the leash. The horse was unhurt. Another stranger, a man, had pulled over in his car and volunteered to take care of her dogs. "There are a lot of really nice people in this world," she said with a shake of her head. "That's something easy to forget sometimes."

The rest of this story is a jumbled and shadowy dream. Linda was taken briefly to Martin Memorial Hospital and then transported that afternoon to a major hospital in Orlando. The next day, the surgeon operated. The crushing weight of the horse had shattered the ball socket in her pelvis into pieces. The tip of the leg bone was just floating in the bone fragments of the socket.

Five days later, Linda was taken to her Sebastian home for a lengthy convalescence. In late August, while being interviewed for this piece, she was getting around on crutches and hoped to be walking without assistance in a few more months.

Of course, her devoted guardian and companion Bubba is still at Linda's side. There is an invisible bond linking dog and human, a cord made of love, caring, and communication more subtle and, in ways, more powerful and eloquent than any spoken language.

"We're family," Linda said, those pale green eyes bright with pleasure as she smiled at the big, handsome dog crouched by her lawn chair. Bubba seemed to understand too, his dark eyes focused intently on the bright face of the most important person in his life.

Was it just instinct or coincidence that Bubba had sought help for his injured mistress and guided Lieutenant Wilson to her side? Some may think so, but not Linda Mikesh. She knows in her heart that it was love that inspired Bubba's race for help, and that his actions were guided by intelligence and a deep imponderable devotion that cannot be analyzed or even measured.

Chapter 13:
A Woman's Place
Is in the Woods

Officer Margaret "Peggy" Park
(1958–1984)

Do not stand at my grave and weep.
I am not there. I do not sleep.
I am a thousand winds that blow.
I am the sawgrass marsh you know.
When you awaken in the morning's hush,
Of quiet birds in circled flight.
I am the soft stars that shine at night.
Do not stand at my grave and cry.
I am not there. I did not die.

—Anonymous

Screams like echoes of a nightmare crackled across the airwaves early on the evening of December 13, 1984, while the sheriff's radio dispatcher listened in horrified disbelief. At that very moment, in an isolated, wooded area near Tarpon Springs, a twenty-six-year-old woman game warden was fighting for her life against a powerful and vicious assailant. The open radio mike in her patrol car transmitted the unrelenting shrieks of that desperate, savage, and unseen struggle.

Blue lights flashing in the falling darkness and sirens wailing, sheriff's deputies and game wardens were soon racing to the embattled warden's aid. Now the dispatcher could only wait, listen, and pray. Then the thunder of a single gunshot followed by silence: deep, awesome, eternal. . . .

Murdered in the Line of Duty. *Game Warden Margaret "Peggy" Park, 26, was killed by a paroled felon on December 13, 1984. She is the first female conservation officer slain while on patrol. (Florida Game and Fish Commission)*

"Even when she was a child, Margaret Elizabeth Park—Peggy to her friends—knew her place was with nature," wrote Henry Cabbage, GFC spokesman and news writer. "The . . . wildlife officer lived and played and worked amid the wonders of the outdoors. That's where she died."

Since the age of twenty, the Columbus, Ohio, native knew she must become a park ranger or equivalent and spend her life defending the wilderness and the wild creatures dwelling there. On family vacations to Canada, little Peggy wandered for miles through the forests: watching, listening, learning. She loved camping, canoeing, and swimming.

Everglades Lawmen

Peggy studied wildlife management at Ohio State University and graduated with a bachelor's degree in 1981. New opportunities had opened up for young, adventurous women who were entering traditionally male career fields in growing numbers. And it was the lure of adventure and the love of wilderness that led Peggy to choose a life as a Florida game warden.

The physically rigorous and mentally challenging regimen at the Florida Wildlife Officer Academy near Quincy didn't faze Peggy, who gave every promise of becoming a fine officer. The diminutive officer—five feet, two inches and around 112 pounds—had an easy and generous smile and outgoing personality.

Game Warden Treece Hughson was Peggy's academy roommate. They became good friends, and Treece would later remember Peggy's closeness with her parents, who were career educators back in the Midwest, and her love for her sister and brother. Also apparent was Peggy's sincere and deep-felt concern for the nation's threatened and endangered wildlife.

"She talked about how frustrating it was that so much of the habitat for wild animals is disappearing and there was nothing she could single-handedly do about it," Hughson said. "She called it the 'concrete jungle.' "

Peggy knew the risks that came with the badge and gun, but she didn't waste valuable time worrying. Another friend at the academy recalled discussing the dangers of the game warden life with Peggy on several occasions. "We talked about it, but we didn't dwell on it," the friend said. "Even so, Peggy was a careful person."

Assigned to Pinellas County near St. Petersburg-Tampa, Peggy soon moved into a little trailer in the woods. She lived there with Alex, her golden retriever; Nicholas, a black Labrador retriever; and two Siamese cats.

Her commitment wasn't just nine-to-five. Nature was her life, as reflected in her membership in the Wildlife Society, the Cousteau Society, and the Nature Conservancy. She often said that being a game warden wasn't just a job, rather it was a calling. "Protecting nature was everything to her," said Lt. Col. Brantley Goodson, the state's top game warden.

Pinellas County's surviving remnants of wilderness were green islands encircled by massive development. The wild animals that clung to a precarious existence needed all the help they could get,

and Peggy was just the person for the task. Patrol duties were shared
with Game Warden Michael Keever, a thirty-five-year-old with
several years with the agency. Sometimes they worked together, but
more often each worked alone. They could cover the county more
effectively by patrolling different days, times, and locations.

"Peggy had little patience with people who littered," Lt. Col.
Goodson said. "She wrote lots of littering citations." Nobody was
going to dump trash in the woods or swamp if Game Warden Peggy
Park was around. Bald eagles also were a priority. The regal, winged
giants held a special fascination. Peggy soon could proudly state
that she knew the location of every eagle nest in northern Pinellas
County. The eagles were her birds, and she was very protective of
them and their nests.

Nights were always busy. That's when the fire hunters came out
with their spotlights and high-powered rifles. But you never knew
what or whom you might encounter on those lonely country roads.
A game warden might cite a man for a fishing or hunting violation,
only to learn that the individual was wanted on warrants for felony
crimes. That's when the game could turn dangerous. Working alone
and at night makes the game warden a vulnerable target. Help is
usually a long way off; and the woods and swamps after dark sometimes hide human predators far more dangerous than gators and
rattlesnakes.

Deer season was under way, and fire hunting cases were on the
rise in late fall of 1984. Park and her partner, Mike Keever, were also
looking for "wire burners." These criminals pulled down high-
tension lines, burned off the rubber insulation, and sold the copper
wire at a tidy profit.

A little before 8 P.M. on Thursday, December 13, Game Warden
Park turned on her blue lights. She pulled up to a parked van on the
shoulder of the road and questioned the two male occupants.
Perhaps she thought they were "wire burners," or night hunters. But
something, in Peggy's eyes, just didn't look right.

Inside the van were Martin Grossman, 19, and his friend, Thayne
N. Taylor, 17. Both were from nearby New Port Richey. Park ordered
them out of the van and asked Grossman if he had any firearms. He
said no. Park then searched the vehicle and quickly discovered a
9mm German Lugar automatic under the driver's seat. She placed
Grossman under arrest for having a concealed firearm and escorted

him back to her patrol vehicle.

She took his driver's license and requested radio dispatch run a check through the National Criminal Information Center (NCIC) computer. Grossman stood six feet, four inches and weighed around 220 pounds. He had been paroled from prison not long before, after serving one year on a burglary conviction. He knew that a felon on probation was forbidden to own or use firearms. Once Game Warden Park finished reading his driver's license number to the dispatcher, it would take the dispatcher only a few minutes to confirm his status. That meant a return to prison, perhaps for a very long time.

The big man jumped the much smaller officer, grabbed her heavy flashlight, and beat her in the head, cracking her skull. She fought back with desperate courage and groped for the .357 Magnum revolver in her holster. Grossman called to his friend for help. For a few moments both men struggled with the officer. Then Park kicked Taylor in the groin, knocking him back. She finally pulled out her revolver, firing one shot that grazed Taylor's left hand and forehead.

The more powerful Grossman, according to Taylor's later courtroom testimony, tore the revolver from Park's grasp, placed the barrel against her head, and killed the game warden with one shot to the brain.

The killer and his accomplice had fled when law enforcement officers arrived minutes later. The blue lights of Park's patrol vehicle were still flashing. Peggy's body lay near the driver's door in a pool of blood. The murder had occurred only six miles from her home.

They called Peggy's partner at home. Keever donned his uniform and buckled on his holster while his wife pleaded with him not to go. She was convinced that Peggy's killer or killers might still be out there and take her husband's life as well.

"That night it was all I could do to get away from the house," Game Warden Keever later told a reporter. "She didn't want me to leave." Sometimes a young wife doesn't understand that when his partner goes down, a man just doesn't have a choice. You have to go.

Keever rolled up to the murder scene where Peggy's body still lay. There is perhaps nothing more sobering than the body of a murdered officer on a lonely and dark road. And this was no stranger. Keever had walked the woods with this young woman, depended upon her, and respected her. Now she was gone forever.

Three weeks later Keever told a reporter: "Whenever I think about her that whole scene . . . flashes through my mind. . . . I'd like to get it out of my mind forever, to see Peggy as I used to see her."

On Christmas Day, an informant who lived in the killer's home led officers to a patch of woods where Peggy's revolver and the Lugar had been buried. He told investigators how Grossman and Taylor had come to the house that night soaked in blood and admitted they had killed a woman game warden.

A jury found Grossman guilty of first-degree murder. Today, he still waits on death row for the 1984 slaying of Game Warden Peggy Park. His accomplice was also found guilty as an accessory to murder and drew a long prison sentence.

The ashes of the nation's first female conservation officer slain in the line of duty were scattered from a hovering helicopter over one of her bald eagle nests.

•   •   •

The caravan of huge swamp buggies came snorting out the vast heart of the Big Cypress wilderness, a half-million acres of swamp and pine flatwoods located north and west of the Everglades and due east of Naples. This is wild country rich in deer, wild turkey, wading birds, bobcats, gators, and even an occasional endangered Florida panther.

Game Warden Julie Jones watched the oncoming pack of monster buggies snake their way toward her. The ponderous machines rocked and swayed over the rugged terrain like ships in a rough sea, easily forded a flooded field, and plowed through the palmettos.

This was deer season of 1984, and Ma Bagget's clan was coming out of the woods, probably twenty-five Baggets of both sexes and all ages, from toddlers to the clan's undisputed matriarch, who must have been in her '70s. And for every kid atop the yawning buggies, there was a nondescript dog, mostly what country folks call a cur dog.

Jones waited patiently. She had information that the Baggets were taking wild turkeys illegally and planned to search their buggies before they left the boundaries of the Big Cypress National Wildlife Refuge. Good old boys sometimes like to put a "skeer" into a young and green game warden, especially a woman. Jones knew that but wasn't particularly concerned. She was a large, strong woman in her mid-twenties, weighing about 165 pounds and standing five foot ten.

When the lead buggy made its way onto the road, Jones left her patrol vehicle and held up her hand, bringing the little caravan to a halt. The rag-tag, sunburned Baggets jumped or climbed to the ground, depending on age and dexterity, and soon surrounded the warden.

Not surprisingly, Ma Bagget did most of the talking. Although a bit stooped and at least seventy years old, the old lady was spry and liked things her way. Even her three sons, all in their thirties and forties, didn't say much. The old lady was the boss. That was clear. Rail-thin, red-faced, her gray hair tied in a bun, Ma Bagget could prove cantankerous.

"Good morning, ma'am," Jones said with a smile. "I'm going to have to search your buggies. It won't take long."

Ma Bagget placed her bony hands on her hips. The pale blue eyes squinted in the noontime glare. She was a strong-featured woman, and the decades had written their passing with a legacy of furrowed wrinkles.

"What if we won't let you go poking through our stuff for no good reason?" the old woman rasped.

While Jones explained the law justified her request, Ma Bagget smirked and exchanged glances with her brawny boys, big, bearded men in T-shirts, jeans, and scuffed boots. One of them wore a holstered revolver. That wasn't unusual, as many hunters packed a snake gun. After Jones finished her explanation, the old lady crossed her bony arms across her chest and turned her head as she surveyed the clot of blood family gathered there in the blinding bright sunlight.

"It seems to me, boys, that there are a lot more of us than this one girl. Are we going to let some woman pretendin' to be a game warden put her nose in our business?"

Jones kept calm. The Baggets weren't the kind to murder an officer. But they would test you and would probably enjoy making a raw game warden look foolish.

The old lady flashed a wicked grin with her store teeth and said: "We could take her pretty easy, couldn't we, boys?"

Jones rested one hand on the butt of her holstered revolver and grinned back.

"Yes, ma'am, I believe you're right," Jones said. "You could take me. But just remember, the bullet in my number one cylinder is for you."

Ma Bagget broke into cackling laughter. "Why, you're all right, honey," Ma Bagget said and waved one arm to clear a way for the game warden, who carefully searched each of the buggies. Jones didn't find any hidden wild turkeys that day, but she did win the grudging admiration of a tough old lady and laid the foundation for a reputation.

Jones had passed the test.

Those who know her will tell you that Julie Jones speaks her mind, has good judgment, and possesses knowledge drawn from the field as well as the college classroom. She has the quiet confidence of someone who knows her job well and takes pride in it.

Jones grew up in the metropolitan corridor clinging to Florida's eastern shoreline. She loved the outdoors and became an enthusiastic angler during family fishing trips. Soon she became fascinated with wildlife, the wilderness, and the biological sciences. She majored in biology at Florida Atlantic University in Boca Raton, eventually earning both a bachelor's degree and master's degree in the field. But it took some time. Jones put herself through school, working for a time as a finisher in an auto body shop. Jones related well to her male coworkers. She had always been mechanically inclined and shared the boys' curiosity about how things worked. All the boys in the body shop were "country," loved hunting and fishing, and most owned an airboat.

This intrigued Jones. She liked the idea of piloting one of those powerful machines across the expansive marsh of the nearby Everglades. One of the shop guys took her out and showed her the basics. Julie was hooked. Soon she became conspicuous as probably the only female student at the university who trailered an airboat behind her pickup.

When she wasn't "framming" around the Glades in her airboat or studying, Jones was working as a part-time biological field researcher for the GFC and the Florida Department of Natural Resources. The jobs involved "crawling in and out of the swamps," and Jones loved it. She catalogued plants and studied mink and otter in Fakahatchee Strand State Park, carried out bird surveys, collected bugs, and trapped mice. Soon she would have her master's degree in biology, but field biology jobs were hard to find in a market glutted with qualified applicants.

Out in the field, Jones often encountered game wardens and struck up a friendship with Sgt. John Reed. He encouraged this capable and confident young woman to apply to the Florida Wildlife Officer Academy. After passing the interview board, Jones found herself the sole woman recruit in her class of thirty-four. She wasn't intimidated. Fellow recruits learned quickly that this woman with the deep brown eyes was serious, wanted to earn the game warden badge in the worst way, didn't complain, and pulled her weight.

"I always tell young women considering a career in law enforcement not to expect or demand special treatment," Jones said. "And the worst thing is to try to act like a man. Be yourself, but let them know you are a serious professional. That's the road to acceptance and success."

When she got into the field, that up-front, take-me-as-I-am attitude and her willingness to get dirt under her nails won Jones respect from the old timers who'd been patrolling the woods when she was still in diapers.

Again she was the only female. She patrolled the remote Big Cypress and back roads of Hendry and Collier Counties with Lt. Ken Pickles, Lt. Greg Taminosian, Eddie Lee Henderson, Don Crabtree, Ray Green, and Rudy Wiggins. All were country boys, a decade or more older. Some might describe them as set in their ways. And they certainly weren't politically correct. Yet they quickly accepted this young woman officer. It was readily apparent that she liked roaming around the boonies on a swamp buggy, wasn't worried about snakes or gators, and did her job without whining or asking for special favors.

Those were the days when Pickles would lead his boys out into the woods and swamp for three and four days at a stretch during the hunting season. On one occasion, Julie and Ray Green went for twenty-four hours straight without any sleep. A game warden learned to ignore fatigue, the oppressive heat, and the bugs. There were always plenty of bugs.

Yet it was fun, an adventure. Jones liked the camaraderie and the shared hardships. When they stayed overnight at the Two Palms camp in the Big Cypress, Julie was always the first to go to bed and the first up. That way everybody had his or her privacy. Actually, Jones recalls few significant problems or adjustments.

Pickles and the boys especially appreciated that Jones knew a carburetor from a generator and was handy with tools. Those old buggies were always breaking down. Hell, a big part of being a game warden was knowing how to fix stuff. "Man, if you went out for several days without breaking down, you hadn't been patrolling," she said with a laugh. "That wasn't a patrol. That was a Sunday excursion." The buggies always carried a good supply of bailing wire, tools of every sort, and lots of spare parts. Even so, Jones remembers that on several occasions the chopper flew in to airdrop the stranded wardens parts they'd either forgotten to pack along or didn't have room to carry.

If any of the boys had any doubts about this female warden, they lost them quickly. Jones recalls with fondness the wire-thin Ken Pickles, a chaw usually bulging out one cheek, and how he'd ruminate on life, taxes, and the art of catching poachers. She calls him the "old Cracker philosopher."

Jones was always learning and discovering. Some of her best teachers and wisest advisors didn't have college degrees. A person didn't have to go to school to acquire a sense of history, a code of behavior, or wisdom. Of course, a Cracker wouldn't call it wisdom, more like horse sense or knowin' enough to come in out of the rain.

Lloyd Austin had probably never seen the inside of a college classroom, but in Jones's estimation he was one of the best teachers she had ever had, a professor of life and a student of nature. When she met him back in 1984, Lloyd was in his seventies and lived in a junk-filled cabin out in the Big Cypress where he ran some cattle. Towers of old newspapers and magazines stood in corners. The old pack rat detested throwing away anything.

She affectionately describes Lloyd as "classic Cracker." She always looked forward to stopping by his cabin, where she often shared lunch and listened intently to the old man's yarns about the old times. He was a robust, barrel-chested man, heavyset and silver haired. Lloyd had grown up in the Florida woods, had been married once, but now lived alone except for trips to Immokalee where, she'd heard, he had a girlfriend.

Lloyd taught the young game warden where the wild turkeys could be found and how to drive a buggy without hardly ever gettin' stuck, even in the worst bog. Or, if you did get stuck, how to get unstuck. One day Lloyd was aghast at discovering that Julie didn't know how to make hoe cake and, for that matter, didn't even know what hoe cake was. It was near eatin' time anyway, so Lloyd decided this was an opportune time for Julie to learn the fine art of Cracker cuisine.

You didn't get hoe cake out of a box bought at some fancy supermarket. Lloyd showed her how the old-timers made it when he was a kid during the 1920s, revealing the tricks of using a little flour, baking soda, and cornmeal and transforming it into mouthwatering hoe cake after a few minutes in a cast-iron frying pan over an open fire.

That was a long time ago, but Jones, now a forty-one-year-old lieutenant colonel in Lake City with responsibility for fourteen counties, still remembers that day vividly. She loved that old man and the vanishing country culture that had shaped and formed him. The only time Jones ever cried during her many years of wearing a badge was the day she learned Lloyd Austin had died. Not only had she lost a good friend, a precious piece of Big Cypress history was gone as well.

Some people wouldn't or couldn't deal with the tragedy and grim realities that are a part of the game warden's world. Jones will always remember the terror and revulsion in the eyes of one young man who had seen his friend die a terrible and violent death on a beautiful sunny day, the blue sky white with drifting clouds.

The young men were both in their twenties and had come to the marsh for a day of fun. The airboat had only one seat for the operator. No problem. One drove and his buddy sat directly behind him, resting his weight on the metal cage enclosing the engine and whirling propeller blade. As they sped though the marsh with the wind blowing in their faces and the engine roaring in their ears, the caging suddenly sagged and gave way. In an instant, the propeller blade chewed through the metal and chopped the passenger in half.

When Jones arrived on the scene, the survivor was pale, shaky, and pretty rattled. The two parts of the victim's body were linked only by a shred of skin from the stomach. Nobody gets used to this sort of horror, but Jones found that she could deal with it. Bad things sometimes happened in the wilderness; you just couldn't dwell on it.

Another fact was that the wilderness sometimes became a cemetery for victims of urban violence. Murderers liked wild and lonely places to dump bodies. Nobody really knows how many missing persons end up as food for the gators, but on several occasions game wardens have recovered the victims of drug deals gone bad, family squabbles, or jealousy.

Jones recalls her first, a "biker dude" from Ft. Myers. The victim had been dumped into a canal linked to the Gulf. A bad mistake. The tide went out and Jones and Officer Doug Gonzalez discovered the decaying body weighted down with cement blocks. Investigators eventually pinned a murder rap on the dead biker's girlfriend.

Another time Don Crabtree spotted a large suitcase sitting on the edge of Alligator Alley. He and Jones pulled over to investigate. Stuffed inside the crumbling suitcase were the putrefying, almost-liquid remains of a human body. Wild hogs had rooted out the suitcase in the swamp, where it had been hastily dumped, and had chewed through the sides. The victim's skull rested a few feet away.

"The medical examiner recovered a photograph showing two young Latin women posing behind a car with Pennsylvania plates," Jones said. "Investigators could read the numbers and traced it to the woman's sister, the other person in the picture.

"The woman had flown up from her native Colombia to visit with her sister's family and was going back home after several weeks. During the return flight the aircraft made a brief stop-over at Miami International Airport and the woman vanished. The killers chopped up the body and stuffed the woman in her own suitcase," she said. "Who killed her and why remains unknown to this day."

On another night the killers weren't so lucky. Jones was up in the GFC aircraft piloted by Sgt. Jan Spangler. She spotted the lights of a vehicle way out in the Big Cypress boonies. Something wasn't right. There was no reason for somebody to be way out there at this hour. They shadowed the vehicle and notified Warden Crabtree on the ground to intercept. Soon afterwards, he stopped a van containing two men. They looked suspicious, but Crabtree couldn't charge them with anything except illegal entry. Of course, he ran the van's

Everglades Lawmen

tag before letting them proceed. Should something turn up later, it would be fairly easy to track them down.

On the next day, an employee of the National Park Service stumbled onto the body of a recently murdered woman right where Jones had originally spotted the van lights. Crabtree's license tag check led investigators to the suspects, who were charged, tried, and found guilty of murder. Investigators concluded that the killers had picked up a prostitute in Ft. Lauderdale, murdered her, and dumped the body in the Big Cypress. Of course, Jones and Crabtree wish they could have prevented the murder, but at least they had the satisfaction of helping send the killers to prison.

Today, after being the first woman officer to wear the silver clusters of a lieutenant colonel, Jones rarely gets out into the woods. Promotion has brought with it reams of paperwork, long meetings, trips to Tallahassee headquarters, and endless administrative chores.

Despite the satisfaction in playing a key leadership role in the agency, Jones admits that her happiest days were spent "bouncing around in a swamp buggy" in the Big Cypress, trying to outwit poachers, rescuing lost sportsmen, and listening to the "Cracker philosopher" lecture on life's absurdities.

• • •

Where had all those years gone? He couldn't be that old, could he? But here was Archie Maynard's kid standing there in uniform and gunbelt and wearing a game warden's badge just like the old man so many years before.

Game Warden Rudy Wiggins jokingly told Maynard's kid that he knew for sure it was time to retire now. Hell, this green recruit's dad had walked the woods with Rudy when people still used manual typewriters, the phones were black and had dials, and coke was something kids drank from a bottle.

Now this kid was stepping into the father's boots. This sawed-off recruit hadn't been walking and talking when Archie gave up the game warden life. Wiggins had started out with the old man and had worked with him seven or eight years before Archie left to become a sheriff's deputy.

This young game warden was Archie's kid for sure. The rookie liked a little Copenhagen and carried a spit cup just like the father. The kid backed up a boat trailer with ease and precision. Knew the

Chip Off the Old Block. *Game Warden Pam Maynard Thorn is following in her father's footsteps. Before becoming a county deputy sheriff attached to the agricultural crime division, Archie Maynard was a Florida game warden. Pam grew up hearing that it was the best job anyone could ever have. (Pam Maynard Thorn)*

woods. Lived to fish. Had hunted deer a bit too. Target shooter in high school. Chip off the old block. Like father, like son. That's what you might say about young Maynard.

Only one problem: the new officer wasn't Archie's boy, wasn't a man by any stretch of the imagination. Game Warden Pam Maynard was Archie's only daughter. She stood a hair under five feet tall and, even with boots and gunbelt, probably didn't weigh much more than a hundred pounds. But she had common sense, didn't fear hard work, and apparently didn't think twice about working the woods alone at night.

Times were changing. Pam just might do. Hell, she was Archie's kid, wasn't she?

Maybe Pam became a game warden because of all those stories her dad had told her and her two brothers when they were growing up. Riding in the woods as a game warden was the best job he'd ever had, he told his children. Or maybe the game warden life was just in her blood. Who could tell? Growing up in West Palm Beach and Okeechobee, Pam never really thought about being a game warden. But she liked fishing, went deer hunting with her brothers, and was pretty much a tomboy who liked to be outside and active.

She was a fair hand with an M-14 rifle from age twelve on up, competing against other youngsters at target shoots all over the country. The range officer weighted the rifle's butt down with lead so it wouldn't punish Pam's shoulder too much. A .308 caliber has a mule's kick. Pam also rode the high school rodeo circuit while a student at Okeechobee High School, competing most often in barrel racing atop a nimble quarter horse. She went to the state rodeo finals in Ocala in 1988. As an officer with the Future Farmers of America (FFA), Pam also got to attend a luncheon with then–Vice President Dan Quayle.

Along the way, she developed an interest in law enforcement and ultimately became a volunteer game warden with the agency's Reservist program. As a reservist, the nineteen-year-old went with a regular game warden one night chasing fire hunters in the boonies. After that, she knew exactly what she wanted to become and never turned back. She was one of three women in the 1994 Wildlife Academy class of twenty-two. One or two of the male recruits had an attitude. However, the majority didn't just tolerate their female classmates; they were supportive and treated them with respect.

A small person, Pam found the physical defense fights a challenge. One day she was the lucky recruit who got to put the handcuffs on Lt. Paul Ouellette, a former college football star and weight lifter who could lift the equivalent of three and a half Pam Maynards over his head without breaking sweat.

Ironically, it had been Lieutenant Ouellette who'd recruited Pam for the Reserve program and encouraged her ambition to become a game warden. Why, Pam thought, did she have to be the lucky recruit to arrest this tall and thick tree of a man?

"I was scared to death," she admits. "But I wasn't a quitter and finally got the handcuffs on my suspect. To do it, though, I had to order Paul to get on his knees."

After graduation, she reported to Hendry County just as her father had so many years before. The payoff came not long afterwards when she tracked a fire hunter down a deserted country road, her running lights out as she crept up on the unsuspecting lawbreaker. Once she had the poacher cold, she flicked on the flashing blues and tried to control her intense excitement at nailing a bad guy for the first time. The suspect didn't run, but he didn't pull over right away either. What was his problem?

Finally, the fire hunter stopped and got out of his truck. When Pam rolled up nearby, the bearded man in his twenties came storming up to the open driver's window. This guy was raging like a madman, shouting profanities, and leaning so close against the patrol vehicle that Pam couldn't get the door open. Later, she would learn that this burly two-hundred-pounder was determined that no woman game warden was going to take him to jail.

"Back off!" Pam snapped.

"I probably told him he was going to get his ass shot off if he didn't walk away and wait by the road," she said. "He was really a big guy and his violent reaction scared me. Guess I didn't show it, though, because he calmed down right then and there."

Those first few years were interesting and exciting as Pam learned her trade and developed the skills required to nab game poachers. If any of her male peers had doubts about a woman game warden, those vanished one night in September 1996, when Pam teamed up with Game Warden Cathy Rogalny. The two wardens tracked and stalked some night hunters for three straight hours long after midnight in wild, swampy terrain.

Game Warden Tom Hayworth was spotting in the aircraft and reported spot lighters a few miles from where the two women wardens sat in their patrol vehicle. Lt. John Reed was on the other side of the county, so this would be a woman's job from the start.

The poacher's light came on intermittently as Pam and Cathy drove across the rugged terrain with their own headlights doused. Once in awhile, they risked turning on their "sneak light" mounted on the front bumper. Getting stuck in a bog was one thing, but there was the grimmer possibility of plunging into an unseen canal.

When the light beam ahead appeared close, they stopped and proceeded on foot, wading through water and mud and plagued by mosquitoes and no-see-ums. There was always the danger of stumbling over a big gator or a nest of cottonmouths.

The light was much farther away than it appeared. The women walked back to the vehicle and resumed the slow pursuit. In the next three hours they repeated the process several times without success. The elusive light never seemed to be any closer as they crept through the tangled woods. But finally they drove out onto a dirt road, and the bandit swamp buggy materialized from the shadows. The officers flicked on their lights and illuminated three men atop the buggy.

"They were startled to find they weren't alone at this time of night so far out in the woods," Pam said. "They looked shocked and not too happy." All were dressed in T-shirts, jeans, and boots, and one wore a baseball cap. Two were in their twenties; the other was a few years older. The game wardens walked up with their flashlights in hand. Right off they saw that the men's shirts were soaked with blood.

"You got any guns?" Pam asked.

One of the suspects handed her a .22 rifle wrapped in a blood-stained blanket. She informed them that they were under arrest and told them to dismount the track. The suspects were ordered to stand about twenty feet away from the buggy, blinking in the glare of the patrol vehicle's headlights.

Pam joined her partner standing at the rear of the buggy. Rogalny pointed to the splashes of blood on the ladder. While Pam kept an eye on the suspects, Rogalny climbed onto the buggy's platform. She found what appeared to be freshly killed deer meat hidden under a layer of beer cans in a cooler.

By the time Lieutenant Reed drove on the scene, there really wasn't much left to do. "Cathy and Pam had everything under control," he said. "They were cool, calm, and collected."

Pam is proud that she and Cathy had met the test and showed that women game wardens weren't just tokens or ornaments. Also satisfying was the judge's confiscation order after the three men were found guilty of night hunting. Their buggy, valued at $7,000, is doing good service for the game wardens patrolling the J. W. Corbett wilderness near West Palm Beach.

A few years back, Pam married a cowboy from LaBelle. They live in the woods with their three-year-old daughter, Kaitlin, who refuses to go outside unless dressed in camouflaged hunting attire. "She's all boy," Pam Maynard Thorn said.

Should Kaitlin become a game warden someday, Mom has no qualms.

"Best job in the world," Pam said. "Just like Daddy always told me."

• • •

Kathy Chidsey creeps through the dark Martin County cane field, lights off on her Chevy Blazer and a thick jacket blanketing the glow of the dashboard," wrote *Palm Beach Post* reporter Angie Scharnhorst. The writer, a Kansas native and formerly with the Kansas City Star, was new to south Florida. She was intrigued with this thirty-one-year-old, petite blond who spent nights prowling the countryside for poachers.

"Features of the rough land are shrouded in the damp night air and Chidsey knows from experience that she is scant inches from plunging into a canal she cannot see," Scharnhorst wrote. "Somewhere ahead of her she has reason to believe there is a light shining in the cane fields. . . . Her only chance of catching poachers is to employ an element of surprise, so she inches quietly forward.

"A soft voice breaks the silence—a muted sound from Chidsey's police radio.

" 'Keep going south,' the voice tells Chidsey.

"The voice belongs to Lt. Dan Angles, a . . . pilot in a single-engine plane overhead. The light that Angles describes is not yet visible to Chidsey on the ground. But from the air, the beam slashes through the humidity in an opaque arc. It is Angles' job to guide Chidsey to it.

"Though Chidsey's Blazer seems to crawl down a bumpy track . . . her adrenaline is soaring. At any moment something could materialize out of the blackness: a deer, a canal or a poacher.

" 'It really is exciting when Danny puts you on a light and you have to run dark through some of these fields going after them,' she said in a low voice.

" 'It can get pretty scary.' "

That night the suspected poachers turned out to be some boys legally frogging. But on other nights, Chidsey has jumped armed poachers and arrested them. She knows the risks but also knows that Florida's wildlife would vanish if the poachers could operate unrestrained. Like her fellow game wardens, she takes pride in doing a job that makes a difference. And Kathy likes interesting jobs. She was a 9-1-1 emergency operator for ten years and worked part-time

Everglades Lawmen

The Times, They Are A'changin'. *Officers Kathy Chidsey (left) and Cathy Rogalny reflect the diversity of today's Florida game wardens. Many wardens are female, African-American, Hispanic, and college educated. Despite their differences, they all share with their predecessors the same commitment to defending wild Florida. (Jim Huffstodt)*

as a dolphin and otter trainer at Ft. Lauderdale's Ocean World before applying to become a game warden.

Not long ago, Chidsey was in the headlines after making a historic deer poaching case where DNA analysis was used for the first time by Florida game wardens in a wildlife conservation investigation. The defendant had told Chidsey that the deer meat she discovered in his pickup was taken legally weeks before in another area and that the meat came from bucks, not does. Proving the opposite was possible only by DNA analysis.

Chidsey's case, supported by the results of the tests performed at the University of Florida lab in Gainesville, held up in court. The poacher was found guilty, and Florida game wardens gained a new and potentially powerful weapon.

Women are still a minority among Florida's game wardens, but their numbers are growing. Now the agency has a crop of young women eager to walk the path blazed by Officer Peggy Park, Lt. Col. Julie Jones, and other trailblazers. Most are married, have youngsters at home, and, when out of uniform with their hair down, will turn heads at a party. With a few rare exceptions, the women have won the admiration and respect of their male peers.

Camille Soveral is a slender blonde with the figure and sophisticated good looks of a Paris runway model. This college graduate studied business and worked several years as a financial advisor. But something was missing. The thirty-one-year-old abandoned the office world for the freedom and beauty of Florida's wilderness.

Today she faces challenges far removed from financial statements and investment portfolios. Camille showed her imagination and spunk one day in the field when she spotted an illegal hunter prowling Lennar Grove in Palm Beach County. Unfortunately, the suspect melted into the woods, and a deep canal lay between the game warden and her prey.

She would have swum across, holding her gunbelt above her head if she'd had to, and to hell with the gators. But another alternative came to mind. With the assistance of a nearby resident, she dragged a plastic hot tub cover down to the canal bank, turned it upside down, and slid it into the water. This was undoubtedly the first time a game warden pursued a poacher atop a hot tub cover. Swamp buggies, aircraft, helicopters, tracks, ATVs, horses, boats, jet-skis—yes, but hot tub covers?

Soveral paddled across the canal and observed the poacher illegally kill a wild hog and spread a camouflage screen over the carcass for later pickup. He then crossed back over the canal in his canoe and posed as an innocent angler. When darkness fell, the poacher would paddle back to the grove and retrieve his trophy without anyone being the wiser. At least that's what he thought, until Soveral appeared to break the bad news.

Yes, the times they are a'changing.

Author's Note: The name of the Bagget clan has been changed to protect the family's identity.

Chapter 14:
Everglades Sunset

Defending Florida's wilderness heritage and wildlife treasures isn't without risk. Sometimes the good guys don't win. Sometimes they don't come home. Author Ernest Hemingway once wrote that all true stories end in death. The writer, adventurer, big game hunter, and marlin fisherman would have also understood why game wardens risk injury and death. They are guardians of a rich natural treasure, a fragile legacy for succeeding generations. At stake is the marsh, the woods, the savannahs, the swamps, and all the varied creatures that dwell there. It is a prize worth defending.

In closing this account of Florida's wilderness game wardens, it seems appropriate and fitting to remember and honor those slain in performance of their duty by ruthless outlaws and those killed in tragic accidents while on patrol. We venerate those remarkable men and women in green who gave their lives for the Florida wilderness and wildlife conservation.

If you seek their monument, journey deep into the Everglades and watch the orange sun sink below the western horizon at the close of another day. Listen and you will hear the melody of the marsh: the buzz of insects, the croaking of pig frogs, the splash of an alligator sliding into the water. If you concentrate, you may hear the distant voices of Everglades lawmen, the echoes of those who lost their lives in defense of wild things and wild places. This is their eternal shrine, nature's cathedral, a living memorial. Think of them when you see a bald eagle soar into the shining sky or when a doe and fawn come floating out of the woods at dawn.

Watch. Listen. Remember.

Explosion of Wings. *Quail are released in south Florida by an unidentified game warden (left) and wildlife biologist Carlton Chappell, circa 1965. (Florida Game and Fish Commission)*

Roll of Honor

George T. Sharpe, *killed in a plane crash, 1946*

James Fields, *killed by a turkey hunter, 1950*

Johnny Ingram, *killed in a plane crash, 1951*

Bud Smith, *killed by gunshot, 1954*

Marvin Albritton, *killed in a boating accident, 1966*

Jimmy Thompson, *electrocuted while repairing an airboat, 1968*

Leon Walker, *killed in a high-speed chase after night hunters, 1971*

Harry Chapin, *killed by gunshot while pursuing night hunters, 1972*

Jim Cook, *drowned on water patrol, 1972*

Dan Crowder, *shot and killed while attempting to apprehend a night hunter, 1974*

Margaret "Peggy" Park, *shot and killed by an inmate on parole, 1984*

Ray Lynn Barnes, *shot and killed by a night hunter, 1987*

Sources

Books and Periodicals

Ashton, Ray E., and Patricia S. Ashton. *Handbook of Reptiles and Amphibians of Florida, Part 2*. Miami: Windward Publishing, Inc., 1985.

Bartram, William. *Travels*. New York: Penguin Books USA, Inc., 1988. Originally published 1791.

Beach, Lee. "Weidenhamer Alligator Attack Investigation Summary." *Official GFC Report*. June 19 to June 24, 1993.

Blissett, Steven R. "A Pipeline of Smuggled Florida Wildlife— Operation Brooklyn." *Official GFC Report*. Undated.

Brook Van Meter, Victoria. *Florida's Alligators and Crocodiles*. Miami: Florida Power and Light Publication, 1987.

Buckow, Edwin C., and A. J. McClane, ed. "Airboat." *McClane's Standard Fishing Encyclopedia*. New York: Holt, Reinhardt and Winston, 1965.

Cabbage, Henry. "Protecting Nature Was Everything to Her." *Florida Wildlife*. January/February 1985.

Carle, William. "Alligators Really Do Attack!" *Florida Wildlife*. September 1948.

Chapman, Frank M. *Camps and Cruises of an Ornithologist*. New York: D. Appleton and Company, 1908.

Douglas, Marjory Stoneman. *Everglades: River of Grass*. Sarasota, FL: Pineapple Press, Inc., 1997. First published 1947.

Florida Game and Fresh Water Fish Commission. *A Quarter Century of Progress: 1943–1968*. Tallahassee: GFC Publications, July 1968.

Hastings, Donald L. "When No Choice is Left." *International Game Warden*. Spring 1985.

Everglades Lawmen

Hines, T. C., and K. D. Keenlyne. "Two Incidents of Alligator Attacks on Humans in Florida." *Copeia*. November 25, 1977.

Huffstodt, James T. "Across the Everglades by Canoe." *Florida Wildlife*. November/December 1997.

———. "Yesterday's Dream—Airboats." *Florida Wildlife*. July/August 1994.

———. "Reign of the Plume Hunters." *Florida Wildlife*. March/April 1992.

———. "A Legacy of Wonderful Words." *Florida Wildlife*. May/June 1997.

———. "Drugs and Lions." *Florida Wildlife*. March/April 1989.

———. "Marine Turtle Trade Suddenly Looks Like a Bad Risk." *International Game Warden*. Summer 1989.

———. "Wildlife Officers Raid Crack House to Save Endangered Sea Turtles." *International Game Warden*. Winter 1988-89.

———. "The Discovery of Gingerbread Camp." *International Game Warden*. Spring 1988.

———. "Changes and Challenges: The Brantly Years." *Florida Game and Fish*. July 1995.

Jackson, Donald D. "Old Bigtooth Returns." *Smithsonian*. January 1987.

Job, Herbert K. *Wild Wings*. New York: Houghton Mifflin and Company, 1905.

Kirkland, Stanley H. "You Can't Hide from These Wildlife Officers." *Florida Wildlife*. July/August 1997.

Knapp, Dale. "Summary of Events Following Alligator Attack at Riverside Park, Port St. Lucie." *Official GFC Report*. August 6, 1984.

Lee, Stony. "Alligator Attack Summary." *Official GFC Report*. August 7, 1984.

Loftin, Jan P. "In the Wake of Hurricane Andrew." *Florida Water*. Winter 1993.

McIver, Stuart. *True Tales of the Everglades*. Miami: Florida Flair Books, 1989.

Oppel, Frank. *Tales of Old Florida*. Secaucus, NJ: Castle Publishing Company, 1987.

Palmer, James L. *Game Wardens Versus Poachers—Tickets Still Available*. Iola, WI: Krause Publications, Inc.,1993.

Perrero, Laurie. *Alligators and Crocodiles of the World—The*

Sources

Disappearing Dragons. Miami: Windward Publishing, Inc., 1975.

Ray, Janisse. "Changing Uniforms." *Florida Wildlife*. Special 50th Anniversary Edition. November/December 1993.

Ries, James. "Hurricane Andrew Detail after Action Report." *Official GFC Report*. August 24– November 15, 1992.

Roseberry, C. R. *Glenn Curtiss—Pioneer of Flight*. New York: Doubleday and Company, 1972.

Simmons, Glen, and Laura Ogden. *Gladesmen: Gator Hunters, Moonshiners, and Skiffers*. Gainesville: University Press of Florida, 1998.

Stermen, David. "The Disaster of Value Jet Flight 592." *Official GFC Report*. May 20, 1996.

Toops, Connie. *The Florida Everglades*. Stillwater, MN: Voyageur Press, 1989.

Vislocky, Kevin M. "Protecting Florida's Resources—The Florida Game and Fresh Water Fish Commission." *Air Beat*. September/October 1988.

Watkins, T. H. "Thin Green Line." *Audubon*. September 1980.

Williams, Ada C. *Florida's Ashley Gang*. Port Salerno, FL: Florida Classics Library, 1996.

Willoughby, Hugh L. *Across the Everglades: A Canoe Journey of Exploration*. Port Salerno, FL: Florida Classics Library, 1898.

Newspapers

Ft. Lauderdale Sun-Sentinel, Ft. Pierce–Port St. Lucie Tribune, Jupiter Courier, Miami Herald, Palm Beach Post, Stuart News.

Interviews

Lt. Bill Ashley, Capt. Steven Blissett, Lt. Col. (Ret.) J. O. Brown, Officer (Ret.) Conley Campbell, Officer (Ret.) J. K. Davis, Fisheries Biologist Jon Fury, Officer Tom Haworth, Officer Allan Hofmeister, Lt. Col. Julie Jones, Sgt. Bruce Lawless, Lt. Dick Lawrence, Officer (Ret.) Roy Martinez, Officer (Ret.) Richie Obach, former alligator poacher Norman Padgett, Capt. Ken Parramore, Lt. Tom Quinn, Lt. John Reed, Maj. Jim Ries, Capt. David Stermen, Officer Pam Maynard Thorn, Lt. John West, and Capt. (Ret.) Eddie Wheeler.

Here are some other books from Pineapple Press on related topics. For a complete catalog, write to Pineapple Press, P.O. Box 3889, Sarasota, Florida 34230-3889, or call (800) 746-3275. Or visit our website at www.pineapplepress.com.

Everglades: River of Grass, 60th Anniversary Edition by Marjory Stoneman Douglas with an update by Michael Grunwald. Before 1947, when Marjory Stoneman Douglas named the Everglades a "river of grass," most people considered the area worthless. She brought the world's attention to the need to preserve the Everglades. In the Afterword, Michael Grunwald tells us what has happened to them since then. (hb)

Everglades: An Ecosystem Facing Choices and Challenges by Anne E. Ake. Reveals the diversity of plant and animal life in the unique ecosystem of the slow-moving waters of the Everglades. Explains how and why this system is in trouble from the diverting and draining of the water. Tells of the many attempts to save the Everglades and why it's worth saving. (hb)

Iguana Invasion: Exotic Pets Gone Wild in Florida by Virginia Aronson and Allyn Szejko. Green Iguanas, Burmese Pythons, Nile Monitor Lizards, Rhesus Monkeys, and many more kinds of non-native animals are rapidly increasing in population in subtropical Florida. This full-color book provides scientific information, exciting wildlife stories, and identification photos for the most common exotic animals on the loose—most of them offspring of abandoned pets. (hb & pb)

Pythons in the Glades by Larry Perez. A ranger in Everglades National Park describes on of the most significant biological disasters in our nation—the invasion of potentially tens of thousands of nonnative Burmese pythons. Nowhere else on the planet has a species of snake so large, up to 200 pounds, established itself beyond its native range. They have already consumed dozens of species of birds, mammals and reptiles in south Florida—several of them threatened or endangered. (pb)

Marjory Stoneman Douglas: Voice of the River—An Autobiography with John Rothchild by Marjory Stoneman Douglas. This is the story of an influential life told in a unique and spirited voice. Marjory Stoneman Douglas, nationally known as the first lady of conservation and the woman who "saved" the Everglades, was the founder of Friends of the Everglades, a feminist, a fighter for racial justice, and always a writer. (pb)

Florida Magnificent Wilderness: State Lands, Parks, and Natural Areas by James Valentine and D. Bruce Means. Photographer James Valentine captures environmental art images of the state's remote wilderness places. Dr. D. Bruce Means covers the wildlife and natural ecosystems of Florida. An introduction to each section is written by a highly respected Florida writer and conservationist, including Al Burt, Manley Fuller, Steve Gatewood, Victoria Tschinkel, and Bernie Yokel. (hb)

Florida's Rivers by Charles R. Boning. An overview of Florida's waterways and detailed information on 60 of Florida's rivers, covering each from its source to the end. From the Blackwater River in the western panhandle to the Miami River in the southern peninsula. (pb)

Florida's Birds, 2nd Edition by David S. Maehr and Herbert W. Kale II. Illustrated by Karl Karalus. This new edition is a major event for Florida birders. Each section of the book is updated, and 30 new species are added. Also added are range maps and color coded guides to months when the bird is present and/or breeding in Florida. Color throughout. (pb)

Myakka by Paula Benshoff. Discover the story of the land of Myakka. This book takes you into shady hammocks of twisted oaks and up into aerial gardens, down the wild and scenic river, and across a variegated canvas of prairies, piney woods, and wetlands—all located in Myakka River State Park, the largest state park in Florida. (pb)

Priceless Florida by Ellie Whitney, D. Bruce Means, and Anne Rudloe. An extensive guide (432 pages, 800 color photos) to the incomparable ecological riches of this unique region, presented in a way that will appeal to young and old, laypersons and scientists. Complete with maps, charts, and species lists. (hb, pb)

The Trees of Florida, 2nd Edition, by Gil Nelson. The only comprehensive guide to Florida's amazing variety of tree species, this book serves as both a reference and a field guide. (hb, pb)

The Springs of Florida, 2nd Edition, by Doug Stamm. Take a guided tour of Florida's fascinating springs in this beautiful book featuring detailed descriptions, maps, and rare underwater photography. Learn how to enjoy these natural wonders while swimming, diving, canoeing, and tubing. (hb, pb)

St. Johns River Guidebook by Kevin M. McCarthy. From any point of view—historical, commercial, or recreational—the St. Johns River is the most important river in Florida. This guide describes the history, major towns and cities along the way, wildlife, and personages associated with the river. (pb)

Suwannee River Guidebook by Kevin M. McCarthy. A leisurely trip down one of the best-known and most beloved rivers in the country, from the Okefenokee Swamp in Georgia to the Gulf of Mexico in Florida. (pb)

Hillsborough River Guidebook by Kevin M. McCarthy. The Hillsborough River is not long, but has played an important role in Florida commerce and history. This essential guidebook is both a history and a guide to the river.